# A NEW COMMAND

## The Life of Bruce Medaris, Major General, USA, Retired

GORDON HARRIS

LOGOS INTERNATIONAL
Plainfield, New Jersey

A NEW COMMAND

Printed in the United States of America
International Standard Book Numbers: 0-88270-181-9 (softcover)
Library of Congress Catalog Card Number: 76-10533
Published by Logos International, Plainfield, New Jersey 07061

## CONTENTS

## PREFACE

I am deeply indebted to Father Bruce Medaris for his patience, frankness, counsel and time given to many interviews essential to this story. I was associated with him as the army commander responsible for missiles and space programs during the 1956-1960 period and came to love and respect him. At his request this statement precedes the account of his remarkable career:

> "The extent of events during my immaturity has been treated lightly because old wounds must not be reopened nor healed sores caused again to hurt. Driven by a need to prove something, one only proves the opposite."

The author accepts full responsibility for the abbreviated accounts of events which took place more than half a century ago. I enjoyed the full cooperation of Mrs. Virginia Medaris, the loyal wife who stood by and supported her husband in sickness and in health, in near poverty and in brilliant successes; and of Mrs. Marilyn Medaris Stillings and Mrs. Marta Medaris Smith, their daughters. Many others contributed, among them Father Al Durrance, Mrs. Betty Ezelle, Bishop William H. Folwell, Miss Florence Hood of Good Shepherd Church. Source material was obtained from the Medaris Papers in the library of Florida Institute of Technology, Melbourne, Florida; *History of the First U.S. Army,* an official publication; documents made available by Mrs. Helen Joyner, historian of the Army Missile Command, Redstone Arsenal, Alabama; files of the Huntsville Public Library and City Clerk's office. Colonel Henry Magill, U.S. Army (ret.), Colonel Charles Patterson, U.S. Army (ret.), and Mrs. Louise Parker Nesbitt of Huntsville, Alabama provided valuable insights. For the 1958-1960 period information was also obtained from the official history of the National Aeronautics and Space Administration.

Father Bruce was the inspiration for this story of a truly gifted leader who accomplished much for his country in war and peace and is now committed totally to the service of God. As the reader will discover, this is a story without end.

# A NEW COMMAND

# 1

# SOLDIER AND PRIEST

Leaving Orlando, Florida, northbound on U.S. Highway 17-92, a motorist drives through Winter Park and enters the city of Maitland in the course of a few miles. Within a block of the busy, four-lane highway, on Lake Avenue in Maitland, stands a California redwood church that grows in beauty with the passing years. It is the Church of the Good Shepherd, Protestant Episcopal, with a congregation of 1,100 many of whom are senior citizens who chose this part of Central Florida for retirement.

The parish was founded by Benjamin Whipple, Bishop of Minnesota, affectionately known as "Apostle to the Indians" in his northern diocese. He sponsored the construction of a lovely, white chapel, that has survived for nine decades since its consecration March 17, 1883. Tall southern pines shelter the white frame building next to the church which advanced from mission status in 1963.

Entering the church Sunday mornings or on other days of

the week, a visitor may see before the altar vested priests celebrating Communion or reciting the office of morning prayer. One of the ministers will be the associate rector, Bruce Medaris, who retired from the Army as a major general in 1960 to enter business, and, a few years later, began a new career as priest at the age of sixty-eight. The roles of soldier and cleric seem incongruous. But in war and peace, in uniform and mufti, in health and under sentence of death, Bruce Medaris was never far from God, whose grace spared him in World Wars I and II through tribulations and dangers that ultimately awakened this proud man to his great neediness. When Father Bruce intones, "The grace of our Lord Jesus Christ, and the love of God, and the fellowship of the Holy Ghost be with us all evermore," the solemn words take on special meaning in the light of the incredible sequence of events that brought him to his current assignment.

Associates during his distinguished military years saw little evidence of faith in Medaris. For much of his life he did not acknowledge his need of God. But the Almighty's will was not thwarted. As an abject convert he became a deacon of his church in 1969 and entered the priesthood a year later.

Some mocked. Some considered it a temporary aberration. Some refused to accept his profession of faith. General Medaris gave his country its first Earth satellite. His seemingly boundless self-confidence revealed an ego so imbued with a belief of invincibility that he could never be wrong. He would say, "I may not always be right, but I am never in doubt." How could such a man become a servant of the crucified carpenter from Galilee?

After retiring from the Army he wrote a book, *Countdown for Decision*, when he believed the nation's future and indeed that of the human race were at stake. He said that decision is the key to success, the way to survival and the only assurance of preserving the American way of life. And he put the case bluntly in words that betrayed the inner man: "The countdown for survival is God's direct challenge to the mankind He created and to whom He gave the power of choice."

The army had discovered early in World War II that he was a crack and fearless trouble shooter with a persuasive yet compelling personality that could influence the Congress, win over recalcitrant industry and inspire those who worked with him. He fought in Tunisia, Sicily, Normandy, the Ardennes and Rhineland, in the halls of the Pentagon, on Capitol Hill and lastly at the rocket development center in northern Alabama where he achieved his greatest success in uniform.

The army pushed him into priority enterprises or political situations where the pressures were relentless and the stakes were high. His roughshod methods earned resentment from some associates who nonetheless respected his tremendous capacity for work, his rare talents as a mover and shaker, and his innate courage and perseverance. They called him the "Big M," his immediate staff spoke of "the Boss." Newsmen found him "outspoken," "dashing," "blunt," and "tough." He was all of these.

But the years of historic achievements had to end. When President Dwight D. Eisenhower, his top commander in Europe, divested the army of its missile team and turned the organization over to a new space agency, Medaris elected to take off his uniform for the last time. The army dangled a third star if he would return to Washington, but he was tired and frustrated, concluding that he had done all that he could for the army and his country. Others would pick up the exploration of space that began under his leadership.

He became president of the Lionel Corporation, best known for the toy trains that bear the firm's name. He bowed out two years later when corporate policy clashed with his high principles. So he left New York for Florida and built a home in Maitland, fifty miles from Cape Canaveral where his army missiles were launched. He organized a management consultant business with such clients as General Electric and the National Aeronautics and Space Administration. With Ginny, as his wife is known to friends, he joined the congregation of the Good Shepherd mission in the chapel built by Bishop Whipple.

That was the situation in 1964 when an old enemy attacked him for a second time in his life. Bone cancer threatened the end. Physicians gave him a year or two more at the most. He put his affairs in order and chose his pall bearers.

What occurred thereafter is the high point in the story of Bruce Medaris, engineer, officer, diplomat, manager, businessman, minister of God. The words of Isaiah gave the answer: "I will raise me up a faithful priest, that shall do according to that which is in mine heart and my mind."

His Creator had helped him perform great deeds in the army but now, in his sixth decade, he finally understood the ultimate reason for which he was spared.

# 2

# GROWING UP

Springfield, Ohio typified mid-America at the dawn of the twentieth century. Rich farmland surrounded the city twenty-five miles east of Dayton in west central Ohio. Its factories produced diesel engines, machine tools, chemicals, leather goods, drilling rigs, trucks and other manufactured products. It was the home of Wittenberg University founded by the Lutheran Church from which Sherwood Anderson, who immortalized small-town Ohio in his stories, was graduated at the turn of the century. The old National Road, now U.S. Route 40, ran through Springfield on its way from Atlantic City, New Jersey to San Francisco, California.

Bruce Medaris grew to early manhood in this community. He was the only child in a home shattered by divorce while he was an infant. William Roudebush Medaris, his father, practiced law, became active in state politics and served for a time as Assistant Attorney General. The boy was born

May 12, 1902 in Milford and named for his father's law partner, John E. Bruce. The family name traces back to two brothers from the Azores who arrived in Carolina in the 1600's. Since they could not read or write, a registrar entered what he heard in the record. One became Medaris, the other Medearis. Their descendants sometimes chose other spellings like Maderis, Medariz and Maderiz. When Bruce was born the Medaris, Wright and Patterson families owned much of Claremont County, Ohio. His mother, Jessie LeSourd, came from a family that began in the United States with Jean Pierre LeSourd, a French soldier who served with General Lafayette in the American Revolution and stayed on when peace came. Bruce Medaris had forebears of Dutch, English, French, and Basque origins.

His parents separated when he was four years old and finally divorced because Jessie Medaris could not tolerate her husband's dalliances. She moved with her son and mother to Springfield. A strikingly handsome woman with firm Puritanic principles, she reflected the strong influence of her mother. Her father, Elisha G. LeSourd, enlisted at the age of seventeen in the 83rd Regiment, Ohio Infantry Volunteers at the outbreak of the Civil War, served with General Ulysses Grant in the campaigns along the Mississippi River, and was discharged as sergeant on July 24, 1865 at Galveston, Texas. He died of the long-term effects of his war wounds in 1895.

A school teacher, Jessie studied accountancy in Springfield and entered the business world, a daring step for her sex at the time. She became chief accountant and treasurer of a manufacturing firm. Grandmother LeSourd managed the small house and the boy, whose character was shaped by the two women and influenced more by the absence of his father than would have occurred in his presence. As he played with other children, he was constantly reminded there was something different about his family. Divorce was a subject whispered behind raised hands. A fatherless child was a rarity in the neighborhood. As grandmother and mother told him, he was the man of the house. He resented the patronizing comments of callers who spoke of the "poor little fellow" and the "little man" in a home without a man. In later years Bruce recalled with deep feeling his association with his grandmother: "She ran the house and me to my eternal profit. She let me do anything constructive. She believed in creating independence."

He fled the house often to escape well-meant visitor sympathy, finding more exciting things to occupy a boy's attention. Like following an ice wagon down the quiet block, snitching morsels as the vendor chipped blocks to fit his customers' ice boxes. Or on special occasions to watch workmen repairing the roofs of nearby houses, popping bits of tar into his mouth instead of chewing gum. He played with children older than himself because he grew tall for his age, games like hide and seek that sometimes involved girls; or stick ball, strictly for boys. He could knuckle down and drive marbles out of rings drawn in the dirt with his favorite shooter.

An adventurous boy could time his comings and goings so that Grandmother LeSourd didn't ask hard questions. Sometimes he wandered as far as the river to watch fishermen haul out mudcats with slender cane poles or admire boats plying the tawny current. He could explore, run and chase, filch cherries and apples from unsuspecting neighbors, experiment with corn silk cigarettes, risk an occasional scolding, since all of these activities required no money. And money was a scarce commodity. His family lived respectably at a near-poverty level.

He had less freedom when his mother returned from work. After supper she taught him to read and write, to draw and to cipher. When Jessie Medaris took Bruce to school she gave his birth date as May 12, 1900. She expected him to be well ahead of his classmates and wanted to spare him the stigma of being the "class baby." He advanced to second grade in three months, spent four months in third grade the next fall and was promoted to fourth grade. Not until she was dying in 1940 did his mother tell Bruce of the falsified birth record. He obtained a copy of the true birth certificate from an Ohio court and the army corrected his age in the official records.

A devout Methodist, his mother enrolled Bruce in Sunday school. He dutifully spent three hours in church every Sabbath, won attendance pins, and marched reluctantly in anti-drink parades staged by the Women's Christian Temperance Union. Reluctantly not because of childhood fondness for liquor, but because participation subjected him to the cruel humor of other children. His religious duties meant little to him other than a weary succession of "thou shalt nots" which, if anything, had the reverse effect. However, his church association brought him under the benign influence of a man who became foster father to Bruce, and to other boys, and a lifelong friend. A confirmed bachelor, Roy "Pop" Wagner worked with boys in the Methodist school and the Young Men's Christian Association. His timely and effective guidance kept young Medaris out of serious trouble more than once when his rebellious nature surfaced away from the watchful eyes of grandmother and mother.

Understanding growing boys' curiosity and energy, Wagner planned activities to channel their enthusiasm through useful outlets. He refrained from preaching, instead he tried reason, reminding his charges that they might permanently jeopardize their health and future success by indulging in harmful pursuits. He came upon Bruce and several friends as they were about to shove candy into pockets while diverting the store's proprietor. "Pop" didn't scold. He simply told them softly that such acts would not profit them; instead, he bought sweets and passed them out. Even silent disapproval from "Pop" was enough to change a young mind.

"Pop" spoke of God as a friend, not as a stern judge waiting to vent his wrath upon a young offender who strayed from Methodism's narrow path. Bruce held him in lasting esteem.

He saw his father rarely. When Jessie thought the boy old enough to understand divorce, she explained what had led her to break the marriage without recrimination and without placing all the guilt on her husband. The boy came to believe that his parents might have worked out the problem if others in the family left them alone. No one felt the separation more acutely than this sensitive child, but it was a subject painful to his mother and he didn't discuss it.

William Medaris contributed as little to the family as the divorce terms permitted, perhaps feeling misjudged by his former wife. Acute need and that fiery independence of spirit nourished by Grandmother LeSourd prompted Bruce to become a newsboy while in elementary school. To operate a newspaper route, delivering papers twice daily to customers, he needed a bicycle and he had to buy an established route from a carrier. He figured potential earnings against the required investment, forty dollars for the route, thirty-five dollars for the bike. The total was no meager sum in a period when the richest man in his part of Springfield earned five thousand dollars per year while neighbors supported families on wages of one hundred dollars per month.

Bruce told his mother about his plan. She listened attentively and explained that banks sometimes loaned money which must be repaid with interest. If a banker considered his scheme favorably, he might loan the seventy-five dollars.

She suggested that he talk with Nelson Milander at Springfield National Bank. After classes next day he boarded a trolley car in front of school and rode downtown to see Milander. Entering the marble-floored bank he asked the uniformed guard directions and followed his pointing finger to the banker's desk. Milander motioned to a chair.

"I am Bruce Medaris," he began. "I want to borrow enough money to buy a paper route and a bicycle."

"How much is enough?" Milander inquired.

"Well," the boy replied, "I think seventy-five dollars will cover what I need. Here," and he unfolded a page of ruled paper, "are the figures. With that many customers in the morning and those on the afternoon route, I figured my weekly income will be this much so I can pay the bank and make a dollar or two."

"You understand what is meant by interest?" Milander asked.

"Yes," Bruce answered. "I guess you want me to pay four percent interest. In thirty weeks, I could return the seventy-five dollars and the interest."

"All right, you have the loan," Milander said gravely. He filled out a promissory note form, handed it to Bruce who signed the paper and gave the boy his money.

"Good luck," Milander added. "We'll expect you in here every Saturday morning with the weekly payment."

Bruce nodded and walked out, his heart pounding with excitement. He had done it and now he could hold up his head a little more proudly because he was in business. He bought a shiny, red bicycle and then acquired his paper route. In six months he added forty more customers and paid off his debt. Ten years passed before he learned that his mother made the arrangements with Milander and guaranteed the loan, believing this would teach Bruce the importance of repaying borrowed money. He never forgot the lesson.

Pedaling along the streets twice daily, before and after school, Bruce struck up an acquaintance with a lamp lighter who turned on gas lamps along the curbs in the evening and turned them off next morning. The lighting system belonged to the city. Lamp lighters bid for contracts district by district. Bruce's friend wanted out, he was aging and the long walks were too exhausting. To the boy this offered a new opportunity. He figured he could handle newspapers and street lamps in the same district and make more money. So he submitted a bid to the city and got the contract. At eleven years of age he was a rising young entrepreneur. As he rode down the street carrying newspapers in baskets attached to the cycle, he balanced a snuffer on the handlebars. He grabbed each lamp post without dismounting, pushed the snuffer inside the lens, opened a valve and lit the Wellsbach mantle from a taper. Next morning he repeated his rounds, simply turning off the flow of gas. He kept both jobs successfully until he entered Springfield High School when he sold the paper route at a profit and surrendered his lamp lighting contract. His business interests had provided an added bonus. They had extricated him from those prohibition parades.

Springfield High offered an excellent curriculum that included four years of English, mathematics, foreign languages and science with elective courses in woodworking, foundry practice and metalworking attuned to the labor needs of local industry. Bruce studied English and mathematics, zoology, physics, chemistry, Latin, Spanish, woodworking and foundry. He also learned touch-typing, a skill that he employed profitably in later life. A voracious reader and quick learner, he had no trouble with studies. He joined a junior military organization, one of the school's extracurricular activities, wore a uniform and drilled one hour daily with a .22-caliber rifle.

But the family needed money and he prized his ability to earn it. An uncle managed the Big Four Railroad Station and offered him a job handling mail. Bruce worked from 6:00 P.M. to 6:00 A.M., piling mail sacks on hand-drawn, iron-tired trucks, tossing sacks into mail cars on arriving trains and removing other sacks for delivery in the Springfield area. Once each month when the Crowell Publishing Company issued its magazine he put in a hard night's labor because these sacks weighed a hundred pounds apiece and there were many of them. On other nights he could catnap by stretching out on piles of sacks. As incoming trains reached the switching area, a mile and a half from Springfield's station, engineers blew their whistles. That was sufficient to waken him and by the time the train wheezed to a stop in the station he was ready to handle mail.

Bruce had few close friends. His days were spent at school, his nights in the station. While he resented the circumstances which robbed him of the pleasures of boyhood, his stubborn pride bottled these emotions. He loved mother and grandmother, who worried about the kind of pace he lived.

It was during those high school days that he began, inwardly, to shift the blame for his parents' divorce—the cause of his hardship—from his father to relatives and friends who persuaded his mother to leave her husband and insist upon the divorce. To Bruce some of their opinions about adultery smacked of the "shalt nots" of Methodism. He chalked up one more black mark against the influence of the church.

War broke out in Europe in August, 1914, when Austria, Hungary and Germany attacked Belgium and Serbia. Russia, England and France were quickly drawn into the conflict. Bruce scanned headlines and heard much talk of possible U. S. involvement at school, in the home and among railroad workers. The name of Kaiser Wilhelm, the German ruler, became a popular epithet. Many of Springfield's citizens were former Germans who kept their counsel as emotion ran high among other residents.

Meantime Bruce learned that taxi drivers operating out of the Big Four station earned more than he did. They boarded passengers from incoming trains or delivered other travelers leaving Springfield to the rail terminal. He managed to talk a friend into allowing him to practice driving an automobile and persuaded the taxi owner to take him on as a driver, quitting the mail job. Drivers' licenses were unheard of and age was of little importance. So he continued in school and drove a cab all night. Other drivers knew his situation. When he arrived to take his place at the end of the taxi line he could nap at the wheel, knowing the next cab would gently push his forward until he reached the lead position. Then the drivers woke him up.

At fourteen and entering the third year of high school he changed jobs again to increase earnings. He became a uniformed conductor on the Springfield Street Railway System, working a night run from 3:30 P.M. until 11:30 P.M. for which he was paid twelve hundred dollars a year. He made more money and had more time for sleep. But there was a drawback. He ended the shift at the midcity car barns from where he walked a mile and a half home. On wintry nights he stopped in a saloon en route to warm himself with half a pint of whiskey, getting rid of the bottle before reaching the house so that his mother was spared the knowledge.

The kindness of his English teacher, Ruth Hessler, left an indelible memory. She understood his circumstances and assigned a seat in the rear of the classroom. As he reported first to her class each day, Bruce knew that he could recite immediately and then put his head down on the desk and sleep. Miss Hessler tested his progress by recitation. Satisfied, she would warn others to "let Bruce alone, he works." Thanks to a photographic memory and unflagging curiosity he continued to do well with little outside study. Athletics interested him only as a means of physical exercise. After his last class he jumped aboard a trolley car and arrived at the downtown office in time to begin his shift at 3:30 P.M.

The pace of business and industry quickened in Springfield and in countless cities across the country as the titanic struggle between Allied and Central Powers engulfed Europe. President Woodrow Wilson chose Brigadier General John J. Pershing to lead a punitive force into Mexico when a rebellion spilled over into Texas and New Mexico. Tensions eased somewhat when President Carranza restored peace in Mexico, but German submarine attacks on Allied and U. S. shipping aroused more controversy. Preparedness became the new catchword. Congress doubled the size of the army, increased the National Guard and expanded the navy. Liberty bonds and savings stamps were sold in the schools. Bruce enlisted in the Home Guard.

Early in 1917 Germany announced unrestricted submarine warfare. Former President Theodore Roosevelt demanded a declaration of war against the Hun. Wilson called up the National Guard and convened a special session of Congress. He asked for a resolution placing America in the war on the Allied side with the historic statement that "the world must be made safe for democracy." The United States entered the war when its land forces comprised 127,000 army troops, about the size of little Belgium's army, 13,000 marines and 80,000 national guardsmen. The first U.S. detachment landed in France that June as Wilson promised two million soldiers and marines in Europe by the end of 1918.

With two classmates Bruce talked excitedly about the war. For him it was an opportunity to further prove his manhood. He had shown that he could keep up with his schooling while earning a man's wages. Firm in that belief he arranged to miss school and secretly went on to a marine corps recruiting station in Dayton. He strode up to a weather-scarred corporal whose chest ribbons hinted of exciting, faraway places.

"I want to enlist," he said firmly.

The marine looked at this teen-ager, nearly six feet tall, erect in stature and with a pleasing, ruddy complexion.

"What's your age?" he asked.

"I was eighteen on May 12," Bruce replied. Since it was now May 20 he believed that he had passed the minimum age required for voluntary enlistment. The corporal filled out forms as Bruce answered questions. He signed the documents and was told the Corps would notify him by letter where and when to report in the next few days. He left Dayton tingling with anticipation. Without mentioning the trip, he continued riding his trolley and collecting fares.

Two days later his mother received a telegram from the Marine Corps asking her to confirm his age and give her consent to the enlistment. When Bruce returned home that night he was surprised to find her seated in the tiny sitting room. As he entered she looked up.

"Bruce, I have this telegram," her voice choking with emotion. "It says that you enlisted. How could you do this to me? I can't let you do it. You know that war killed your grandfather. I don't want to lose my only son."

He was not prepared for her tears. He hesitated as she

sobbed, then he gently answered: "Mother, I must go. I have thought about nothing else for weeks. I have got to do my part. I am not going to be killed, and I'll make sure my pay comes home."

She shook her head. "You don't understand," she said. "It isn't money, it's you I am worried about. You aren't through high school. I hoped we could find a way to send you to college. Everything in life is ahead of you, and now you want to throw it away."

"I've got to do it," he insisted. "I don't want to hurt you, but this is something I must do."

They talked on but his mother was unable to shake his resolve. Finally and tearfully, she agreed to consent. He went upstairs to his bedroom shaken by her grief but determined to leave. Years afterward, when his mother disclosed his true age, he realized that she could have stopped him simply by telling the Marine Corps he was only sixteen. She hadn't. He left for Columbus, the state capital, a week later for enlistment, having said goodbye to mother, grandmother, Roy Wagner and his classmates. He didn't tell anybody then, but he also said goodbye forever to his mother's church. With other enlistees he traveled by train to Parris Island, South Carolina, for boot training.

A strong body, self-confidence and resolution carried him safely through the tough discipline and arduous physical stress of those days. Now his grandmother's teaching stood him in good stead. He respected authority, and that was about the only brake on an otherwise rebellious nature. Sheer exhaustion felled him several times during long drills and marches, prompting dire mutterings from the training cadre. As the cycle neared its end, his company marched to the rifle range to fire for record. Handling the heavy weapon easily Bruce put eight shots in the bullseye on the last series at six hundred yards, then heard a gunnery sergeant's whisper: "Two more like that and you'll spend the war here as an instructor." The next two shots were deliberately wild. He received an expert rifleman's badge on July 12, 1918.

By one of those odd circumstances that occurred again and again in later years, Bruce did not accompany his outfit to France. A marine working in the post store patronized by recruits came under suspicion of stealing. Recruit Medaris reported to a sergeant that he bought some things and paid cash without a receipt and noticed the clerk failed to ring up the sale on his cash register. So he was detained as a witness for the thief's court-martial which delayed him three weeks. He attended reveille daily, made up his bunk for inspection and read all the books he could find, as many as three per day. When the trial finished he left for Quantico, Virginia, to join Company B of the Thirteenth Regiment. Some time later he learned that only two of the men with whom he trained survived combat, one permanently crippled, the other seriously wounded. The rest died in bloody fighting at Belleau Wood. He credited his escape to luck. Back home his mother received his diploma at Springfield High School's commencement. E. W. Tiffany, the principal, gave Bruce "the very highest recommendations."

Arriving in France, his company and the Eleventh Regiment formed the Sixth Marine Brigade. The Fourth Brigade had been heavily engaged since October, 1917, fighting alongside army troops and the hard-pressed French along the Marne River. The German command was unpleasantly surprised by the fighting qualities of the Americans. His brigade marched up and down the cobblestone roads, usually in support positions behind the front and sometimes within range of enemy artillery. Once Bruce sat down and leaned against a tree during a halt, slipped out of his sixty-pound back pack, and then for no reason, got up and walked across the road. Seconds later a shell burst where he had been standing. He escaped injury, once again believing that luck was with him.

The French commander, Marshal Foch, launched a counterattack on July 17 with American army and marine units integrated into four French armies. They mauled the Germans at St. Mihiel and in the Meuse-Argonne campaign. By fall the invaders were in full retreat. An armistice ended fighting on November 11. In four years, nearly five million Allies and three million men in armies of the Central Powers perished.

Since his regiment had not engaged in combat, it was assigned to military-police duty at Bordeaux where the Yanks boarded ships to return home. Bruce became assistant to the provost marshal, responsible for keeping American soldiers out of trouble in a district filled with bawdy houses and saloons, the home of thieves, pimps and prostitutes. Temptation was too much for a seventeen-year-old with an active libido and he fell prey to the ladies of the night. Sex had been a taboo in Springfield. It was a part of his nature that couldn't be discussed even with "Pop" Wagner. Now he was immersed in it.

Between the marine encampment and the city, the army housed stevedore companies composed of negroes assigned to load U.S. shipping. Frequently a lone marine headed for Bordeaux and its many fleshpots was waylaid, beaten and robbed. Bruce was on duty in his district one night when angry marines erupted, tore up the stevedore barracks and killed six black men. Next day the regiment was ordered to form a hollow square around a platform from which the marine commander, Colonel Smedley Butler, decried the vicious attack and concluded with a peremptory command: "I want every man who took part in this disgraceful incident to step forward." Standing in the front row, Bruce heard Butler add in an undertone, "and if you do, I'll punish you!" Not a man moved. That ended the trouble.

Bruce returned to Hampton Roads, Virginia, on August 8, 1919, received an honorable discharge, mustering-out pay and train fare for the 692-mile trip to Springfield. The marine certificate described him as 69½ inches tall, with hazel eyes, dark brown hair and ruddy complexion. He rated "excellent" in military efficiency, obedience and sobriety. The Corps commended his "honest and faithful service." His mother's prayers for his safety had been answered. Two years later the marines sent him a good conduct medal.

He found a new and unexpected situation awaiting him at home. His mother had married Emil Opferkuck in his absence. His new stepfather was a diesel engine specialist and widower who had brought two young children with him. Bruce was hurt and angry. He had been displaced in his own home. Opferkuck was initially cordial, but, as Bruce quickly learned, he brooked no disagreement with his opinions. So he decided to leave home and enroll in Ohio State University at Columbus, forty miles away, to study mechanical and electrical engineering.

He visited his father in Toledo, where William Medaris had become an insurance attorney. Understandably proud of his son's achievements, William readily agreed to finance his education. But there was one condition. He must study law. Bruce refused. Only then did he reluctantly turn to his stepfather for help. Opferkuck assented but he, too, stated terms. He would select Bruce's clothing and his living quarters. Not for a proud and self-reliant ex-marine who had come this far with little assistance and was not about to appear at the university in the kind of clothes Emil wore. So he resolved to work his way through college, scarcely a novel decision in his life. He found a room in a boarding house and worked at part time jobs. Because of his marine service he was immediately admitted to the senior Reserve Officers Training Corps and became company commander at the beginning of the school year in 1920.

Despite a busy schedule, there was time on weekends for fun. This handsome fellow who had been in France and possessed boundless vitality had no trouble attracting the girls. In those days girls of easy virtue were called "round heels." In time he encountered a much different young woman, Gwendolyn Hunter of Bellefontaine, Ohio, an only child and two years older than Bruce. She was a little shorter than he, blond and well proportioned. He courted her steadily, risking the displeasure of her parents who considered him too young for marriage and hoped for a more mature suitor. Ignoring their misgivings, he persuaded Gwendolyn to marry him. A justice of the peace performed the simple ceremony May 19, 1920 as the college term neared its close.

They set up housekeeping in a small apartment while Bruce found a job with the Bonney Floyd Foundry as draftsman, working twelve hours a day, six days a week for the annual salary of $1,320. He continued his studies in chemistry, drawing, mathematics, French and military science, maintaining a good scholastic record. As the new term approached, an opportunity to increase his earnings came during a wildcat strike by Pennsylvania Railroad workers. To break the unauthorized walkout, their union, the Brotherhood of Railway Trainmen, sought replacements. Bruce signed up, carrying a union card for the only time in his life, and became a brakeman. He worked from 3:30 P.M. to 11:30 P.M. and boosted his income to $2,300 per year. Strikers threw rocks; brake chains were severed on rail cars, but he came through unscathed.

Midway in his second year in college, Major Robert Thompson, who taught military science, announced that the army would conduct a nationwide competition to select 110 candidates for officer commissions. Only members of the army and National Guard were eligible. Bruce hurried to the apartment and excitedly explained the opportunity to Gwen. He had decided to enter the competition. Gwen naively thought it might be fun.

With Thompson's help, Bruce enlisted in Troop B, 107th Cavalry, Ohio National Guard in the fall of 1920 in order to qualify. He missed work at the railroad yards one or two days weekly to maintain Guard status. He learned to ride a horse, although one time his mount broke into a gallop, ignoring his yells, and came to a halt in the midst of busy Columbus traffic. As the written examinations for officer candidacy neared, Bruce found that he would be tested on one of four subjects, none of which he had studied. Undismayed, he bought a descriptive geometry text, carried it to work and mastered the subject in sixty days. When he took the examination he ranked among the first ten in the nation. He spent part of the summer of 1921 in the National Guard camp at Camp Perry, Ohio.

He finally stood before a board of officers at Fort Hayes, in Columbus, with an endorsement from Lieutenant Colonel C. F. Leonard, the senior officer at Ohio State, which certified him "extremely energetic, of good military appearance, an expert rifleman, and although young, a man of mature appearance and experience, having served for about two years in the Marine Corps. I believe him to be fitted for commission in the Army of the United States." The board accepted him, believing Bruce was twenty-one years old.

An army truck carried the young couple and their few belongings to Chillicothe, Ohio, September 3, 1921. He took the oath as lieutenant of infantry with pay of less than two hundred dollars a month. The army provided an apartment. Bruce joined the 19th Infantry Regiment at Camp Sherman as the outfit returned from strike duty in the Midwest coal fields. When the regiment transferred to San Francisco shortly, he was moved to the 29th Regiment at Fort Benning, Georgia, home of the infantry school, and served with a mule-drawn machine gun company.

# 3

# THE LEAVENING PROCESS

Fort Benning sprawled across southern pine forests in the red clay belt of southwest Georgia near the city of Columbus. For newly commissioned officers and their wives, fresh from another kind of life, the harsh environment of the post was a trial. Gwendolyn tried to be good-humored about their primitive quarters which contrasted sharply with her comfortable Ohio home. They lived in four pyramidal tents with wood floors and walls. A small enclosure in the rear housed shower, basin and toilet. Two galvanized washtubs and a kerosene stove, with a few pieces of furniture chosen by quartermasters for utility rather than beauty, completed their first home. In these raw surroundings the young bride cooked, washed and sought to make the best of a trying situation.

For Bruce, this was all part of the challenge. He was out to build a reputation as one of the infantry's promising lieutenants. Duty came first, as he frequently reminded his wife. Their life together had to be relegated to off-hours. His uniforms had to be spotless and crisply ironed. He studied constantly, reading texts on infantry tactics and weapons, borrowing works by Clausewitz and others from the post library to bring himself up to the technical level of career officers from West Point and the Citadel. But, more importantly—because of his marine experience and those years of hard work—he could lead men.

The average private soldier of that era had little education and drew meager pay plus some allowances for rations. He did some soldiering, but more often was called on as a handyman. Bruce came to terms with his men by making it clear that he would allow no disobedience. Their lives off duty were their own, but he expected them at their stations on time and in condition to work.

Marches and maneuvers kept him away from home frequently. He enjoyed these expeditions which brought him close to the troops as they bivouacked in the deep forest. Promotion required total commitment, so he reasoned, and he was more than willing to do whatever he could to achieve that goal.

Lieutenant and Mrs. Medaris exchanged social calls with other couples at the fort, having learned the tradition that "you must return a visit even if you can only afford baked beans." Officers were expected to drink. Liquor was illegal but available from bootleggers. Bruce played bridge and polo, displaying an inconsiderate and arrogant personality which he felt typified a rising young military sportsman and quickly earned the cordial dislike of their friends. Gwendolyn learned that army wives must not complain; in fact, they, too, became part of the army and subject to its traditions.

Her daughter's letters, cheerful as Gwendolyn tried to make them, shocked Mrs. Hunter. Living in tents seemed cruel and inhuman, particularly in view of her condition—she was pregnant.

But things improved in time. A frame building that once housed bachelor officers was converted into makeshift apartments. Bruce drew a four-room unit divided by a common hall. A potbellied, coal-burning stove furnished the only heat during the surprisingly rigorous Georgia winter. A curtain hung across the hall supposedly assured privacy but had a nasty way of blowing aside at inopportune moments.

When Bruce arose in the morning, he stirred the stove to warm the place, dressed, mounted his horse—brought to the door by an orderly—and galloped across the parade ground to join his company. Gwendolyn spent her days with the other wives, sewing and collecting things for the baby, feeling that to the army, wives were little better than camp followers. They served a useful purpose but should not expect more than their husbands' positions merited. Her drab existence was momentarily brightened when she gave birth to a daughter, Marilyn, on July 2, 1922 in the Benning hospital. Gwendolyn knew Bruce would have preferred a son.

But he quickly allayed her fears and showered genuine affection on the baby. It was a profound experience for the normally cocksure lieutenant who, in the emotion of the moment, offered a prayer of thanks.

Marilyn entitled the young couple to new quarters which boasted two bedrooms, a kitchen, bathroom, living room and greatest prize of all, steam heat. Bruce soon found a Boston terrier puppy for his daughter. He himself had never owned a pet. Marilyn and that terrier became inseparable companions for 13 years. An Irish setter and stray cat of uncertain parentage joined the menage, uninvited but welcome. Stretching his scanty resources Bruce also acquired his first automobile, a Durant Star.

A few months later, when Gwendolyn felt the baby could stand the trip, they drove to Ohio so the grandparents might become acquainted with Marilyn. They followed the U.S. Route 25 trace, having been assured by other military travelers that rivers could be forded safely. In those days, bridges were few and far between and the only paved streets were found in cities. They crossed the hills of northern Georgia into neighboring Tennessee, over ground once drenched with the blood of men waging civil war. Climbing a long grade, Bruce stopped to allow the terrier a short run. When he had called in the dog, he took the crank to the front end.

"Gwen, you won't believe this," he called. "The blasted crank doesn't fit!"

Bruce walked dejectedly back, put down the crank, and announced, "Well, we have one choice. This is where we take our stand until another car comes along to tow us up the hill. I can start the engine by coasting down the other side, but there is no way to get there without help."

They soon laughed at their misfortune, two young souls enjoying the novelty of their plight. Gwendolyn placed the baby on the seat and helped Bruce pull out side curtains and button them in place. Then they settled down to await rescue; if no help arrived by morning, Bruce told her that he'd just have to walk to the nearest farm.

At daybreak a carload of coal miners en route to their pit roared up the hill. Bruce signaled and the vehicle halted. He explained the problem and, good-naturedly, the men lashed a stout tow rope to the Durant, teasing Bruce and Gwen gently as they worked. They pulled the Star to the hilltop, released the tow line and insisted on waiting until certain the travelers were out of trouble. Bruce let his car run downhill until the engine fired, waved his thanks and reached the next town where he swapped cranks. They completed the long drive to Bellefontaine without further mishap. Bruce never again stopped the car on an uphill slope.

After a brief stay, Bruce drove back to Benning alone. The Hunters were determined not to subject Gwendolyn and her child to the return trip. Instead they came later by train.

Thirty years later, Bruce returned again to the fort as a major general to address infantry officers of another generation. He described conditions of the early twenties as they laughed and shook their heads.

"I did not realize that I was being abused in those days," he concluded. "So far as we were concerned, I had been given a place to sleep, to put down my bed, to take care of my family. The army had done the best it could. It was a challenge to prove that I was man enough to do it the hard way. I was very young, very eager and a very ignorant lieutenant. The test of command ability was whether I could raise my voice enough to be heard from the beginning to the end of the mule train. I was able to do so. Here the traditions of the infantry became part and parcel of my life. I founded my future in the traditions of the 'Queen of Battle.' Nothing can ever detract from the final importance of the foot soldier who, weapon in hand, feet planted on a piece of ground wrested from an enemy with his own sweat and blood, is the symbol of victory for our arms."

Those words probably characterize Bruce's attitude in those early years as well. But Gwendolyn did not share his bravado. Facing loneliness, hardship and deprivation, she struggled valiantly to meet the army's terms but never became fully reconciled. The rigid caste system separated lieutenants even from captains, let alone the majors and other field officers. It was a cruel segregation that ignited resentment in more than one army wife. Gwendolyn did her best to satisfy Bruce's high expectations, but, apart from their family life, there was little about Benning to remember kindly.

Two years passed during which he learned the art and techniques of ground war. He played with Marilyn as a pleasant diversion. She accompanied him on walks and trotted to keep up with daddy's long strides. Bruce displayed her proudly to friends. The young officer who never experienced a father demanded total obedience; if Marilyn misbehaved, he punished her. Gwendolyn winced at his strictness and willingness to spank. She might scold on occasion but never struck her daughter. Almost from infancy, Bruce treated Marilyn as a small adult rather than a child and included her in their social activities.

In 1924, Lieutenant Medaris and his dependents were transferred to the Department of the Caribbean, specifically Fort Clayton in the Panama Canal Zone. Bruce was exuberant since Panama was a choice overseas post in a shrunken army that had little to offer elsewhere. He rushed home with the news.

Gwendolyn heard him out and joyfully clapped her hands.

"That's wonderful, Bruce," she exclaimed. "I'll be happy to leave Benning even though it means taking the baby into a strange country thousands of miles from Bellefontaine. Will there be doctors, or fresh milk for Marilyn?"

He reassured her that the army looked after its own and painted a colorful picture of Panama, its tropical climate and the new experiences they would share. An overseas tour was mandatory for a career officer and Panama was by far the best anyone might expect, a kind of plum by army standards.

Gwendolyn's happiness changed to concern as she thought of her parents. "I know mother will be terrified," she murmured. "She will worry that we may never see her again."

"That is utter nonsense," Bruce retorted. "Your parents know I have to go where the army sends me. There's no sense fretting about this, we are going to Panama and we'll enjoy it."

Bruce wrote his mother, explaining that he would be away three or more years. But Mrs. Opferkuck was more easily assuaged than Gwendolyn's mother. Her reaction bore out Gwendolyn's fears. She was heartbroken and tried to persuade her to come home while Bruce went off alone. Gwendolyn refused to consider that alternative. She would never leave her husband. So the little family, with the spunky Boston terrier, sailed on an army transport to Cristobal on the Atlantic side of the Panama Canal.

In the military tradition, a fellow officer and his wife greeted them and looked after their needs until the young family was established in quarters at Clayton. Their new home was a pleasant, ground-floor apartment with stucco exterior in a relatively new infantry post. All the quarters were raised off the ground to keep out dampness, insects and snakes. Clayton was of classic design. Regimental headquarters formed one side of a hollow square, battalion barracks bounded the other sides. Officers lived in quarters behind headquarters which were arrayed in a semicircle, seniors occupying those in the middle flanked by their juniors. Garrison life followed a well-defined pattern. Morning troop inspections preceded special details, boards and courts conducted by officers. One day each week was set aside for athletics and recreation. Bruce did well on the rifle range, winning a gold medal in departmental matches and a leg on a Distinguished Rifleman's badge.

Detailed as one of two regimental scout officers for the 33rd Infantry, he explored much of the Canal Zone, riding over obscure trails through lush forests, surveying and mapping new routes of travel. Vast stretches of dense rain forest, banana, sugar and rubber plantations, interspersed among rugged volcanic peaks, covered the Isthmus outside the Zone. He rode horse or mule, choosing a mount suited to the terrain. He took part in an expedition that crossed the Zone on the old Morgan Trail named for the British buccaneer, Sir Henry Morgan, who raided Spanish galleons carrying off Inca treasures and destroyed Panama City in 1671. For these trips which kept him away days at a time Bruce dosed himself with quinine, the drug that enabled armies of workers to build the Canal and the only known protection against dread malaria.

Drenched in sweat crossing lowlands, stung with penetrating cold in higher elevations, the troop retraced their route after reaching the Pacific Ocean. They had covered half the distance to Clayton when Captain Hilliard Jackson, the commander, fell victim to malaria. Bruce ordered the men to pitch camp, administered quinine and wrapped the officer in heated blankets as his body shook in muscular spasms. A night and day of agony passed slowly. Suddenly Jackson quieted. Bruce realized that he was dying and with bowed head spoke a prayer dredged up from his Sunday school days. He could never erase that memory. Bundling the body in tarpaulins, they placed the dead commander on a mule and brought him home. Riding at the head of the small column, Bruce pondered the meaning of this human tragedy and found no ready answer. The regiment buried Captain Jackson with military honors. His wife and children sailed home to the States.

Infantry soldiers gave their mules loving care because the hardy animals carried their food, weapons and ammunition on marches. They patiently trained the animals not to thrash about when trapped by quicksand, an ever-present danger in the jungle-like countryside. When a mule bogged down, ropes were employed to haul the animal free from the thick ooze. Bruce looked on approvingly as Pappy, the boss mule who carried a lighter load befitting his station, trotted up and down the caravan, driving recalcitrant mules back in line with flying hooves. When the train returned to Clayton and the animals were unpacked, the bell mule led them into twin barns in file where each animal took his assigned stall. Sometimes Bruce rode up the hillside overlooking the post to watch mules as they gamboled in the pasture like carefree children.

He maintained the same relations with his men as he did at Benning. For several days after assuming command, he patiently explained what he expected of them and made it unmistakably clear that if they failed to measure up, in dress or performance, punishment would be meted out promptly and equitably. They stood inspection before passes were issued allowing them to leave the post. If they did not pass muster, the first sergeant, who followed Bruce as he walked along the files, noted discrepancies and refused liberty until infractions were corrected. If a man failed to return on time and did not call in a reasonable excuse, he lost the pass privilege for a stated period. Their officer knew that if the men understood the ground rules and accepted the fact that all must obey, they might gripe but they would accept the discipline. In the long run that made for a contented troop.

Gwendolyn found life at Clayton more pleasant than she had anticipated. There were bridge parties, sewing classes and other planned activities to occupy wives in the closely knit society while officer-husbands were on duty. Servants cost little and Bruce insisted that his wife must have more help than required. He encouraged her to dress well, citing the importance of appearances to a man's status. Neither worried about expense with the inevitable result that debts began to accumulate. Marilyn emerged as a pretty child with quick intelligence, her mother's affectionate nature and some of her father's will. She ran off several times, refusing to play behind the home, until Bruce fastened a rope around her waist and lashed it to a tree. Taunted by playmates with cries of "look at the little puppy, her daddy put a leash on her," she cried in humiliation. But while he applied discipline, this vibrant father also shared love. Once Bruce and Gwendolyn traveled into the interior with another couple, riding horses on the rough trails, and Bruce insisted the child must accompany them. Since they couldn't safely drink from the many streams they crossed, Marilyn sipped beer when she became thirsty. It was a memorable holiday for the child as she watched her father manage the expedition.

Perhaps life at Clayton became too predictable for his ambitions. In the second year of his four-year tour, Lieutenant Medaris applied for transfer to the ordnance corps, an elite branch of the army responsible for vehicles, weapons, aircraft, bombs and ammunition. There were only 305 ordnance officers in the peacetime army. Before an officer could apply for this detail he must have completed four years of line service. Bruce qualified on that score. If accepted he must spend four years in trial status after which ordnance decided whether to keep him or send him back to infantry, armor or artillery. Ordnance officers could look forward to an important bonus, the chance to acquire a master's degree in engineering at Massachusetts Institute of Technology. The flaming ordnance bomb worn on his uniform identified him as a specialist. Regardless of rank he could order a commander not to fire a suspected weapon. Senior members of the corps, ordnance inspectors, possessed absolute authority to condemn unsafe weapons. The army respected them as professionals who knew the technical and tactical capabilities of firepower.

The detail was approved on January 27, 1927. This began an association which continued in active and reserve duty for more than thirty years until Bruce attained the office of assistant chief of ordnance. His new career started with an interview with Major O. J. Gatchell, deputy ordnance officer for the Canal Zone.

"Welcome to the corps, Bruce," Gatchell greeted him in an office where two ceiling fans stirred warm, damp air. As he sat down, Gatchell reviewed events since World War I, warned that guns and equipment were almost priceless because the army had little money for replacements, and stressed the heavy responsibility to assure the safe maintenance and handling of deadly materiel.

"There is one lesson you must remember," the major added. "We have trouble with people who don't know how to spell ordnance. They confuse the term with ordinance. God help us, the twain shall never meet! But I want you to understand the full meaning of my words when I tell you, forgetting that bad joke, that there is no 'I' in ordnance. We are a team and don't you ever forget it."

The major's statement became a cardinal tenet of his philosophy. He did not forget.

Now it was time for another move. Bruce, Gwendolyn, Marilyn and her terrier occupied quarters at Corozal Ordnance Depot where he commanded three companies of a hundred men each. First sergeants looked after company details while Lieutenant Medaris conducted inspections, and functioned as property officer, summary court officer to mete out penalties for minor offenses, and manager of the post exchange, freeing his seniors for more important tasks such as inspecting harbor defenses at Ancon and Balboa. He won acquittals for several enlisted men as defense counsel in courts-martial. As a result the command turned him around by naming Bruce prosecutor or trial judge advocate. He was learning military customs.

Bruce decided to perfect his Spanish believing that a second language would benefit his career, perhaps subconsciously drawn to the tongue spoken by his Basque forebears. He acquired understanding of the grammar and sentence structure from a Springfield High School teacher who spent several years in the University of Madrid. He visited the Union Club regularly with two Panamanians of his age, read the daily newspaper aloud to them as they corrected his pronunciation and talked in Spanish. That facility would win him an unusual assignment later.

Chile and Peru had disputed forty years the control of the provinces of Tacna and Arica which were once part of Peru and bordered Chile on the north. The Treaty of Ancon in 1883 ceded them to Chile for ten years after which a plebiscite would decide which nation the people wished to join. Eventually both agreed to accept arbitration by the president of the United States. Spanish speaking officers were required to assist in conducting the plebiscite. Bruce was one of those chosen. He welcomed the task since he would receive compensation from the Tacna-Arica Commission as well as army pay and that offered opportunity to reduce his debts.

He worked for the commission eight months in the high mountains, serving as president of an election board made up of three Chileans, three Peruvians and an army sergeant from Puerto Rico who spoke only Spanish. A laborious search of church records as to birth and parentage determined voters' eligibility. Bruce soon found reason for cynicism about the honesty of priests when he encountered obviously falsified records. In many cases the mother's name was followed by the words: "Father not known."

He rode horseback occasionally twenty-five miles over mountain trails to La Paz, Bolivia and descended 8,000 feet via cogwheel railway to the port of Arica where an American cruiser lay at anchor for books and supplies. These infrequent visits were the only occasions when he spoke English. He thought in Spanish and had become bilingual when the plebiscite ended. He also retained a suspicious attitude toward the church, sure that in many of those "Father not named" cases, a priest did a small favor for a señor who knew when to be generous.

Bruce returned to Corozal for a warm reunion with Gwendolyn and Babe as he called Marilyn ever afterward. The child had brunette hair, brown eyes, a slender figure and an affectionate disposition. She strongly resembled her father. But the happiness of their reunion was short lived. Gwendolyn became ill and her physician told Bruce he suspected tuberculosis which meant that she must leave Panama immediately. He sent mother and child home to Ohio where Gwendolyn's parents looked after Babe while her mother underwent treatment at Fitzsimmons Army Hospital. A long convalescence followed before she could rejoin Bruce.

Still trying to clean up obligations, Bruce looked about for part time jobs to increase his earnings. He umpired in the Panama Baseball League and became a judge at a dog racing track where the chicanery soured him on gamblers and heightened his growing cynicism. He wrote a column titled "The Periscope" for the Panama American, a daily English language newspaper, in which he analyzed and commented upon national and international affairs, giving voice to his strongly critical opinions. He tried to mask his identity under a pen name but army intelligence tracked him down when he attacked U. S. foreign policy.

Called to account, Bruce listened to a stern reprimand and was ordered to stop writing. "I caught unshirted hell," he told friends.

Gwendolyn returned with Babe and found a confused and unhappy husband. With little chance of promotion, only death or retirement opened up pitifully few opportunities; he could only expect more years in some post back in the States at the same rank and pay. This was a bleak prospect for his restless, driving ambition. While he did not blame the army, knowing full well that the service operated on a barebones budget, he resented the lack of foresight in national leadership, believing the United States must lose its position as a great power unless the military establishment expanded. As to his family, he knew that Gwendolyn longed for a more permanent home. They could afford very little luxury on his officer's income. He did manage a surprise gift for Gwendolyn's birthday, a carved ivory jewel box, and there was a huge bouquet of roses. Bruce explained that they were ordered for a funeral and cancelled, so he was able to get them at half price.

He began to think seriously of an option. His fluency in Spanish, known to the American business colony, attracted job offers from companies opening business ventures in South America. General Motors Export Corporation dangled an attractive proposition. A dealer in Cali, Colombia, 150 miles inland from the nearest seaport, needed a manager. Colombia possessed an abundance of wealth based on coffee and sugar. Bruce talked about the prospects with his wife.

"It sounds good to me," he said. "We'd have enough money to live comfortably, more than I could hope to earn in the army for a long time. I think you and Babe would like the change; it's a much higher elevation and better for your health. There is a small American and English colony and

I'm told the Colombian people are sincerely hospitable."

Gwendolyn welcomed the change. She wrote her mother a cheerful, chatty letter, explaining that Bruce would leave the army. "He has learned," she wrote, "that hard work and success in the army bring no more reward than the army gives to slackers who dodge their responsibility." They would live in Cali, 3,000 feet above sea level, in a beautiful valley. The city's population of 100,000 included only twenty American and English families. "Babe and I will have to learn Spanish, Bruce speaks fluently, prices are high but so are wages." She assured her mother that she would visit Bellefontaine with Babe the following summer.

Bruce visited Cali to firm up his employment and was pleased when the Colombian dealer offered a base salary of ten thousand dollars, three times his military pay, and an overriding bonus if he increased business. Army regulations provided that an officer could resign his commission and apply for reinstatement within two years, meanwhile holding a reserve commission. That settled it. While he had no intention of a permanent break, he wanted to pile up a quick stake and return to the service, keeping this resolve to himself. The army accepted his resignation.

The English-speaking colony welcomed the attractive Yankee couple. Bruce's versatility in the two languages brought him instant success in business and in social circles. They shared the luxurious life of Colombian planters who accepted Señor Medaris as one of their culture. For the next year they enjoyed a dizzying round of parties, frequent visits to a large plantation in the mountains, an electric refrigerator, servants and abundant gifts. Bruce found auction bridge games played by planters and exporters entertaining and profitable. He piled up more income, thanks to that bonus arrangement, than his employer took from the automobile business.

After an evening or weekend in a hill plantation, the child sleeping in the car as they returned to the city, Bruce would nudge her gently as they reached a height overlooking Cali. "Wake up, Babe," he would say. "Here is Fairyland," as they looked out on the bright lights in the valley below.

Gwendolyn prepared her daughter to enter school, asking Grandmother Opferkuck to send primary books while her own mother arranged subscriptions for magazines, the *Saturday Evening Post*, *Collier's*, *Liberty* and the *Woman's Home Companion*, none of which could be purchased in Cali.

Their idyllic existence began to sour, however, in more ways than one. When Gwendolyn took the child to Ohio for the promised summer visit, Bruce took advantage of their absence to find other company—women found his magnetic charm irresistible. And he was feeling sorry for himself. His employer had changed his mind about their business deal. Bruce would stay on another year at the same salary, but with a sharp cut in the bonus pay. Meanwhile Congress changed the law concerning officer reinstatement. When this news reached Cali, Bruce immediately applied for active duty, but without success.

When she returned to Colombia, Gwendolyn learned that Bruce had been unfaithful. Shocked and bewildered, she confronted him: "How could you cheapen yourself in this way?" she cried. "How could you do this to me?"

Shamed, repentant and disgusted with himself, Bruce blamed his loneliness and business disappointment, but his wife could not accept his easy virtue.

"I won't have Babe subjected to this kind of situation," Gwendolyn declared. "You can play as you wish, I'm taking my daughter back home!"

The hateful exchange was carefully hidden from the child. Gwendolyn explained they would return to Bellefontaine so that Babe could enter school. The child assumed daddy would follow shortly.

Spurned by his wife, turned down by the army, his pride hurt by the drastic change in his business situation, Bruce stubbornly hung on for a time, negotiating for a position in the States. The Baker Kellogg Company, a New York investment house specializing in South American securities, offered employment. He seized the opportunity to get out of South America and also avoid returning to Ohio since a short, angry note from his mother placed her on Gwendolyn's side in the quarrel. How all of this would end, he did not know.

# 4

# PROUD IN HEART

At twenty-seven Bruce Medaris was suddenly looking into an uncertain future. In recent years he had known nothing but success, first as a marine and then in turn as an army officer, linguist, diplomat and businessman. Now his world was in dismal semi-collapse. Gwendolyn and Babe were gone. He was locked out of the army and struggling to stay ahead in business.

How did he feel about all this? Whatever pain he experienced was quickly suppressed and concealed. He didn't want to know why these things had happened to him; he wanted only to get back on his feet and forget about them. He blamed Gwen for refusing to forgive him. He wasn't ready to take a hard look at himself as a proud, ambitious and self-righteous man who was perhaps getting a much-needed rap on the knuckles.

Leasing a New York apartment, Bruce undertook to convince his new employers that they gained a valuable resource in this representative who understood South American psychology and the growing importance of those nations in hemispheric economics. So it came as something of a shock to discover that bond markets respond to forces that were beyond his control. When demand for these securities bottomed, Kellogg let go most of the company's staff, including Bruce. His self-esteem wounded, he refused to consider other employment in the metropolis. He decided to return to Ohio perhaps to make amends and a new start with Gwendolyn, taking along a distrust of the city which he harbored for many years.

Bruce found a job with the Curtiss Wright Flying Service at Columbus airport. As the heart of a machine tool industry, Columbus supported hundreds of manufacturing plants. The airport was a busy terminal even in those early days of commercial flying. Bruce promptly learned to fly and became passionately devoted to aviation.

Soon he met with Gwendolyn and talked persuasively about a reunion. Despite misgivings of parents and friends, but pushed by Marilyn's longing for the father she feared and loved, she wanted to resume their marriage. Babe was overjoyed when mother announced they were leaving Bellefontaine halfway through her first year in school to live with Bruce in Columbus.

Listening to heady talk of business friends, Bruce began buying and selling stocks, hungry to get in on the "easy money" they talked about. He could buy stocks on margin with as little as a ten percent down payment, sell when the shares increased in price, buy more and repeat the process while taking profits. This raised his income several thousand dollars, and like other young and inexpert financiers, Bruce believed in living it up. Gwendolyn got clothes, servants and money whether or not she wanted them.

Returning from a business trip in the summer of 1929, Bruce called his stock broker and received a highly favorable report. Prices were going sky high on the New York Exchange. An investor who bought American Telephone and Telegraph shares in 1928 for $175 watched in glee as the stock climbed to $335. Similar incredible advances inflated other industrial stocks. Few paid heed to the warning of Roger Babson, a financial prophet, who predicted a depression. Bruce amassed a paper fortune of $100,000.

He embraced Gwendolyn and Babe as he entered their home. His wife nervously promised to share a secret later. In the privacy of their bedroom Gwendolyn told him that she had undergone minor surgery in a military hospital. Someone had been careless in the operating room as a result of which there was serious doubt that she could bear children.

Bruce had difficulty concealing his anger.

"My God, Gwen, do you understand what this means?" he asked bitterly.

"I did it because the doctor recommended an operation," she replied quietly. "He assured me the procedure was fairly routine and I need not be concerned about any problem. Not until I went back for a checkup did the truth emerge."

"I can't believe it," he snapped. A surgeon's mistake had apparently cheated him of the son he wanted so much. He resented Gwendolyn for submitting to an operation without talking to him. As she sobbed, he stalked from the house. Hours later he returned to calm her grief, while inwardly he remained resentful. Whether Gwendolyn feared childbirth because of her tuberculosis experience or subconsciously chose this course because of his unfaithfulness, Bruce never knew. From that moment on their marriage was doomed.

He flew to Ontario in mid October to fish for black bass with two friends. They stayed in a wilderness lodge, caught fish, ate and drank heartily and relaxed in the remote setting. They were on the lake on October 24, a day that became infamous as "Black Thursday." At dinner that evening another guest remarked that he heard disturbing news by radio about a panic in Wall Street. It was the first hint that something had gone wrong. Bruce flew the plane back to Columbus next day and drove into the city to confront his broker.

"What in God's name happened?" he asked Dan Overton, who handled his account.

Dan shook his head. "I can't believe it, Bruce," he replied grimly. "The bottom fell out of the stock market. My New York office bombarded me with calls demanding more money on margin accounts. The ticker went crazy. We couldn't keep up with falling prices. I tried my best to reach you but when the airport said you were in Canada, there was nothing left to do but close your account. Maybe if I could have reached you in time and if you were able to come up with money, we could have saved a little. If it makes you feel better, I've lost my shirt and so have most of my customers."

Bruce tried to speak, but only waggled his head and slumped into a chair. "What's left?" he inquired. Dan leafed through a ledger, jotted figures on a pad and said, "I hate to tell you this but you have exactly sixty-nine dollars coming." Bruce waited silently while the broker wrote out the check.

His world in shambles, his dreams of fortune shattered, Bruce walked across the street to a haberdashery. He picked out a business suit, hat, shoes, socks and shirt and endorsed the check. He was well dressed and flat broke. More bad news quickly followed. Curtiss Wright virtually closed its flying service and wiped out his job. The spectre of the Great Depression stalked the land.

One link remained to a less glamorous but more certain past, he was still a first lieutenant in the army reserve. Although he could not possibly guess the future in his bleak despondency, that link would become the most important fact in his life.

At home he told Gwendolyn the harsh truth. They were penniless. "I can't believe this could happen," she tearfully rebuked him. "Why did you put everything we had in the stock market? You gambled and didn't stop to think what this could mean to Babe and me!"

Acutely conscious of his mistaken judgment but too proud to confess it, Bruce poured out hot words. Heartsick, almost consumed by guilt, he stormed out. There would be recurring scenes in the weeks of bare existence that followed. He resorted to selling appliances door-to-door, earning just enough to pay rent and buy food. His clothing became shabby. Gwendolyn scrimped and reworked dresses for herself and the child, somehow keeping the home together more through faith than substance. The bitterness, which divided husband and wife, festered like a running sore. She began to suspect that some of his frequent absences at night hinted at more infidelities.

He came home one evening to find an empty house. A note on the kitchen table caught his eye. He picked it up and read, "Bruce, I've taken Babe with me to Bellefontaine. I can't stand any more of the torture I've endured for months. I tried to make you happy but you have changed. What you are doing now is apparently what you prefer. So this is goodbye."

First failure, now desertion. The stark fact struck him like a hammer blow. He poured Scotch, crumpled the note and tossed it in a waste basket, noting wryly that it fell in on the first throw. His heart told him that Gwendolyn had ample reason, but his stubborn pride refused to accept total responsibility. He would show her that she walked out on a man who could not be defeated by fate or whatever it was that dogged him since leaving the army. He rented a smaller apartment, kept on selling and sent money to Gwendolyn when he could.

Marilyn did not understand the separation, loving her father as she did. One night her mother entered the bedroom and softly announced, "Daddy will not be living with us anymore." The child removed a signet ring from her finger, a gift from Bruce, and placed it under a pillow. She entered third grade in Bellefontaine's school that fall. Ten years elapsed before she learned what happened, protected from the unpleasant truth by the conspiratorial silence of mother and grandparents. Gwendolyn did nothing to affect the child's love for Bruce while she grew to young womanhood.

The Hunters provided a home but lacked resources to do more for their unhappy daughter. She found employment in the Florence Crittenden Home for Unwed Mothers in Columbus, a job that kept her away three weeks each month. Mother Opferkuck disapproved of her son's misconduct as strongly as she had his father's and readily sided with Gwendolyn. She did up her own hair and washed the family car, putting the equivalent money aside covertly to aid her daughter-in-law. Bruce visited Babe occasionally, receiving a loud welcome from the terrier and his daughter. He never saw Gwendolyn who absented herself on these painful visits. Hoping for a reconciliation, the child at length persuaded her mother to have dinner with Bruce in the hope he could pay more support and find her a better job. Hating his plight, he explained that he could do no more. A year later Gwendolyn sued for divorce and custody of their child. Bruce did not contest the action.

Grieving more than he cared to admit, he left Columbus where there was too much to remind him of his difficulties. He moved to Cincinnati, the larger city, at the urging of a lifelong friend, Paul Bell, who represented the American Automobile Association. He shared Paul's apartment in the Broadway Hotel. Door-to-door sales brought enough income to contribute to their food bills, but he enjoyed few pleasures. He tried to find jobs, but there was no opening for a man whose primary skills were in the military field. Selling became a hardship as bread lines grew longer and the Roosevelt administration opened public works projects to stave off economic collapse.

Low in spirit, he returned to the hotel one evening to find Paul playing contract bridge with two young ladies of good families. Bruce pulled up a chair behind Virginia Smith, the daughter of a Cincinnati banker. As an expert in the technicalities of the game, he offered advice while attracted by her brunette beauty. He soon began calling her "Ginny," but his straitened circumstances prevented him from pursuing a warmer friendship.

Plodding the streets, weary of turndowns, he accidentally met Colonel C. O. Sherrill, an officer whom he had known at Fort Benning years before. They shook hands vigorously. Sherrill was now retired and in business. Bruce described his tour in Panama and his ill-fated gamble in Colombia.

Sherrill nodded gravely. "That was bad news when Congress removed the option to return to duty," he agreed. "What are you doing these days?"

"I'm selling door-to-door only the doors aren't opening any more," Bruce answered. "It's a losing proposition but I've not found anything better."

"That's not for you," Sherrill snorted. "You come to my office in the morning. I want to talk more."

Next day he visited the general offices of the Kroger Baking Company. Sherrill was vice-president for personnel of the firm which operated retail grocery stores in the Midwest. He lost no time in getting to the point.

"Bruce, Kroger is a big, growing and stable firm," Sherrill explained. "I think you should join us. Never mind the depression. People have to eat and it's our business to get good food to them where it is convenient at prices they can afford. We're doing just that. I can assure you plenty of work, adequate wages and real opportunity for advancement. If you show us the same kind of enthusiasm and energy you showed me at Benning, I can guarantee that you will never regret your decision to come aboard."

Bruce took him at his word. "I'll join right now," he replied, feeling that this was the opening he wanted.

He started work with Sherrill in the Cincinnati headquarters and soon learned corporate policy and management procedures. Breaking in as a store clerk and manager, the long hours and hard work occupied his mind to the exclusion of painful memories. Sherrill placed few restrictions on Kroger's young executives. He could work as long as stores were open and that meant as long as sixty hours weekly in most locations. Saturdays were peak shopping days when he spent fourteen hours or more watching customers select goods, spotting new lines where traffic was heavier, inventing new procedures to increase sales. He derived immense satisfaction from managing people and things.

With restored confidence, Bruce began circulating again. He visited friends, squired women attracted by his flashing smile, handsome appearance and charm. If anything, he found it all too easy to satisfy his physical appetite as well as his need of companionship. But he frequently thought of Ginny in a far different light. Bell urged him to escort a girl to a dance celebrating the opening of a new hotel. His first thought was of Ginny Smith. Picking up the phone he called the Smith home and asked for her. When she answered Bruce said "Ginny, this is Bruce Medaris. You remember, I hope, that we met at Paul's apartment where I taught you to play contract." That sally provoked laughter. "Well, I have to admit, you already played a pretty good game," he acknowledged. "I'd like to take you to the dance at the new hotel. Paul is going with Betty. Will you come?"

Hesitating momentarily, Virginia accepted the invitation. They shared a happy evening. Bruce learned that she had spent a year in the university, then taken a full course at the Cincinnati Conservatory and become an accomplished pianist. He was drawn to this pert, vivacious girl with a sharp mind, ready to question and, it seemed to him, interested in his happiness. He invented excuses to call her. They danced and played bridge. Sometimes they talked and Ginny learned more about the kind of life this unusual man had lived. R. Clifford Smith was not about to see his daughter swept away by an undeserving fellow, so he quietly made inquiries and the responses were reassuring. Conservative Cincinnati society did not readily accept divorced men without explanation.

Bruce accorded Ginny great respect. He realized that he must have a wife at his side as he moved up the ranks in the Kroger company. His affection was sincere. Ginny Smith could fill the void in his life and serve as a check on his impulsive nature.

As they dined in a riverside club one evening he said quietly "Ginny, you know all there is about me. I made a mess of one marriage for which I have deep regret. My mistakes have been costly but they are behind me. You know how much I care for you. Will you marry me?"

Ginny touched his hand. "Bruce, I do care for you, but I want a little more time to think. We don't always agree and I won't surrender my right to think as I believe. You must know that I will never blindly submit, but I want to share your life."

He kissed her gently. Ginny left shortly with her family to

spend the summer at their second home in Traverse City, Michigan. Bruce visited her frequently and she gave him the answer he wanted. They were married August 29, 1931 in Traverse City with the warm blessing of her parents. Bruce left shortly afterward for Cleveland where he took the post of personnel director for Kroger in that territory and leased an apartment on the west side for his bride. Later they moved into a larger flat which they both considered their first home. Two years passed during which Bruce earned a sound reputation in Kroger as an innovative executive. Early in 1933 the company ordered him back to Cincinnati for intensive management training during which he learned the grocery business from the ground up. Next Bruce was appointed assistant in the corporate merchandising department.

The first child of the marriage, Marta Virginia, was born in Cincinnati December 26, 1933. Now Bruce had another daughter to share his affections while driving to Bellefontaine occasionally to see Marilyn. She cherished these visits. He would take the child for a ride, gravely explaining that she must learn to drive for her own safety and allowing her to steer the car on little used byroads.

Despite bright prospects with his employer, Bruce talked often of his longing for the military life. Ginny understood his need and urged him to try for reinstatement. He wrote the Adjutant General in Washington May 25, 1935, explaining that he had faithfully discharged his obligations as a reserve officer since leaving the army and frankly admitting that he solicited the help of friendly congressmen. Senator Bulkley and Congressman W. E. Hess of Ohio introduced an unusual bill in the 74th Congress to return Bruce to the regular army as a lieutenant. To his dismay the War Department opposed the bill, not on his merits as an officer but on the ground that if reinstated he would be entitled to back pay and allowances since his resignation in Panama. Bruce countered by assuring Congress and the army that he would make no such claim. His letter revealed the depth of his commitment:

"I realize that my entire background, training and temperament are such that I cannot ever reach my highest sphere of usefulness or personal contentment except in the military service. I can sincerely pledge myself to make my record such that the army can always feel the action was justified." Time would confirm that pledge. He went to Washington to plead his case, but the War Department was adamant. And Congress refused to pass a personal bill against the judgment of the Secretary of War.

If the army didn't want him, Kroger did. He was promoted to district manager in Wisconsin and moved Ginny and Marta to Madison, supervising stores west to the Mississippi River, traveling about his territory by auto. Ginny's solid encouragement, the home she maintained, and their little daughter enriched his life. He took his wife and baby on some of his less arduous trips. They liked Madison. Bruce kept up his reserve activities and studied army correspondence courses. The winter of 1935-36 brought the heaviest snows Wisconsin had experienced in many years. Frequently Bruce was forced to remain in small towns when drifts blocked highways. But he opened new stores, aggressively pushed more lines of commodities and kept his district high up in Kroger's esteem. Next winter brought a series of ice storms that again crippled transportation. He organized convoys to deliver foodstuffs and kept his stores well supplied.

Ginny delighted him with a son, John Bruce, Jr., born in Madison November 10, 1936, despite serious complications. The child was premature and physicians despaired for his survival. Bruce fought to save the baby, visiting the hospital twice daily to bring containers of life-sustaining milk from the baby's own mother. While Ginny remained despondent, he never lost faith and at length was able to bring the child home. For months they struggled to build their son's health, slowly winning the battle.

With a growing family and assured future, Bruce should have been content, but the conviction grew that unless he forced a change he would move up in the Kroger ranks and spend the rest of his life selling groceries. Prosperity and stability were not enough, he wanted something more.

With no better reason than inner discontent, he decided to leave Kroger and take over a Cleveland trade school whose proprietor held out glowing promises of lucrative returns if Bruce would manage the enterprise. Bruce journeyed to Cleveland, leaving the family in Madison until he established another home. In a short time he discovered that his associate was a confirmed alcoholic while the school's financial structure was so shaky that it could not survive. He got out of the deal embarrassed and disgruntled with new reason to question his faith in other people.

Bruce and Ginny moved to Cincinnati where a competent pediatrician took charge of their tiny son and started him on the road to health. Ginny worried about dwindling savings and the impact of the school's collapse on her husband's morale. "It's not the end of the world," she reminded Bruce. "You couldn't possibly get at the truth of that mess. That man was a liar and a cheat."

He took a position as general manager of a Chrysler automobile dealership and planned an ambitious sales campaign. An uncle promised to give Bruce his fleet business, turning over a large number of vehicles each year. Their affairs took a turn for the better.

Marilyn paid a surprise visit, persuading friends to drive her into town to see daddy. She had met Ginny for the first time shortly after Marta's birth when Bruce took his new family to Bellefontaine. When Ginny saw her at the door she immediately called to Marta and Bruce, "Your sister is here!" That recognition was important to Marilyn and she responded to Ginny's warm affection. Later Bruce told his wife, "That was a wonderful thing you did for Babe."

"She's our daughter now," Ginny firmly replied.

The prospects of the fleet business vanished overnight when his uncle died of a heart attack. The used car market fell off while creditors tightened their grip on the automobile dealership. Soon the firm was thrown into bankruptcy and Bruce found himself ten thousand dollars in debt because he had personally signed loan agreements. It was the worst dilemma of his business experience. He borrowed money to pay off some creditors by pledging household furniture as security and promised others that he would make good whatever it cost him. With Ginny's untiring help, eight long and lean years were required to retire the debts and clear his name.

At this juncture Marilyn wanted a bicycle, but her mother and grandparents could not afford to buy one. Recalling Bruce's promise to help her if he could, she appealed to him. Despite his financial problems, Bruce shipped the bicycle. He could not disappoint Babe although the gift incurred Gwendolyn's displeasure.

"If my child is injured on that thing, I will never forgive him," she told her mother.

Once again Bruce resorted to selling to housewives in order to support his family. Once more he fought himself, keenly aware that he threw over a promising career with Kroger only to encounter failure. Somehow he must find a solution for the problems his selfishness brought upon Ginny and their children. He looked up Paul Bell in need of a sympathetic ear.

"What is the matter with me?" he asked. "Everything I attempt winds up in trouble. No matter how hard I work luck runs against me."

"I really don't know what to tell you," his friend said. "You have the intelligence and energy to do big things, Bruce, but I must say that your business judgment could be improved. Look at the success you had with Kroger. That's in your favor. Why didn't you apply some of that experience before rushing into these other deals?"

Bruce threw up his hands. "I just trusted other people, Paul, that's my only excuse. I've got to find something worthwhile or the results of my mistakes will hurt Ginny and our children."

At this low point friends came to the rescue by recommending Bruce to the Dictaphone Corporation which manufactured office equipment. He became senior salesman for the area, plunging into the new job enthusiastically, and turned the corner.

Gwendolyn remarried. Her husband was one of the small group of Americans they had played bridge with in Colombia. Bruce felt relief that someone would provide a home for his former wife and daughter. Now in her teens, Marilyn elected to become a Presbyterian and was baptized in that church. The news pleased her father.

Less pleasant news came from Europe. Adolf Hitler was creating a mighty war machine. Benito Mussolini was embarking upon a mad scheme to rebuild the Roman Empire. Japan was slowly strangling China. As Britain and France looked to their defenses, the United States began to produce weapons, ammunition and ships. Cincinnati's plants converted to war production. Bruce concluded that war in Europe must come as the only means of checking Hitler's ambitions. The army announced on July 1, 1939, that Congress had authorized it to expand the officer corps by calling up selected reservists.

Ginny read the signs correctly. She listened to Bruce's animated talk, watched as he pored over columns of news daily, understanding the urgency of his desire to share in what was happening. "If they ask me, Ginny, you know that I will have to say yes and return to the army," Bruce told her as he waited impatiently for a summons. His reserve activity had won him earlier the presidency of Cincinnati Chapter Reserve Officers Association, and honorary membership in Scabbard and Blade, a military society of the University of Cincinnati.

Bruce talked to Colonel Frederick McMahon, chief of the Cincinnati ordnance district, an army procurement organization which maintained supply contracts with midwestern plants.

"I've got a lot to offer the army and I want to be called up," Bruce said.

McMahon grabbed his hand. "I can use you right now," he replied. "No one knows how big this thing will become, but all the signs point to mobilization whether or not we are drawn into war. We'll have more business than my office can handle with our small staff. So I'll endorse your request, Bruce, and get it off to Washington in the next mail."

The orders he longed for arrived within a week. He was recalled in the rank of captain and ordered to one year's active duty effective July 1. Doubts and indecision were shucked off. He was his former self, sure, positive, already planning how to expand the district staff, moving with a powerful sense of urgency.

What seemed old and familiar to him, however, was new, exciting and somewhat frightening to Ginny who plied him with anxious questions about the kind of security the army offered. Where would they live? How would they be accepted by career officers and their wives?

"We'll move into a house close to Fort Thomas," Bruce assured her. "There are no government quarters available at the fort, but we'll be part of the post while I'm on duty in Cincinnati. You'll like army people, Ginny, they look after each other. My work will require some travel, but most of it will likely be within the district boundaries so I don't expect long absences. Meanwhile the post will provide a fine environment for you and the children."

He wrote his mother and Marilyn, telling them he was returning to the military life and sending his love. To Babe he added, "If you need something, and if it's possible for me to help, I will."

After eleven years of civilian life, Bruce Medaris had come home to the army.

# 5

# A MAN UNDER AUTHORITY

Sixty-one days after Bruce donned the uniform, Nazi armies drove into Poland in a fierce blitzkrieg, destroying cities and helpless populations on a colossal scale. The Second World War had begun.

Soviet forces crossed Poland's eastern frontier on September 17, 1939, and the small nation capitulated on October 5th. Mankind had never witnessed this kind of fighting, total war. Honoring their treaties with Poland, Great Britain and France declared war two days after the attack began but could do little more than rail against Hitler's duplicity. President Franklin D. Roosevelt summoned Congress into special session to amend the Neutrality Act and authorize the sale of war materiel to the Allies on a cash and carry basis. Leaders of both major parties declared that America would not otherwise become involved in the awesome struggle.

A NEW COMMAND

Captain John B. Medaris (the army insisted that an officer must use his first name) and his family occupied a home near Fort Thomas, Kentucky, across the river from his office in the Cincinnati Ordnance District where he was appointed executive officer. Ginny and the children adjusted happily to the quiet life of the small garrison.

There was much to occupy his boundless energy. Lacking specific guidance from Washington about what would be required, Bruce assumed there would be unprecedented demands for production to support Allied armies, navies and air fleets. He tackled two major tasks: first, to enlarge the district staff which consisted of only seven employees and train newcomers in the complex procurement activities; second, to assess and recruit the productive capacity of industries large and small in Kentucky, Tennessee and southern Ohio. He drew up plans for an office of 1,000. When he left Cincinnati a year later the work force had grown to 200. The most urgent need concerned inspection of manufactured items to make sure that contractors used specified materials and followed government engineering specifications so that the army got what it paid for.

It was not only a matter of economics. The lives of men who would use the weapons and ammunition were at stake. If the products did not perform as expected against an enemy, defective material could endanger its users. So competent men and women had to be found and trained who appreciated the importance of reliability and safety.

The situation in Europe steadily deteriorated in the spring of 1940. Soviet armies overran Finland, German panzer columns rolled into Denmark and Norway, then Belgium, the Netherlands and France. The French capitulated on June 25. Italy invaded Greece.

Aware of the success of the Cincinnati district in building its staff and enlisting the willing participation of industry,

Brigadier General A. B. Quinton, Jr., chief of all ordnance districts, called Bruce to Washington with the goal of accelerating the same expansion in other parts of the country. He would soon be promoted to major and extended on active duty for another year. The grand piano he presented to Ginny on their second anniversary and household effects were loaded into a van for Washington. The family drove first to Springfield where Bruce visited his mother in a hospital. He was shocked to find her gravely ill.

There was a tense scene when he accosted his stepfather in a corridor. "Why didn't you tell me?" he demanded. Opferkuck shook him off. "You are a busy man," he replied, "and I have my work. Besides, there is nothing you could have done. Jessie is dying."

"Have you told her?" Bruce asked. "No, I have not," Opferkuck answered. "And I forbid you to say anything about it to her. I don't believe that God wants that woman to lose hope."

"But there is no hope," Bruce angrily retorted. "No matter," Opferkuck said. "She doesn't know and you are not to tell her. She is my wife."

Bruce spent as much time as permitted at his mother's bedside. Fighting to control his grief, he told her that they were en route to Washington but he would return soon to be with her again.

"I have something to tell you, Bruce, which I should have said years ago," Jessie said softly. "You are two years younger than you know because I did not give the school your correct birth date when you enrolled."

His mother slowly and painfully explained why she misrepresented his age. As a school teacher, she had seen what happened to the youngest member of a class and it was that childish but cruel teasing that she hoped to spare him.

"You must not worry about it, mother," Bruce assured

her. "I can straighten out the records. Now you must think about getting well again."

She looked into his eyes as she replied. "I'm not sure about that, Bruce. God may have other plans. But I want you to know that I have always been proud of my son. I think Virginia is a good wife and mother and I'm happy that she will be with you."

He kissed her goodbye and left the room, the tears came as he took Ginny in his arms and held her tightly.

They went on to Washington where Bruce talked a builder into renting him a small house near Fort Myer, just ahead of the moving van. Two days later, on July 4, 1940, he returned to Springfield to bury his mother.

War fever seized the nation. Britain stood alone, surrounded by German U-boats draining her supply line. The Luftwaffe carried out saturation bombing raids on English cities. Congress hurriedly authorized large appropriations for guns and ammunition. General Quinton and Major Medaris were directed to speed up the placing of production contracts and to increase the tonnage for the embattled British. Bruce took his orders literally earning these comments from his superior: "If being too aggressive, Major Medaris has that fault. He is impatient with stupid people but in this critical situation, that enhances his value." Wealth or position failed to awe Bruce, his country needed help and he would do whatever he could to provide it regardless of others.

The army sought the production capacity of the J. I. Case Company, a leading producer of farm machinery, which resisted military contracts. The firm's lawyer insisted upon conditions and escape clauses which were unacceptable to the government. Quinton ordered Bruce to Chicago to beard the lion. Meeting the president and attorney, he explained that army contracts followed the letter of the law and appealed to Case to accept government terms. The manufacturer refused.

At this, Bruce arose and delivered an ultimatum.

"I don't care what you think of me," he said. "Either your company signs that contract or you will get no orders from the army. Your country needs your production facilities desperately and before this war is over, the J. I. Case Company will need the support of the country.

"I am not going to waste time in further discussion. I will return to my hotel, and you will have two hours before my train leaves for Washington to make up your mind. I'll return if you ask me to do so but only if he," and he pointed at the lawyer, "has already left for New York."

No one had ever addressed Case in this summary fashion. The president fumed, thought of calling Washington to register a complaint, listened briefly to the attorney's bitter reaction and finally told him to get out. Calling the hotel, he asked Bruce to return. They completed negotiations in forty-five minutes, shook hands, and Case joined the army.

His ability to unravel touchy situations projected Bruce into similar predicaments within as well as outside the army structure. Judge Robert Patterson, under secretary of war, borrowed him to help spread millions of dollars worth of contracts equitably in the face of intense pressure from senators and congressmen who wanted some of the vast sums allotted to their states and districts. While engaged in this work, politically sensitive even in a country on war footing, Bruce came up against an acute shortage of TNT, an explosive packed in bombs and shells, which threatened to cut shipments to Britain and limit munitions stocks building up in the United States. There was a TNT plant owned by the Mexican government that stood idle. Two attempts to persuade Mexico to put it in production failed miserably.

Edwin N. Clark of the secretary's staff told Bruce, "We

must have that plant but I don't know what more we can do." Bruce suggested another try, in secrecy since Mexico was a hotbed of German spies. Clark approved the idea.

Bruce informed Ginny that he would be out of touch for some time. She had long since understood why he talked little about his activities at home. He obtained the help of a TNT production expert, Dr. C. G. Storm of Picatinny Arsenal, and, together with Clark, they left by train for Brownsville, Texas, where the cars were switched to a Mexican railroad. They wore civilian attire and masqueraded as American businessmen looking for investment opportunities in neutral Mexico.

When they reached Mexico City, Bruce enlisted the help of a military attache in the American embassy who arranged for him to speak privately with the Mexican chief of staff.

Speaking Spanish behind closed doors, Bruce told the Mexican leader of his mission. "I am speaking for General Marshall as one officer to another officer," he went on. "My country urgently requires TNT for the duration of the war and we are prepared to negotiate terms favorable to both sides."

"I understand your need," his host answered. "You will return to your hotel and await further contact."

Next day an unmarked sedan picked up the three men and drove to the ministry of war where they were courteously greeted and escorted to a closely guarded conference room.

"Major Medaris, you speak our language fluently," the officer said with whom they would deal. Bruce explained his tour in Panama and with the Tacna-Arica Commission. They chatted easily. Clark understood very little Spanish, Dr. Storm none at all.

"It is possible," the officer said, "that the plant could be restored to production. However, we have no toluene," naming the basic chemical required.

"We have ample supplies," Bruce answered, "and I will commit rail tank cars to deliver the toluene at whatever times and in whatever quantities are required."

They agreed that Mexico would contribute sixty percent of the operating costs while the United States would pay forty percent. The host explained that for a given quantity of toluene, Mexico would produce so many pounds of TNT. Bruce jotted down the figures, showed them to Storm and explained their meaning. Storm loudly protested that they were being asked for twenty-five percent more toluene than required. Bruce quieted the engineer and initialed the agreement.

The Mexican officer smilingly observed, "Your friend understands TNT. He does not understand diplomacy." The two men laughed. The chief of staff approved the pact and the U. S. gained a source of supply that operated for the remainder of the war. In return, Mexico gained sufficient toluene to produce TNT for its own needs.

Rumania joined the Axis, assuring Hitler oil for his mechanized armies, air squadrons and submarines. Japan pressed its expansion in the Far East. President Roosevelt called up the national guard to strengthen the army. General George Marshall persuaded Congress to increase the army manpower from 191,000 to 280,000 men. Plants across the land shut down civilian production to build tanks, aircraft, trucks, ships, guns and ammunition. Britain's dogged resistance under fierce aerial attacks bought two years' time during which America mobilized the industrial power that would eventually overwhelm the Axis partners.

A letter from Marilyn, attending business school in San Francisco, upset Bruce. He wrote his daughter telling her that he felt living in the city was not a safe place for a young woman, and invited her to come to Washington and stay with them. Ginny followed up with a warm letter. Welcoming the chance to know her father better, Marilyn sent off a letter to her mother who was living in Mexico. Gwendolyn was deeply offended, but Ginny was pleased and accepted her at once as a member of the family. Marta and little Bruce enjoyed her companionship.

A young man Marilyn knew in high school turned up at Quantico, the Marine Corps training base not far from Washington. He got in touch with his schoolmate and she asked him to visit the family.

"Better talk to dad," Ginny advised. "He's all army, and has firm ideas about enlisted men."

"I don't like to disappoint you," Bruce told her, "but you must remember that this is an officer's home and officer families do not fraternize with enlisted men."

Mindful that the father lecturing her sternly had once been a marine private, Marilyn kept silent. A Medaris, she would have her way, lecture or no lecture. She arranged to meet her friend several times away from home. Some of Bruce's fellow officers came to her defense, arguing that draftees entering the armed services were a cut above the career enlisted men of the old days. He relented and told Babe to bring the marine home where he regaled the visitor with stories of his own stint with the corps.

Bruce and Ginny took Marilyn to the officer's club for dinner frequently and introduced many lieutenants who heard them affectionally call her "Babe." The name stuck, and sometimes, as she walked about in Washington, young officers greeted her with "Hi, Babe!" leaving Marilyn to guess if it was someone she had met at the club or just a particularly bold flirt. Her wavy brown hair and slender figure attracted notice. But Marilyn didn't mind. She handled the encounters deftly and saw no reason to ask for daddy's help. In time her independence and youthful exuberance caused some tension in the family. Bruce talked over the situation with Marilyn and they agreed that she would take a room nearby. She worked in Washington and visited the family occasionally, until Bruce left for overseas duty. Then she returned to Columbus to enroll in Ohio State University.

Back at the office Bruce was getting even busier. Production of war materiel assumed flood proportions and created immediate need for some kind of traffic control. Bruce organized an ammunition regulating station which scheduled shipments across the nation. Traffic experts determined the routes and tracked freight cars from source to destination. In this mad scramble the delay of vitally needed parts on rail sidings could not be tolerated. A teletype network connected the Washington control office with parts manufacturers and loading plants. The system functioned effectively throughout the war.

More subtle problems required attention. The army received bids for a large metal parts order of a critically important fuze, the device that causes a bomb or shell to explode. To evaluate proposals Bruce obtained prices from earlier buys. Three firms wanted the contract, unaware that the quantities involved were so huge that all would eventually share the work. Two bids were comparable, the third was much lower. Bruce calculated that the low bidder must default in time or find himself bankrupt. He struggled alone with the moral question, knowing that he dared not reveal competitive bids, and concluded that the military need was paramount regardless of economics. He phoned an executive of the low bid company, and asked if he was familiar with the proposal.

"Yes, I am, Major Medaris," he answered. "As a matter of fact, I worked up some of the costs in developing our bid but haven't seen the price we quoted. Is there something wrong with our quotation?"

"I can't say that," Bruce replied. He did not have to say more. The man examined the documents and found the error. Two anxious wires followed shortly requesting permission to withdraw the bid and submit another. The permission was granted and the contracts placed at prices that protected both the government and producers. Bruce knew that he bent the rules. When questioned, he told a superior: "We needed production, not a bankrupt contractor. Money wouldn't make up for fuzes we didn't possess."

Hitler struck at Russia in June 1941, tearing up a nonaggression treaty, planning to outdo Napoleon. The Japanese destroyed the U.S. Pacific fleet at Pearl Harbor on December 7. The United States declared war next day. Now time for preparation was over, the nation was committed to wage two wars. Production goals were doubled and redoubled to supply American and Allied forces.

Ginny guessed what was really behind his uneasiness as Bruce drove himself and his associates to keep pace with the relentless demands. He hungered for a place with troops. The army turned down his repeated requests for overseas duty, unwilling to lose his aggressiveness in the Washington melee. Bruce turned to an old friend, Brigadier General Henry Aurand, who organized international missions. One was operating in Egypt where Britain's Eighth Army resisted German advances in North Africa. The American unit channeled British supply requirements to the States and followed up on delivery to combat elements. Aurand was putting together another mission for Iran. Bruce seized the opportunity, although Iran was far removed from the battlefields. He was promoted to lieutenant colonel and placed in charge of the ordnance section.

Ginny intended to remain in Washington for a while and return to her father's home in Cincinnati where the two children would be well cared for. After a brief stay in Aberdeen, Maryland, for a refresher course in tanks, Bruce left for New York City where a tri-motor amphibian plane departed for Iran. Four hundred miles over the Atlantic an engine failed and the pilot turned back, landing the plane safely in New York. Frustrated by this delay he called Aurand for instructions. Then he learned that his orders had been changed since there were enough Americans in Iran. He would return to Washington for another billet. A plaintive cable came from an officer-friend awaiting him overseas, "Have villa and Scotch, where are you?"

Had he completed the trip Bruce would have spent the remainder of the war safely removed from fighting in Africa and Europe. Thinking of the mishap that delayed his arrival in France as a young Marine, which may have spared his life, he reassured himself that a kindly fate intervened again to keep him out of Iran.

Orders arrived for the kind of assignment he wanted. Bruce became commander of an ordnance battalion in II Corps, a large combat organization training in Florida's sparsely settled panhandle country for service in North Africa. His battalion consisted of six companies which provided ammunition and maintained weapons and vehicles. He celebrated his fortieth birthday in May, 1942, as he took over his first field command in fifteen years, accepting congratulations from fellow officers including Colonel Urban Niblo, the corps ordnance officer.

Scouring Jacksonville, the nearest city, which swarmed with navy personnel assigned to a large base, he located a drab, weather-beaten house on a dirt street and rented it for an exorbitant price. Ginny moved down with the children.

"I'll be here until July," Bruce told her. "The corps will go to North Carolina then for maneuvers en route to an overseas destination. I know this house is pretty bad, but there wasn't another to be found. At least we'll have some time together before I leave."

Ginny cleaned up the place, hung blackout curtains since enemy submarines prowled off Florida's coast and there were fears of invasion, and ran splinters into fingers unaccustomed to rough floors. Bruce was surprised and delighted by the improvement she had made in the place. But there was no escape from the muggy blanket of hot air that filled the house in that pre-air conditioning era. The roof leaked and rats scampered about, ignoring traps and poison bait. And Ginny worried when the children played outdoors, fearful of poisonous snakes that might coil under hedges.

They saw Bruce only on weekends. Ginny drove him to a bus stop at 5 A.M. Mondays for the return trip to Camp Blanding. His days were spent in exhaustive training and the endless battle to get supplies and equipment which the battalion must have to support field maneuvers.

One weekend he came home and found Ginny in a state of hysteria. "A huge spider hung over Marta's bed this morning," she cried. "I just can't take any more of this. It isn't fair to me or the children."

"I'm sorry we couldn't do better," Bruce replied. He agreed that his family would be better situated in Cincinnati if Ginny's father could take them. Mrs. Smith had died the previous summer and he was caring for her mother, another aged relative, Ginny's sister who worked and her small child. Clifford Smith actually needed Ginny badly. So it was settled. Bruce helped pack the car and Ginny drove to Ohio with Marta and little Bruce.

Months passed and still Bruce stayed on at Blanding, training a seemingly endless stream of ordnance troops for overseas. Lonely, desperately needing companionship, he struck up acquaintance with a young widow introduced by an officer's wife who hosted parties for unattached women and the plentiful supply of officers cut loose from family responsibilities searching for excitement and pleasure. The attachment grew into a love affair. Bruce found her Jacksonville apartment a welcome change from life in camp. His letters to Ginny became colder and less frequent and she turned to her father for advice.

"Maybe I shouldn't have left Bruce there alone," she said. "I'm worried about him."

"Now, Ginny, you mustn't let your imagination carry you away," Smith countered. "Bruce must be terribly busy and I think that is the explanation."

Hepatitis broke out in virulent form and spread like wildfire through II Corps. The epidemic resulted from a defective supply of yellow fever serum with which all the troops were inoculated. The hospitals were filled with the sick. There were some deaths, others suffered permanent liver damage. The disease infected Bruce who found that patients in the hospital were placed on a low-fat, low-salt diet and that was the sum of medical treatment. If they became very ill, massive vitamin injections and intravenous feedings were ordered. Otherwise they were expected to recover, just when, however, seemed no one's concern. After two days of this regimen, Bruce stormed into the commandant's office and demanded proper medical treatment.

"I cannot and will not do what you are asking for all of these people," the commandant declared.

"Whether you do it for all is on your conscience," Bruce retorted, slamming a clenched fist on the desk, "but you are not going to ruin my life. Either you treat me immediately or you will answer to the corps commander, congress, the inspector general and anyone else I can bring into this mess!"

He got the treatment. In ten days he rejoined his battalion on maneuvers in North Carolina.

The hepatitis had interrupted his love affair and perhaps

caused him to do some thinking. Then Ginny sent a letter which gave Bruce more reason to question his recent behavior. Assuring him the children were doing fine, Ginny continued:

"I have done a lot of soul-searching in an effort to understand why you seem to be growing away from us. Perhaps you think it was selfish of me to leave Florida. I should have stayed and would gladly return if you are going to be there longer and want us with you. There have been times when you seemed so caught up with your work that I thought you didn't need me. That was very wrong. As your wife, I ought to share your problems under all circumstances. So if you can forgive my running off, I'll do my best to make amends and return to you. You know how much I love you and I can only say that our separation has been very hard for me to accept."

Guilt-ridden, Bruce pocketed the letter and delayed his reply.

General Dwight D. Eisenhower opened a front in North Africa in early November, 1942, by placing American and British forces at Casablanca, Oran and Algiers. He wanted to squeeze the German and Italian armies from the west while the British attacked Field Marshal Erwin Rommel's Afrika Korps from the east. II Corps ordered his battalion to Africa but to Bruce's disgust, the orders did not mention him or his headquarters unit. After frantic phone calls he received a wire telling him to report alone to Fort Dix, New Jersey, where he would command the 42nd Ordnance Battalion bound for North Africa.

He called Ginny the day before Thanksgiving. "If you want to see me before I leave, you will have to come to Florida immediately."

"Of course I want to come," Ginny replied, "but tomorrow

is a holiday, Bruce, and I just don't know about reservations. Can I come later?"

"No," he replied. "It must be now or not at all."

Clifford Smith heard Ginny's frantic plea and managed to wangle a reservation on a plane out of Cincinnati later that day which would carry her to Atlanta, Georgia. From there on Ginny must manage by herself. He drove her to the airport just in time to catch the plane only to learn that it was already filled. Ginny begged for a seat. The pilot walked into the terminal and asked her how much she weighed. Then he said the happy words, "O.K., come on with me.'"

She took the last seat beside a man who struck up a conversation and listened attentively while Ginny explained that she must get to Jacksonville to see Bruce before he went overseas.

"Settle back and rest," he said. "I'll help you."

When they reached Atlanta, the pair ran to a taxicab and rode downtown to the railroad station. The ticket window was closed, but her acquaintance discovered the southbound train had not departed. They rushed downstairs and climbed aboard, finding the cars filled to overflowing with troops, some sitting on baggage in the aisles.

Frightened, feeling she could not possibly reach Florida in time, Ginny waited while the stranger hunted down a conductor who located a lower berth for her. She remembered that she hadn't eaten since leaving Cincinnati. The conductor arranged to drop off a telegram which would tell Bruce that she planned to stay in a Jacksonville hotel. Ginny checked into the only available room next morning and waited. Bruce called and instructed her where to board a bus for Camp Blanding to spend Thanksgiving Day.

Seemingly distant and reserved, Bruce met her at the camp. Next day they left by train for Washington, D.C., where he had to leave messages, and continued on to New

Brunswick, New Jersey. They found a room in a third rate hotel filled with newly married brides, sobbing and crying as they said goodbye to husbands bound for Camp Kilmer, the port of embarkation, or Fort Dix for final training.

"I've got to report to camp," Bruce stated curtly. "If you want to stay on, wait here for me. I may get back but on the other hand, they may detain me. If you want to leave, I'll understand."

"Bruce, what is the matter?" she frantically asked. "Why are you treating me like a stranger? It's hard enough for me to think you may be leaving and that I might never see you again."

"I've got to think about my battalion," he muttered, ashamed to tell his wife the truth about his guilt. "It would be better, I guess, if you got back to the children."

Sorrowfully, torn apart by unnamed fears, she decided to return to Washington to spend a few days with friends, trying to regain her composure before going home to Ohio. For a fleeting, terror-sticken moment, she thought of hurling herself under the wheels of the train. The hurt had become almost more than she could bear. But something restrained her. After a brief stay in Washington she took a night train to Cincinnati, surviving the lonely ordeal, filled with doubts about her husband and their marriage. Clifford Smith received a short but kindly note from Bruce asking him to look after his family.

Trying to erase this unpleasant memory, Bruce threw himself into the task of preparing his battalion for embarkation. He begged and persuaded officers at nearby Raritan Arsenal to release needed supplies. He formed classes for officers and enlisted men, teaching them fundamentals they must know to survive in combat. By dint of an all-out effort he whipped the unit into shape to await embarkation in December, 1942.

Facing uncertain destiny, Bruce experienced the disquiet which wracked other men leaving families, sweethearts and careers to risk their lives thousands of miles from home in strange lands. He looked forward to the test of battle, but he also squirmed inwardly at his cruel treatment of Ginny. Before she arrived in Jacksonville, Bruce had made a clean break of his illicit relationship, so that was behind him.

To assuage his troubled conscience, he wrote a farewell letter to his wife:

> Dear Ginny:
>
> We are about to leave. You will probably learn of our destination in the newspapers after we arrive. As we both know, I cannot tell if or when we will return.
>
> I am not happy about our last hours together. Many thoughts were running through my mind which I could not bring myself to discuss and there is no reason to burden you with them. I hope that you and the children will be happy with your father. It is a relief to me that you have him to sustain you.
>
> Recognizing the uncertainties which lie ahead, I want you to try to make a new life without me. You stood up through good times and bad and for that I am truly grateful. But you deserve better and that is why I'm asking you to put me out of your mind. You may find someone who will love you and the children and give you the happiness I failed to provide.

Alarmed by Ginny's despair, Clifford Smith took her to their minister who tried reason and prayer with little success. She approached total collapse and threatened to kill herself. Unable to walk, she consented to see a psychiatrist at her father's urging. The visit started her on the road to health.

"You will drive to my office tomorrow," the physician said.

"I'm not sure that I can make it," she sobbed. "I don't seem to have control of my arms and legs."

"You will try," he ordered.

Somehow she managed the trip. Thereafter she saw the psychiatrist daily for a while, then less frequently. She refused hospital treatment because of the children. Six long and trying months passed before she recovered completely.

Meanwhile at the port, Colonel Medaris received two assignments as the troop ship, *Dorothea L. Dix*, began the hazardous Atlantic crossing. He commanded the ordnance battalion and, as senior army officer, also commanded military police, signal, chemical, medical, anti-aircraft, postal, air corps, and camouflage units and a railway operations battalion. The ship's master, an old-line navy officer, bluntly informed Bruce that he would tolerate no nonsense from the army. His last voyage with troops had been a nightmare.

Bruce talked over the situation with other officers and published ship's orders. Military police would maintain order. Troops must keep messes and personal areas clean. Anti-aircraft gunners stood watch with sailors on the ship's armament. The area occupied by a detachment of army nurses was posted "off limits." Any man found inside the signs would be court-martialed. In a few days the ship's company settled down to a relatively peaceful voyage. Bruce ate two meals daily with the captain but reserved the third for army mess.

As the Sunday before Christmas approached he read army regulations and learned that when no chaplain is available, a troop commander must conduct religious services. So he announced there would be an open-air service on deck. Now his mother's training and those childhood days in Methodist school came in handy. He stood on an upper deck as the battle-dressed soldiers awaited his words.

Motioning with his hands, he led them in singing the familiar hymn, "Abide With Me." Falteringly, at first, the chorus of voices swelled into harmony as the men gave vent to their emotion. They recited the Lord's Prayer in unison. Then he spoke briefly, recalling their common obligation to God and country and urging them to have faith as they came to grips with a powerful enemy.

"With God's help," he continued, "this may be the only time in our lives when we are separated from loved ones because of circumstances beyond our understanding. It will be a strange Christmas for most of us. We must remember the meaning of the birth of the Prince of Peace even as we prepare to meet the unknown. He came into the world to save mankind. We are part of a great army whose mission it is to ensure that the peace for which He gave his life can be restored, and that all men, rich or poor, weak or strong, can live together without fear and enjoy the riches of creation. Let us pray for courage, strength and the help of Almighty God in the days ahead."

As he finished, the strains of "Onward Christian Soldiers" came from the little organ carried to the deck. This time there was no faltering and the men roared the mighty hymn. It was a memorable experience for Bruce, who felt a deep upwelling of emotion. He had touched something he could not comprehend but he treasured the moment.

Nearing Gibraltar, the ship convoy encountered a violent storm. *Dix* was a cargo ship converted to transport service by the installation of metal bunks, three tiers deep, in the holds. Angry waves tossed the ship about like a cork and the relentless pounding tore loose the bunks in a forward hold. Standing beside the captain in the wheelhouse, Bruce heard reports from the lower deck.

"We have an emergency in hold number one. Men were

thrown to the plates, bunks fell on top of them. We have injuries and need assistance!"

"Seasickness in hold number two. Some injuries, much vomiting."

Quickly Bruce barked orders, sending troops who escaped injury to extricate victims, placing the nurses in sick bays and wardrooms converted to rescue stations. Military police stood guard at strategic locations to restore order and avert panic. There was no fatality.

The captain and Bruce agreed to forego deck services on Christmas Day since the convoy had entered submarine-infested waters where they might also come under attack by German bombing planes. Instead the army officers distributed a message to the troops, praying that "our efforts may be directed to make it possible to celebrate the birth of Christ with our families in a free country." Torpedoes sank one ship and damaged another as they neared the port of Oran. *Dix* narrowly escaped a torpedo that ran behind the ship's stern.

When the ship docked, Bruce went ashore, picking his way through rumbling port traffic, tanks, trucks and jeeps mingled with towed artillery, dodging small mountains of crates. He found an army telephone. Lacking any information on the location of II Corps, the outfit with which he trained in Florida, he remembered the ordnance code. Picking up the instrument, he asked the operator for "speedy eight." Within seconds he heard the voice of Colonel Niblo, the corps ordnance officer.

"It's Bruce, Urban," he yelled over the traffic noise. "I've just arrived. Where do you want me to report?"

Niblo told him to wait at the ship. A jeep picked up Bruce and he was soon shaking hands with Niblo. The colonel filled him in on the situation in North Africa, using a wall map to explain the location of II Corps in southern Tunisia with

French and British forces arrayed along a line extending north to the coast. Some ordnance units were with the corps, some at theater headquarters in Algiers, more in the ports of debarkation.

"There's a lot of work ahead, Bruce," Niblo said, "and I'm damned glad you are on hand. You'll find the theater crowd uncooperative, sometimes I wonder if they know there is a war going on. You'll have to help fight to get the stuff the troops need."

Bruce returned to the *Dix* with orders assigning him as Niblo's assistant and directed the unloading of his battalion and its equipment. Now he could feel the ominous excitement that war engenders.

# 6

# A TIME TO FIGHT

Donning the heavy steel helmet he would wear for many months—and often use as a wash basin—Lieutenant Colonel Medaris rode a jeep seven hundred miles eastward from Oran to Constantine across the Atlas Mountains and vast stretches of desert. Romantic notions about steaming Africa vanished quickly in the near zero cold. At way stations troops warmed themselves by burning gasoline in makeshift heaters fashioned out of fuel cans.

Bruce met commanders of three ordnance battalions serving II Corps at his destination. As assistant to Colonel Niblo, he took charge of preparations in Niblo's absence. He relocated headquarters to Tebessa, the main supply base, an ancient walled city served by a narrow-gauge railway that carried one-third of the daily tonnage required by American forces and their French allies. A fleet of six thousand trucks hauled most of the food, fuel, weapons and ammunition.

Engines and parts to keep the huge fleet moving were in short supply. Big guns stood idle for lack of repair parts.

Niblo left Tebessa on Valentine's Day for Algiers, to become ordnance officer of Fifth Army, preparing for the subsequent invasion of Italy, and recommended Bruce as his successor. Thus he became the corps' ordnance officer while waging a running battle with rear headquarters in a desperate effort to speed up supplies.

Bruce marveled at the industry of his mechanics, men from a dozen states and as many backgrounds who fought against shortages, penetrating dust storms and fatigue as they labored around the clock. They cannibalized wrecked vehicles to restore other trucks to service. New parts were hammered out in mobile machine shops. They produced one useful gun from two unserviceable ones. German dive bombers frequently interrupted work in daylight raids and drove the men into slit trenches to escape exploding bombs. Small parties left camp each morning to contact the combat troops at the front to find out what they needed.

Ordnance manuals supposedly provided instructions for all situations. They were singularly inept and hopelessly unreal in this harsh environment where battle lines moved back and forth. "Forget the books!" Bruce told his officers. "We've got to improvise and invent to meet the situation." That policy won favor among the fighting divisions and disfavor with old hats ensconced in Algiers.

American troops sustained a crushing defeat at Kasserine Pass in their first major encounter when the Nazis attacked in late January. With heavy losses of men and equipment, the Americans pulled back, pursued by the enemy. Only the arrival of British and U.S. reinforcements a week later halted the Germans and saved the supply base. News of this debacle shocked the home front.

Bruce renewed his demands for large quantities of tanks

and guns to replace losses. An entire armored division had been virtually wiped out. His estimates were promptly challenged until a visiting officer confirmed their accuracy. Meanwhile General Eisenhower appealed to Washington for more equipment. Eisenhower came to the front and ordered General George S. Patton, then in Morocco, to take over II Corps. Two more U.S. divisions were brought on line.

Patton lost no time in whipping the corps into a fighting machine. In a typical gesture he ordered troops to wear neckties and steel helmets at all times. Asked if this applied to mechanics repairing tanks, Patton roared, "Hell, yes, they're soldiers, too!" Indeed they were. Bruce lost men in combat and took on a commander's most difficult task as he wrote letters to families in the States concerning the deaths of husbands and sons.

General Patton directed his staff to plan an assault on the German flank. Poring over battle maps and equipment reports as he developed the ordnance plan, Bruce was interrupted by a subordinate who told him a strange general was in the shop area. He went out to salute the visitor.

Extending his hand, the stranger said quietly, "I'm Omar Bradley. Tell me about your situation."

They walked about the area, smelling of oil, gasoline and hot metal, while Bruce explained his operations and answered friendly but searching questions. Bradley examined tanks and guns under repair, poked his head into vans, and greeted mechanics cheerfully. There was no ostentation about the man, he wore his stars easily. But he wanted answers and got them: how long were tanks deadlined; how much ammunition was expended daily; how much did consumption increase in the heat of battle; how efficient was the supply line from the port; did Bruce have enough people; how did he maintain contact with the artillery, infantry and armored divisions?

"How long have you been with II Corps?" Bradley asked as they walked towards the command post. Bruce told him of training with the corps in Florida and, encouraged by the general's keen interest, something of his background in Panama, the long break in active service, and his part in the marshalling of industrial production.

"I've heard much about the German 88 millimeter gun, Medaris," Bradley said. "How good is it?"

"It's a fine weapon in this terrain," Bruce explained. "It develops high muzzle velocity and delivers its round with accuracy over a flat trajectory. It is a deadly gun in desert fighting. But our 75s and 105s are more reliable and stand up better. The real question is whether you want a gun suited to one kind of terrain or the greater flexibility of ours."

Bradley's dour face, which belied his warm heart, broke into a grin. "I belong to the school which relies upon specialists like you who can give a commander expert advice on the weapons suited to a plan of battle. That's your job."

His statement delighted Bruce. This was the kind of commander he could respect. Their meeting was to have great meaning for his future. He found a man who had complete faith in his judgment.

It was during this period that he received Ginny's response to that sullen, despondent letter he sent her from Camp Kilmer. He tore open the envelope with apprehension and read it slowly:

> Dear Bruce:
>
> This letter has been long delayed. I am slowly recovering from a breakdown with the loving care of dad and my sister. When we parted, I felt that my world had collapsed and tried to throw myself in front of a train but something, maybe the Almighty, stopped me in time. I

managed to reach home with the help of people I didn't even know.

That cruel letter you sent before you left hurt still more and the result was that dad called in the doctor. Thank God for his help—the children only knew that I was sick.

It's time that I told you some things which I've kept within me too long. Our marriage has not been as happy as might have been since you put your career ahead of everything, including our family and my love. You seem to believe that you can live two lives, one with us when you choose to, the other is one you have never allowed me to enter. We can't be husband and wife on a sometime basis when your schedule permits and your mind isn't full of other things. I admire your dedication but you must share your devotion with us. That has not been your way.

I believe that your ego dictates your behavior not only in the army but also in our home. There have been many times when I had to fight from screaming when you asserted your authority as husband and father with no thought to the effect upon me, Marta and little Bruce.

As to finding that "new life" you suggested, I will never consider such a solution. I want you where you belong but only if you treat us with the love and respect that we have for you. I pray that God will help you find the answer and that He will protect you and bring you home safely.

Stung by her honest assessment, heartsick over the pain he caused, Bruce realized that Ginny had torn away the shell of self-delusion and bared his weakness. He composed the reply carefully, admitting his faults, promising to make amends and asking forgiveness. They would start anew. From then on her letters helped sustain him through campaigns in Africa, Sicily and Europe. He treasured her letter, re-reading it many times, grateful for her courage. "She helped make a man of me," he told intimate friends.

General Patton launched II Corps on a drive to El Guettar, threatening the Axis battle line arrayed in front of the British Eighth Army in the south. Bruce instructed his officers to push supplies as close to the front as possible. "We must not allow any soldier to want for gun or ammunition," he directed.

The attack succeeded and Rommel left Africa, sick and disillusioned. After the battle, Bruce dispatched teams to collect repairable equipment and destroy the remainder. Tons of ammunition were recovered.

When he reported the results of this clean-up effort, Patton's staff told him to search for more. The teams combed the battlefield another week. A second report was also rejected. Bruce now understood that General Patton wanted an inflated list of captured enemy materiel for the American people to counter earlier U.S. losses.

Refusing to change the figures, Medaris told Patton's assistant "This is as complete as the facts justify. I cannot and will not misrepresent." He left, expecting to be ordered home. Instead he earned Patton's grudging respect in the form of a medal.

Praise of American supply came from another quarter. Rommel concluded that "the Americans are fantastically well equipped and we could learn much from their organization." What that meant to a commander can be understood from General Bradley's summary: "In contrast to the enemy who was forced to hoard supplies and equipment, I could spend ours freely to take any objective that merited the cost. We spent tanks, trucks, guns and ammunition to save lives."

Eisenhower recalled Patton to prepare the U. S. Seventh Army for the invasion of Sicily. Bradley succeeded him as II Corps commander. He asked Bruce to continue on his staff, expressing confidence in his performance. That trust would soon be tested.

Both sides prepared for the inevitable showdown as Afrika Korps linked up with the Fifth Panzer Army. German aircraft ferried replacements from Sicily to Tunis. Bruce added a new unit for battlefield recovery of equipment. A visiting officer told Algiers that "these ordnance soldiers of II Corps are tough and experienced front line troops who survived severe combat." They worked whatever hours were necessary; on one occasion repairing in twenty-four hours an entire battery of 90 millimeter guns shot up by German artillery.

At Bradley's insistence, the high command assigned the Americans a specific objective for the final assault. II Corps would take Bizerte while the British assaulted Tunis. Bradley asked his staff how they would move men and machines 200 miles north, crossing the British line, to strike Bizerte. Plans were agreed upon with the British to allow U.S. combat divisions through their line on a fixed timetable. No such agreement covered the supporting elements. The motorized train of ordnance units was much longer than others including shop vans, depot stocks, tanks and guns awaiting repair.

Bruce told his commander that "I have no schedule. We propose to move without telling the British. If we tell them it means delay, possibly the loss of some supplies, and I cannot promise to be in position on time."

"How can you move?" Bradley persisted.

"Sir, you will have to trust me," Bruce answered. "If you tell me when you want my units in position, we'll be there."

Bradley consented. Military records do not mention the

movement since the scheme was never reduced to writing. Colonel Medaris told battalion and company officers his plan:

"Crossing the British supply line is worse than dealing with two committees of Congress. So we will not tell them. I will give each of you the hour when you must leave this area and the day and hour when you must be in the north." He pointed out locations and secondary routes that they might travel. They could not follow the main roads reserved for the combat divisions.

Some of the men went forward to observe supply traffic moving along the British line. Each company broke down its motor train into pieces about a hundred yards long, ignoring convoy regulations in the process, and began the two hundred-mile trek in driving rain. They approached the British zone stealthily, stopping short of being seen. When a gap appeared in the stream of British traffic, one unit would burst out, cross the line and disappear northward. They were in assigned positions on time and repaired damaged artillery during halts. II Corps moved 30,000 vehicles and 110,000 men and equipment without interfering with the British. One ordnance battalion stayed behind to clear an area of 3,000 square miles and rounded up 20,500 tons of ammunition and supplies.

When the joint British-American offensive began on April 23, ordnance units moved 9,000 tons of ammunition to forward supply points. Bizerte fell May 6 when the vaunted Afrika Korps surrendered unconditionally to the Americans whose swift advance cut off Axis supply. The British entered Tunis and the war in North Africa ended.

The British came upon a lone American officer, Captain John Ray, staff ammunition officer for Colonel Medaris, waiting on a street corner and puffing a cigar. Ray had been taken prisoner. Three times he was supposed to have been put aboard a ship carrying captives to Italy but managed to evade his captors within the prison. When he realized surrender was imiment, the German commander turned himself over to Ray who put on a pistol belt, took a cigar and went out to await the British.

The island of Sicily was the next objective for which General Patton organized a task force consisting of I and II Corps supplemented by other units. Men and equipment were ferried across the Mediterranean from Africa for the invasion. Bruce left Tunis when the initial landings occurred and reached the beachhead safely. More ordnance troops arrived for bomb disposal, antiaircraft gun maintenance and to repair a thousand newly developed amphibious vehicles adapted to beach operations. Some of the II Corps staff went ahead with combat teams to locate ammunition supply points and collection sites for materiel. The first units who went ashore disabled Italian coastal guns.

Bruce received news of his promotion to colonel as the Americans advanced northward. Fine lava dust covering narrow roads raised havoc with vehicles, tanks and guns. The telltale cloud enabled enemy gunners to pinpoint the advancing columns. There were other problems. Parts were in short supply, old guns broke down and it became necessary to make new parts in the field to keep equipment operating. Patton's logistics chiefs failed to meet II Corps requirements. Bruce left the First Armored Division at the front to register his protest at Palermo headquarters, expressing his disgust to Colonel Thomas Nixon, the ordnance officer.

"We are in an impossible situation," he asserted, "because someone back here has failed to anticipate our needs. You don't have any place nearer than Palermo to which I can evacuate equipment for major repair. That forces us to drag materiel from one end of the island to the other and I cannot afford the loss of men and time. We're not getting prompt response to requisitions. Where is the stuff? I know damned well it's around here someplace!"

He listened to Nixon's rejoinder. "We're trying to locate the dumps, probably strung out along the beaches," and retorted, "It's a fine thing when headquarters can't find its own supplies."

Piecing together what Nixon told him, Bruce concluded that General Patton had little interest in logistics. Instead his concern was to destroy Germans. Where or how the equipment and supplies reached his units, Patton didn't care. Beach control had been assigned to an engineer brigade totally unfamiliar with ordnance operations. As a result the wrong kinds of ammunition were being sent north to II Corps in the wrong quantities. Ordnance companies on the beaches were not allowed to perform their specialized duties.

As Bruce ran down his list of shortages, Nixon said, "I'll do what I can to help you, but you've got to understand that we have to support other organizations, too."

Bruce left Palermo firmly convinced that ordnance service in the field belonged with corps and divisions who did the fighting and not with rear headquarters.

Following the pattern established in Africa, he pushed his units close behind the artillery and infantry, so close that at times, men working in the shops heard the chatter of small arms fire. The enemy launched short range rockets into the area one night. Bruce looked on unbelievingly when he saw a rocket explode under an officer's bunk, hurling man and blanket into a tree. The victim climbed down unhurt.

Messina fell on August 17. An infantry column from II Corps walked into the city two hours before General Patton arrived in triumph. Italian troops began deserting as the

Americans advanced and the surrenders took on landslide proportions. Many of their German allies escaped to Italy but the Axis had lost 164,000 men including prisoners, the equivalent of ten divisions. The Allies sustained only 16,000 casualties.

As he wrapped up the ordnance effort, Bruce had more suggestions to the command about field service. He recognized the importance of bomb disposal but thought it could be handled better by squads of trained men instead of company-sized units. Similarly, too many troops were assigned to maintain antiaircraft guns. He placed the responsibility for ammunition shortages at the door of the engineers on the beaches, indirectly on General Patton's judgment, and strongly advocated keeping that function in the hands of ordnance personnel. Despite the difficulties, 50,000 tons of ammunition reached Sicily and only 7,500 tons were consumed. The victory came sooner than expected because of the Italian defections.

II Corps headquarters moved into Campo Felice on the north coast of Sicily, most of the officers expecting to join the Fifth Army for the invasion of Italy. Rumors spread that Bradley was going to England to mount the invasion of France. A luncheon was quickly arranged as a farewell tribute. Afterward the general walked down the line, shaking hands with men who served with him in Sicily and Africa. Bruce stood twelfth in line. As Bradley moved along, it was whispered that if he said, "I'll be seeing you," it meant the officer would accompany him to England. If he said, "Thank you for your service," it meant remaining with II Corps and going into Italy.

As he grasped Bruce's hand, Bradley said, "I'll be seeing you, Bruce."

Grateful for Bradley's vote of confidence, Bruce was even happier when he compared notes with the others about what the commander told them. He learned that three of his comrades—the quartet was jokingly called "The Four Musketeers of II Corps"—would also be going to England. They were Colonel Andrew T. McNamara, the quartermaster; Colonel Grant Williams, the signal officer and Colonel William Carter, the corps engineer.

Writing Ginny, Bruce said: "I can't tell you my next assignment but I can say General Bradley has picked me for it. I'm happy that some of the men who served with II Corps in Africa are going along. The chief permitted me to pick four others, I know you will love them dearly as I do when you have the chance to make their acquaintance. Major John Ray, we lost him for a while to the Germans, is my ammunition chief and Major Ralph Atkinson will head up supply. I'm especially pleased that Sergeant Del Sasse stays with me. He is an outstanding soldier and will make a good officer. And my old friend, Sergeant Kintner, my driver since I landed in Oran, will accompany me wherever I go. Give my love to the children, and the family. I miss you all and think of you often. God has carried me safely through two campaigns and I know your prayers will help in the days ahead."

The "Musketeers" enjoyed a brief rest at Taylor Villa in a Tunisian oasis before flying out of Casablanca for the American air base in Prestwick, Scotland. From there they flew in a small plane to East Anglia in a dense fog, stepping out into wet, chilling weather. The drive to Bristol in a command car was too much for Bruce accustomed to the balmier weather of the Mediterranean. He contracted pneumonia and was hospitalized for a week. Then he and McNamara found an apartment in the Mews three blocks from Allied headquarters in London and spent weekends in Bristol with American units.

Eisenhower chose General Bradley to command the U.S. First Army which would spearhead the invasion of France.

As Bradley's ordnance officer, Bruce became responsible for twenty thousand troops formed in four groups or regiments, sixteen battalions and ninety-six companies. His urgent task was to make sure the four hundred officers directing ordnance units in the field could measure up to their assignments. He found that no effort had been made in the States to match officers with specific jobs. Few had any combat experience. As he began screening personnel files to weed out the obviously unfit, the question of command authority came into sharp focus.

First Army headquarters arrived from Governors Island in New York harbor fully expecting to take over. Colonel Joseph O'Hare, the personnel chief, insisted that he would select officers for the technical sections including ordnance. Bruce refused to accept this arrangement. The two men wound up before General Bradley to plead their cases. When they finished, Bradley told O'Hare that he had total confidence in Medaris as a result of operations in Africa and Sicily; therefore Bruce would select his own officers.

The next step was to find a man who could assist in the objective screening process. He found Major E. F. Trevor, who had no ordnance connections, and charged him with the sensitive assignment. Twenty of the four hundred nominees were rejected, there were many transfers, but when it was over, Bruce believed they had found the right men and put them in the right jobs.

He selected Colonel Nelson Lynde as his deputy, putting him in charge of training troops. Colonel F. A. Hansen became his executive officer. Both were regular army officers while Bruce now held a reserve commission. He posted other reservists to key positions since the career army could not possibly furnish enough officers for the massive forces. Bruce wanted to give the few regulars all possible experience to assure competent leadership in the post-war ordnance corps. Lynde and Hansen later became major generals.

First Army commanded as many as five corps and sixteen divisions. The kinds and quantities of guns, ammunition and equipment these legions would require in Europe had to be spelled out. Adhering to the policy laid down in earlier campaigns, Bruce taught his men that their first task was to keep the combat units adequately supplied under all conditions. He published a four-page procedure telling battalions and companies what was expected of them and leaving to them the manner of doing. One group would handle ammunition and move it from rear depots to the front. Another looked after non-divisional elements such as armored cavalry brigades. A third operated depots supplying weapons and parts to infantry and armor divisions while the fourth group performed heavy maintenance and moved up as the front advanced. As the planners struggled with the problem of how to get more tons aboard than the allotted shipping would carry, Bruce joined with the antiaircraft officer, Colonel Charles G. Patterson, in some unusual horse trading, conducted with Bradley's tacit approval. Bruce wanted more trucks but had tracked vehicles to spare. Patterson's battalions were equipped with forty millimeter machine guns towed by trucks. Ordnance crews transferred the guns to tracked vehicles and Patterson released his trucks to Bruce. These were filled with ammunition, food and fuel for the invasion force.

Later, when Lieutenant General Courtney Hodges took over First Army as Bradley moved up, the quintet of Colonels Patterson, Medaris, McNamara, Williams and Carter became known as "Hodges' Forty Thieves" in tribute to their deftness in acquiring equipment and supplies without regard to ownership.

By May 1, 1945, the high command was satisfied that men

and materiel were ready. Bruce spent the next five weeks visiting ordnance units dispersed throughout southwest England, briefing officers on the invasion plan and assessing their state of readiness. Ginny's frequent letters caught up with him from time to time, telling him of the children's progress. For a while at least, her bright, chatty comments took his mind off the grim business which filled long hours. He tried to be as cheerful as possible in his replies, describing the English towns and his adventures in the London fogs. He could not speak of the imminent assault against Normandy. So the time he had for letter writing was an opportunity for reflection. Bruce was growing up on the inside and, in the process, some deep-seated and long-hidden personal needs were beginning to make themselves felt in his life.

Walking aimlessly through the streets of Bristol one dark Sunday morning, alone with his thoughts, wondering as were thousands of other men how he would measure up in the titanic struggle, he passed the stately cathedral of the Church of England and heard music from within. He pushed open a heavy oak door, entered and sat down in a rear pew. He stared in wonder at magnificent stained-glass windows and the vaulted ceiling of the nave. Robed priests celebrated the eucharistic service before the high altar, aglow with glittering candles. A life-sized image of the crucified Christ looked down upon the congregation.

As the celebrant reenacted the Last Supper, saying "He took bread and when He had given thanks, He brake it and gave it to them saying 'This is my body which is given for you' " Bruce felt a surge of emotion. He walked to the communion rail with others to receive bread and wine. He sensed that he belonged there although he belonged to no church. For the first time since boyhood he felt the pain he had so long suppressed. He felt separated and alone—

unloved. After so many years of being strong and independent in the absence of his father, the weak little boy, who was hurt deeply by that absence, began to make himself felt. Bruce didn't understand it; he only knew that he was keenly hungry for what was happening in that church. There was almost a trace of joy as he joined the congregation to pray "Our Father, who art in heaven. . . ."

After the benediction, Bruce walked out onto the street in pensive silence. The fatherless child had felt real solace for the first time.

# 7

# THE TIDE TURNS

An armada of more than three thousand ships carried 176,000 Allied fighting men to the Cotentin shore of France June 6, 1944. Overhead seven thousand planes swept aside German fighters. The Allies had begun to bring the devastation of war home to Germany.

Colonel Medaris and ordnance planners computed the tonnage required to support 55,000 U.S. assault troops whose task was to smash coastal defenses and secure a foothold. During the planning phase, Bruce came to rely heavily upon guidance from the God he had somehow met at Bristol Cathedral, discovering that it came if he asked for it. That realization changed his life thereafter.

He landed on Omaha Beach strewn with wrecked vehicles the day after the initial assault. About five weeks later, as First Army moved inland, fire broke out in a large ammunition storage area on the beach, threatening the loss of vital supplies. The holocaust was touched off when a truckload of captured German ammunition exploded, hurling flaming fragments into piles of land mines.

Speeding to the scene with Colonel Arthur Luce, Bruce found the officer in charge had fled, leaving his men to fend for themselves. It was a frightening spectacle. As explosions continued, metal fragments tore through the air and flames soared as troops watched from a safe distance. Knowing that First Army must have the ammunition stores and that the blazing inferno would attract German bombers when night fell, Bruce immediately assumed command.

"We can't use water," he yelled to men dragging hose, "it will only spread the fire!"

He called them around his jeep and organized fire fighting teams. They found shovels as others brought up bulldozers.

"We've got to cover those stocks with dirt as fast as possible," Bruce directed. He climbed upon a dozer and steered the awkward machine towards the fire, followed by other dozers and shovel crews. Colonel Luce was wounded by shrapnel.

"Get him out fast!" Bruce ordered a jeep driver. "There's an aid station over the hill."

More soldiers returned, their courage restored by the sight of officers and men battling the flames. Bruce put them to work hauling tons of sand. The fire was under control by eleven P.M. Then he sought out the officer who had abandoned his post.

"I'm relieving you of command," he told him. "You will report to headquarters immediately." Next day the offender left for England and home.

If cowardice occurred in extremity, there were others who put the lives of fellow soldiers above their own. Bruce cited several for courage. And General Bradley presented the Soldier's Medal for bravery to Colonel Medaris.

This was a far different war than in Africa. Enemies

fought at close range. Germany had suffered enormous losses to the Soviets on the eastern front. The Nazis threw in youngsters and old men as they struggled desperately to save what was left of their conquests. Now it was their own country the invaders threatened.

The Americans faced a serious dilemma a few weeks later. The makeshift port constructed with great effort on the beach to unload men, equipment and supplies was demolished in a violent Channel storm. Stocks dwindled as General Bradley debated how and when to break German lines in Normandy and thrust into the peninsula to capture the port of Bordeaux which would assure adequate supplies. While Bradley discussed his plan with Major General Troy Middleton, a corps commander, and others, Bruce computed the quantities of ammunition necessary to support the large scale attacks. He concluded that supplies were inadequate and hurried to headquarters with his figures.

General Bradley left the conference to hear Medaris.

"You're recommending that I call off Middleton while going ahead with the other corps into Normandy?" Bradley inquired.

"Yes, sir," Bruce responded, returning his level gaze.

"You know how important this attack is to us?"

"Yes, sir, of course I do."

"You know if we attack now, we'll probably save a good many lives later on?"

"Yes, General Bradley."

"And you still say no?"

"That's my recommendation, sir," Bruce replied. "I don't think we can support both corps."

Bradley released the assault into Normandy and delayed the attack upon Bordeaux until supplies built up. Middleton then succeeded in taking the major seaport.

Reinforced and well supplied, First Army prepared to

shatter enemy lines for a bold drive towards the Seine River while other divisions swung south towards Paris. An unexpected obstacle prevented the attack. Thousands of hedgerows, grown up over centuries, bounded the Normandy fields. Attempts to trample them down with armor failed. Indeed, they were so resilient that the Sherman tanks rode up one side, exposing their soft underbellies to German infantry with anti-tank guns behind the next hedgerow. The tanks' guns were, of course, pointing uselessly towards the sky.

Sergeant Curtis G. Culin, Jr., hit upon the solution. He welded tusklike steel prongs to a tank. The teeth rammed into a hedge, keeping the tank level. Then it burst through in a shower of dirt, roots and stones. Culin received the Legion of Merit for his invention. Four months later he lost a leg in Huertgen Forest.

General Bradley took Bruce with him to witness a demonstration of Culin's tank. Satisfied, Bradley turned to Bruce and said "We've got to have those quickly." Bruce asked one question, "How quick?"

"Two weeks," Bradley replied.

It sounded impossible, but Bruce had an ace up his sleeve. In London, when the invasion was being planned, Bruce was responsible to dispatch supply orders to the States. Trying to make estimates for which there was no precedent, he came upon "rod, welding" in the catalog. How much welding rod would First Army need in Europe? The manual indicated a small quantity, presumably enough to repair vehicles. By then Bruce was distrustful. He had found similar estimates hopelessly inadequate in Africa and Sicily. They were written by men who never fought this kind of war. He wrestled with the problem, but was far from any answer when he retired that night. When he awoke, however, a figure stood out clearly in his mind. He wanted one million pounds of welding rod.

Washington promptly challenged the order. Any such quantity would mean operating plants twenty-four hours a day and for what purpose except to satisfy some eccentric ordnance officer? General Bradley called Bruce to his office.

"You know that I trust you implicitly, Bruce," he said, "But are you sure about this item? It's obvious that Washington thinks you're way off base."

"I am very sure, general," Bruce replied. "I can't explain it, but we'll need that much rod."

"I kinda thought you'd say that," Bradley grinned. "All right, I'll insist."

Now the time had come. Most of the five hundred tons of rod were ashore. Welding crews were summoned by radio and reported to assembly areas where First Army collected eight hundred tanks. Hurried calls to England brought more rod. Bruce dispatched heavy tracked vehicles to the beaches to retrieve steel tetrahedron devices planted by the Germans to punch holes in landing craft coming ashore. Those were cut up to provide the steel tusks. There was delicious irony in using German steel to penetrate those hedgerows. Within ten days the entire fleet of tanks was equipped and Bradley's armored divisions launched the attack. They burst through enemy lines on July 25th, heading for the German frontier while a second thrust proceeded to Paris.

Bruce gave credit to his ordnance units for the tank modifications. And, offhandedly, he felt it had been God who guided him by putting the figure of one million pounds of welding rod in his mind. There were many other occasions when he silently asked help and got it. Eventually Bradley learned that Bruce sought guidance from God. Bradley's logistics chief, General Robert Wilson, knew about it too.

Neither man apparently took exception to this "unmilitary" procedure because they kept their peace.

Ginny sent news clippings of the D-Day invasion of France. Her letter guessed that he was with Bradley. Like thousands of anxious wives, all she had was an army post office number which betrayed nothing of geographical location. Bruce wrote that he was in France and assured her that he was well.

Supplies from coastal depots were reaching First Army much too slowly. Bruce sent teams of expediters to these bases. They combed the growing stockpiles to locate needed materiel. America's wartime supply boss, General Brehon Somervell, visited France to survey his operations. When he met Bradley, Somervell complained about the "Hundred Bulldogs," as the ordnance expediters were called; claiming they interfered with orderly supply procedures and, according to his staff, were unnecessary. Bruce challenged these assertions and cited case after case to prove that Somervell was wrong. He won the argument with Bradley's support, only to find later that his victory had a price. He was recommended for promotion to brigadier general three times, including one endorsement from Eisenhower as supreme commander. Three times the promotion was turned down with Somervell's initials on the rejections. Understandably bitter, Bruce realized much later that the same God who had told him how much welding rod he would need loved him too much to let him believe in his own infallibility. Bruce Medaris would become a general in God's time.

Encouraging innovation, he worked with his staff to perfect firing tables which permitted the army to plan combat operations based upon firm forecasts of ammunition and supplies. With the aid of his colleague, Colonel Williams, a mobile radio network was organized that linked all of the ordnance units. In this way Bruce received nightly reports on the status of major supply items. American tanks reached Paris August 25. Occupying Germans had agreed to pull out in order to spare the historic city. General Hodges had taken over First Army as Bradley moved up to command all U.S. forces in Europe.

"We have a problem, gentlemen," Hodges informed his staff. "We have outrun our supply train. Now we can either sit here and wait for supplies, which will allow the Germans time to regroup, or we must find some other means of bringing up supply."

Colonel Patterson, the antiaircraft chief, placed his truck fleet at the army's disposal. They hauled supplies until fighting ceased the next year, rolling up 2.5 million miles in the process. Bruce struck a deal with a French auto maker in Paris to rebuild truck engines and turn out spare parts, keeping vehicles moving without waiting for shipments from the States. Colonel Nelson Lynde took over this operation and later managed plants in Belgium in support of American forces as the war drew closer to Germany.

On one occasion, a high-ranking antiaircraft officer from the States discovered that First Army ack-ack units employed a sighting bar developed by the British which served its purpose well. Bruce had them made in ordnance shops. A new sight manufactured in the States proved worthless—by the time a gunner lined it up the attacking plane was out of range. Colonel Patterson had left these gadgets in storage.

The visiting general reported this unauthorized use of British gear to General Hodges, said he would send a replacement for Patterson and cite Medaris to the chief of ordnance for due punishment. Hodges listened attentively and replied that First Army had magnificent antiaircraft support. He sent the general on his way.

When the enemy pulled out of Liege, Bruce and Colonel

Nelson Lynde contracted with Engelbert & Cie to recap tires and manufacture tires and tubes for First Army, keeping vehicles moving without waiting for shipments from the States. Fabrique Nationale produced spare parts for vehicles and guns, while another Belgian firm, J. Honrez Artillerie, rebuilt infantry mortars. Having these supply sources close to the lines saved weeks of shipping time for the Allies.

As the fighting continued ever closer to the Rhine a staff inspector found out that Bruce and his ordnance units employed two hundred operators on that radio network which was not authorized by the "book." Called to account, Bruce readily admitted that he was responsible and explained how the system functioned.

"Bruce," General William Kean admonished, "you know that ordnance is supposed to rely on the official communications channels. So this private network will have to go."

"I understand," Bruce told the chief of staff. "I'll stop the transmissions."

He did just that. "Don't talk," he instructed the radio operators. "But make sure you listen around the clock. We'll need you in time."

After losing an entire army in a futile counter attack at Mortain, the Germans launched a massive assault on December 16th against First Army in the Ardennes Forest. They hoped to slash through the Allies, seize the port of Antwerp and break the major supply line from England and the United States. The bold gamble caught American units by surprise.

Colonel Patterson and Bruce were in London enjoying a brief respite and checking up on supplies when General Hodges' aide found them with news of the onslaught and said a light plane was standing by to rush them back to the front. They left within an hour. Bruce hurried to the command post where General Kean asked the location of ammunition supply points that might fall into the hands of German columns. Bruce pointed out the sites on a tactical map. Kean told him to "get the stuff out of there fast!"

"General, it will take at least forty-eight hours to get out the word and remove that ammunition," Bruce said.

Kean looked at him, aware that in all likelihood Medaris kept that forbidden radio network in standby. He grinned.

"Get out of here," he ordered. "Do it your way and don't bring up the subject again!"

The orders were transmitted to forward companies in twenty minutes, and most of the ammunition was safely trucked to new points out of the reach of the Germans. During two weeks of continuous fighting in the First Army sector, ordnance had no other means of communications than the unauthorized radio network.

During brief lulls, Bruce formed technical intelligence units that rounded up enemy weapons and equipment for examination and shipment to the States. In this way the Allies kept abreast of new items available to the Germans and could determine their supply of natural resources by detecting substitutes—known as "ersatz" material. Wreckers patrolled forward areas to return disabled guns and tanks for repair. Bruce persuaded the British army to release 250 American-built tanks in order to re-equip First Army divisions that lost theirs in the historic Battle of the Bulge.

General Bradley relates an incident that occurred as shortages threatened to halt the American sweep toward the Rhine river. He summoned army commanders to review the situation. General Patton appeared with his supply chief. When Patton spotted Medaris and Wilson, he immediately sent for his ordnance officer.

"Look out for that pair," he said, pointing to Bruce and Wilson. "I know them both. They worked for me in Africa. They'll take your teeth!"

"George's caution was not unjustified," Bradley observed. "No one knew better than he that First Army merited its reputation for piracy in supply, maintaining that all was fair in love and war."

Germany's air force, the proud Luftwaffe, once master of the skies over Europe and England, had disappeared as Allied air fleets gained the upper hand. Day and night bomber squadrons roared off English fields to rain destruction on Nazi war plants, railroads and ports. Facing ruin, the Germans unveiled two new weapons in a belated attempt to stave off the end. Hitler called them "Vengeance Weapons." One, a ramjet-powered projectile, was called the "buzz bomb" by the Allies because of the telltale noise of its motor as it sped over distances up to one hundred miles. British radar, antiaircraft gunners and interceptor planes combined to destroy many of the flying bombs, but some penetrated the defenses in England and on the Continent.

The other weapon, known as V-2, presented a far more serious threat. A true rocket, it soared into the upper atmosphere following a ballistic trajectory and fell on its target at supersonic velocity. Bigger and faster than any previous rocket, V-2 could not be intercepted. The ton of high explosives in its warhead and the fact that this weapon struck without warning combined to give it a sinister character. The destruction wrought by V-2 raids on British cities aggravated the multiple problems of the English people. General Eisenhower remarked that if the V-2 had appeared earlier in the war, it might have changed the course of history.

At work in his mobile office one day, Bruce heard a loud explosion followed by a low-pitched thunderous rumble. He guessed that an ammunition dump had blown up. The field telephone rang at his elbow. Picking up the instrument he heard an excited voice, "Colonel, something big and heavy just impacted in a ravine near the cooks' tent and we have casualties!" Hurrying to the scene, Bruce found officers and men assisting the injured, some wandering dazedly. Three required evacuation for shrapnel wounds, eight were "walking wounded." Bruce scrambled down the sloping pit, examining pieces of thin metal, twisted pipe, valves and other fragments.

"What do you make of it, Colonel?" Sergeant Kintner asked, turning over a jagged piece.

"Intelligence reported the Germans were testing a new rocket," Bruce responded. "I think we have the honor of receiving a V-2. Get some shell boxes and collect all of those remnants. I want them examined by the technical people and then we'll route them to SHAEF. The rocket experts will find them interesting."

He phoned a report to General Kean, citing the casualty figures and his plans for disposing of the fragments.

"I'd say this was a wild one," he added. "There is no target in the immediate vicinity of that much interest to the enemy. We know that V-2 was designed as an area weapon to hit targets like London and the Channel ports. Apparently this one fell short. This baby is supposed to fly well over a hundred miles."

Bruce could not then guess that twelve years later he would have daily contact with scientists and engineers who developed the V-2.

The German weapon was created at Peenemuende Rocket Center on the Baltic Sea where Wernher von Braun directed 12,000 specialists in the advancement of rocket technology for the German army.

Even in war the Peenemuende leaders, although under

intense pressure from Hitler's chiefs to complete V-2, dreamed of space exploration, knowing their work laid a foundation to open this new frontier. Hitler's feared Gestapo, the secret police, arrested von Braun and two colleagues in March, 1944, on charges that they planned to use their rockets for space travel instead of destroying England. The military intervened and obtained their release on the ground that without them, there would be no V-2.

As Soviet armies invading from the east threatened to overrun Peenemuende in the spring of 1945, von Braun and his associates faced a hard choice. They could remain and surrender to the Russians with little reason to expect more than quick execution, or flee to Bavaria and take their chances with the Americans. Calling his staff together, von Braun put the question, adding that he intended to move south. Some of the men expressed concern about their families and elected to stay. More than one hundred of the elite accompanied von Braun, taking tons of research documents with them. When they reached Bavaria, von Braun's brother, Magnus, contacted U.S. Army units. They ended up in Fort Bliss, Texas and nearby White Sands Missile Range, New Mexico later that year.

In his next letter home, Bruce mentioned the V-2 briefly to Ginny but devoted most of the missive to describing the towns and cities he visited in Belgium and the warm welcome accorded the Americans by the people. "I attend the chaplain's services when I can, which isn't often," he wrote. "I must say that war makes believers. Major Warren draws a good crowd. I pray for you and the children and that seems to help my loneliness."

As General Hodges worked out plans for invading Germany, Bruce attended a meeting in which he was asked where ordnance supplies could be established in order to support the troops crossing the Rhine. As he looked at the map, one spot seemed to be illuminated. He placed his finger on it and remarked, "That's my position." It later turned out that he had selected a site within ten miles of the Remagen Bridge captured by an American column over which the first Allied troops poured into Germany in late March. Bruce choked back the inner joy he experienced, knowing that once again guidance came when needed.

Keeping pace with the rapid advance as German resistance weakened, Bruce arranged to airlift a hundred tons of ammunition daily. After crossing the Rhine, the Americans penetrated eastward until they reached the Mulde River 400 miles inside the Reich. Ordnance companies took over German shell, explosives and bomb plants. One unit came upon nine complete V-2 rockets hidden in a tunnel. They were shipped to Paris.

As the enemy withdrew, First Army began planning for a new assignment far from the European battlefields. General George Marshall ordered Eisenhower to release First Army headquarters to return to the States. There the staff would regroup to move into the Pacific for the invasion of Japan. Marshall explained that the appearance of a battle-tried army "will have profound effect on the Japanese." Bruce wanted to be thoroughly prepared for this new arena so he studied Japanese military organization, transportation networks, manufacturing centers, weather and terrain. Meantime ordnance set up a large installation in Kassel to service German automobiles and trucks for the U.S. civil affairs and military government teams that would control the American zone of Germany. The Allies controlled a 600-mile long front as they made contact with the Russians on the Elbe River. Their armies shattered, the Germans surrendered on May 6 in Italy and Germany. The last shot was fired at one minute after midnight, May 9. Church bells rang out the news in Cincinnati as in Washington, New York, London, Paris and thousands of cities in Allied countries. Men knelt on foreign soil they had conquered to give thanks for an end to the carnage. The war in devastated Europe was over 335 days after the Normandy landings.

Bruce wrote to Ginny telling her of his return and urging her to arrange for Marta and Bruce to join him in Traverse City, Michigan for a vacation. Ginny dutifully followed his instructions and managed to collect enough rationed gasoline for the drive from Ohio.

General Hodges said goodbye to First Army and left Paris by plane May 10 for the States. To his delight, Bruce accompanied his commander and other staff officers.

There was time for honors to officers and enlisted men who helped make victory possible. Colonel Medaris received the Distinguished Service Medal. General Robert Wilson, the logistics chief with whom he dealt most often with II Corps in Africa and Sicily and with First Army in Europe, summed up Bruce's contribution in these words:

"He was an outstanding organizer and administrator whose thinking was far ahead of anyone else. He was a human dynamo who could get more things done by himself than any two men. He would carry out adverse decisions to the letter even though he disagreed. But he would always argue his position cogently and courageously until it was either accepted or overruled. He was a pioneer in modern ordnance service, there was no book for this type of war. Many, many times he wrote 'the book' and his concepts were always proved sound by actual experience."

They were heady words for a proud man, and Bruce alone knew that he couldn't legitimately take credit for it all.

# 8

# THE PATIENT YEARS

Spring warmed the land when General Hodges and his companions landed near Washington. Each officer received orders to report in forty-five days to Governor's Island, New York. After this recuperation leave they would depart for the Philippine Islands to organize the invasion of Japan.

Bruce had one overriding desire, to see Ginny and their children as soon as possible. He phoned Cincinnati and spoke to his father-in-law, Clifford Smith.

"Dad, is that you?" he fairly shouted. "This is Bruce. I'm back in the States and want to talk to Ginny."

"It's good to hear your voice, Bruce," Smith answered. "Thank God you're home again. Ginny got your letter and has gone up to Traverse City with the kids. They're fine, so don't worry on that score. Let me give you the number of her brother's store. Barron will get in touch with Ginny."

As he jotted down the number, Bruce added, "I'll see you

soon, but you can understand how much I want to be with my family."

With the help of a sympathetic operator, Bruce put through the call to Michigan and talked with his sister-in-law, leaving instructions for his wife.

Meanwhile Ginny unloaded the car at her father's country place, turned on the water heater, and then drove into town for supplies. She stopped in a music store to see her sister-in-law, Barron Smith's wife, who ran towards her with the welcome news, "Ginny, Bruce is in Washington!"

Laughing and crying in relief, Ginny listened to Bruce's plan. Barron would drive her and the children to Grayling at midnight where they would board a train for Detroit, arriving next morning. Then she would check in at the airport and find reservations waiting for a flight to Washington. Her heart filled with joy. Marta and Bruce screamed happily at the word of daddy's return with the added bonus of a train ride and airplane flight to meet him.

Bruce enlisted the help of an army officer in Detroit, explained his family's situation and said he wanted them in Washington. "No problem," the officer replied. "We'll work out the details and have tickets ready for Mrs. Medaris when she reaches the airport. Your family will arrive in Washington about half past eleven tomorrow morning." Bruce found an apartment provided by army for temporary guests. Next day he drove to the airport an hour before the scheduled arrival, impatient for the reunion.

As it turned out, the Detroit-Washington flight was sold out and the airline added a second plane in which Ginny and the children found seats. Bruce met the first plane and was keenly disappointed when his family did not appear. Since he didn't know of the second plane, Bruce rushed to a phone booth trying to get information about Ginny's departure from Detroit. When her flight arrived, she failed to see

Bruce in the crowd of people who were waiting for friends and relatives. Ginny collected the children and walked slowly towards the main building wondering what had gone wrong. As they approached, Bruce left the phone booth. Other travelers smiled understandingly at the wild shouts of recognition, "Daddy!" "Bruce!" The tall uniformed officer beamed as he grasped wife, daughter and son while they smothered him with kisses and a few tears, a scene repeated many times in other cities as fathers and sons returned from Europe.

They spent several fun-filled days celebrating Bruce's forty-third birthday and homecoming, dropping in on friends who wanted to hear all about the war from a father who preferred to talk about his children. Then they rode to Governor's Island where Bruce received instructions about the planned move to the Far East at the conclusion of his leave.

Ginny asked about his next assignment. Bruce explained the situation with a disclaimer from the heart, "Don't worry about that now, I have enough time for a good rest."

They went next to Traverse City where Bruce slowly unwound. He found difficulty in sleeping in the quiet home, still expecting an orderly to awaken him with a hurried message about some problem at the battlefront. It would take a long time to relieve the nervous tension under which he had been living for more than three years.

In fact, Bruce was soon ordered into a hospital by army physicians who found him near the point of exhaustion and collapse. He recovered quickly, though, and the doctors let him go.

Meanwhile dramatic events in the Pacific Theater augured well for the defeat of Japan. Air, sea and ground forces drove the conquerors back to their home islands. General Douglas MacArthur returned to the Philippines.

On August 6, a B-29 bomber dropped the first atomic bomb on Hiroshima, a major Japanese city, creating widespread destruction. Three days later a second bomb destroyed most of Nagasaki, again with a terrible loss of life. Next day the Japanese Cabinet sued for peace, finally accepting the unconditional surrender terms offered by the Allies at Potsdam a month earlier. President Harry Truman directed MacArthur to take the surrender on a U.S. battleship in Tokyo Bay September 2, 1945. The war was over.

No need now for the First Army in the Philippines. Instead Bruce was assigned as ordnance officer of the Fifth Service Command, which managed logistics installations in the Midwest. He moved Ginny and the children into quarters at Fort Hayes in Columbus, Ohio, where he had been commissioned lieutenant twenty-four years before. Marilyn joined them for a while and proudly introduced a suitor, Eugene Stillings, who was pursuing graduate study in horticulture. Bruce and Ginny liked the young man and guessed that marriage would follow shortly.

Now his mission was to help reverse the process which he helped accelerate during the buildup for war. The task required tearing down the nationwide supply system created to support conflicts across two oceans. The army was being dissolved almost overnight. Hundreds of thousands of men were summarily discharged with the thanks of the government. Bruce dutifully worked out plans to close many activities and consolidate others to reduce manpower and costs.

He found the sudden change from a position of great responsibility and authority to a caretaker's role anything but attractive. And there was the very real possibility that with sharply reduced appropriations, the army might simply terminate his services as it had other officers'. Bruce pondered his course. Marta and Bruce needed his attention and love, as did Ginny who was not in good health. Reserve officers had the option of leaving the army to return to civilian occupations, so he decided once more to take off the uniform. This time he would open a management consultant business in Cincinnati, persuaded that his wartime experiences would help business and industry solve their problems. They picked out a house in the suburbs, and Bruce rented an office in the city.

General Bradley wished him well, observing that "if you do as good a job running your business as you did working with me, you will make a grand success of it." The top ordnance officer, Lieutenant General L.H. Campbell, wrote his best wishes, adding that "the high character of your performance marks you as a man of outstanding ability and energy. You leave behind a host of friends who always will hold you in highest regard and respect. Thank you for the very eminent contribution you made to the success of the ordnance mission." This praise was tinged with irony, however, since he was still a colonel when some of his peers had received general's stars.

He picked up clients, largely in the Cincinnati area, and worked hard to help solve their difficulties while building a reputation as a consulting expert. Early in 1946, Ginny accompanied him on a business trip to Washington where they spent some time with officers and their families whom he knew in service. When they got back to Ohio, Bruce faced the stark fact that he could never be completely happy away from the army, the same conclusion he arrived at years earlier. It did not surprise Ginny who agreed that he should return to the ranks.

The army was offering integration into the regular army to a few selected reserve officers. Bruce had maintained his reserve connections while in private business. He applied and was promptly accepted, subject, that is, to one question. A law authorized a seventy-five percent pension for officers with World War I service. Was he returning only to claim that pension? The answer was an unequivocal no.

Receiving orders to report to Washington, Bruce closed his office and put the house up for sale. They moved again, Ginny making the best of it and reassuring the children. For a few days they lived in a duck hunting lodge Bruce found on the Potomac River, complete with wood burning stove, while the army worked out his assignment. He became executive officer for Brigadier General Harold Nisely, ordnance officer of Army Ground Forces at Fort Monroe, Virginia, where the family lived in a large frame house. Marta, a vivacious teen-ager, and young Bruce, approaching his eighth birthday, rode to and from school in a military bus with a guard escort. Before long, Marta had an inkling of her father's reputation on the historic post. As the bus approached their quarters, the escort asked the driver, "Is that where the Big M lives?"

"What did he mean, mother?" she asked Ginny.

Her mother shrugged and smiled. "It's just a nickname, honey," she replied. "Your dad is considered a hard taskmaster by some of the people. Don't let it bother you."

Sharing love and awe for her father, Marta knew then that the firm hand he kept on his children extended beyond the family to his relations with others. "I am right most of the time," he told his son and daughter, "therefore you must understand I am right all of the time."

Teen-age girls were addicted to saddle oxfords which, to achieve the height of current fashion in school circles, had to be scuffed and dirty; it was simply unthinkable to be seen in clean shoes. Marta acquired a pair and tried to explain to her father why she must not clean them. This was to no avail because, as Bruce explained with the ring of authority in his voice, *his* daughter must clean her oxfords daily. None of her arguments about "the fashion" convinced him otherwise. So Marta dutifully complied, wondering at times why he was always right.

Ginny found space in the caverns under the fort which she and other wives decorated and furnished as a recreation center for young people. She played the piano for an octet whose recitals were warmly received by the garrison. No musician, although he liked music, Bruce mixed drinks at these functions.

General Nisely retired. The ground forces commander, General Jacob Devers, known as "the tankers' general," picked Bruce to succeed Nisely. Once more he filled a general's job while a colonel. His duties kept him in close touch with the combat arms: infantry, artillery, armor and antiaircraft. He visited their training centers at Forts Sill, Bragg, Bliss and Benning. This was his first look at the Georgia installation where he originally learned the infantryman's trade. Nearing the end of his brief stay, Bruce drove around the post with another officer, remembering his favorite horse and experience of twenty-five years ago. At Quarters 23 he stopped and got out of the car.

"Funny how our standards change as we grow older," he remarked to his companion. "When I lived here, I thought these were just about the nicest quarters a junior officer could ever enjoy. Now they look drab and unattractive and awfully small."

The peacetime army had two principal missions—to maintain some kind of readiness posture in the event of war and to revamp doctrine, policy and procedures in the light of World War II experience. With missionary zeal, Bruce embarked upon a personal crusade to reform ordnance service and its relationships with the combat arms. There was little enthusiasm in the Pentagon for his ideas. In fact, seniors in ordnance regarded him as a rebel who constantly plagued them wherever he operated. He lectured at the Army War College and Command and General Staff School, hammering away to future commanders at the need for a new ammunition policy.

Some Pentagon officers remembered the problems Bruce created for them in Tunisia, Sicily, England and Europe by insisting upon prompt and adequate support. They questioned his loyalty to ordnance, since he obviously felt that belonged to the field commander. Now he spoke for General Devers, a quantity to be reckoned with but his preachments were largely ignored. His ego allowed no compromise—and received little gratification.

His ordnance associates found other reason to wish he kept to his knitting in Cincinnati. The army would accept the ordnance budget only with the approval of the Ground Forces who, after all, were the principal customers of ordnance supply. Acting for General Devers, Bruce reviewed every item in the new budget with Pentagon officials sent to Fort Monroe for this purpose. After one of these sessions he walked out with a civilian authority who remarked, "You are not very polite." Bruce retorted, "Politeness is nice but takes too damn much time!" That sally made the rounds of the Pentagon as budgeteers groaned at the changes he insisted upon.

The family found much to do at Monroe. Bruce and Ginny fished and crabbed with the children, who were doing very well in school. There was a fine swimming pool and a busy social calendar. They anticipated a happy tour of at least three years.

At this juncture, another of those inexplicable coincidences occurred to interrupt their pleasant sojourn and to remove this otherwise likable thorn from the ordnance planners. The United States maintained excellent relations with Argentina which was growing powerful in South America under dictator Juan Peron. The navy and air force maintained military missions in Buenos Aires. The Argentine army, however, received professional assistance from the Germans prior to World War II. Now there was a vacant chair which the army wanted to occupy but could do so only if invited. General Jose Humberto Sola Molina, the minister of defense, accepted an invitation from Secretary of State George Marshall to visit U.S. military installations. At the same time, the army hoped to negotiate an agreement by which a mission would be accepted by Argentina. A West Point dean of notable linguistic ability was tapped to escort the Argentine party as interpreter. The dean, however, fell seriously ill. The army searched their files for a replacement. The only colonel with sufficient background and fluency in Spanish was J. B. Medaris. General Devers protested that he did not want to lose him. But it was an emergency and Bruce was just the man.

A few days later he rode the harbor pilot's boat out of New York to greet the guests. Completely at ease in their language, with a thorough knowledge of their customs and traditions, he got along with them very well during the tour. There were a few anxious moments when junior officers sought to escape their security escorts in search of female companions, but the minister enjoyed himself. The visit concluded with a buffet at Fort Myers, the home of General Bradley, the chief of staff. Bruce stood by as Bradley chatted with the minister, interpreting for both. When General Bradley asked if Sola Molina was prepared to sign the mission agreement next day, the response caught Bruce off guard.

"We will welcome a United States Army mission in my country," the minister said, "provided Colonel Medaris is the chief."

"Did you know anything about this?" Bradley inquired in an aside.

"No, sir," Bruce replied. "It was not discussed with me."

The minister got his wish. Bruce was ordered to form a mission in three weeks, collect the families, and board ship for Buenos Aires. He picked five officers representing the combat arms, a warrant officer and three enlisted men. General Bruce Clark, Bradley's assistant, sent him off with flattering praise for his work with the visitors.

Bruce wrote Marilyn about their imminent departure, adding that they would be away at least three years. During the nineteen days at sea, Bruce conducted morning classes in conversational Spanish and briefed the men and their wives on the niceties of social conduct in Argentina. They leased a villa in Olivos, a suburb, that filled a quarter of a block with spacious grounds and servants' quarters over a detached garage. His offices were in the War Ministry building downtown.

The family fitted into the pleasant and orderly life of the Argentine capital. Ginny looked after other wives, helping them to adjust but confessing her own problems quietly to Bruce. Giving instructions to servants, doing business with the butcher, grocer, baker or tailor became difficult tasks and troubled Ginny because of her failure to master the language, although she made a valiant effort to learn. She was not alone. None of the other mission officers and only one sergeant could carry on a conversation in Spanish, which placed added burdens on Bruce who became their interpreter as well as their chief. Ginny became well known and liked, however, as the attractive hostess at official receptions tendered by Colonel and Mrs. Medaris. They formed enduring friendships with his Argentine colleagues who welcomed the Americans in the common military tradition.

His religion had become more important to Bruce as a consequence of his personal experiences in England and Europe. While in Ohio and Washington, he attended Episcopal services regularly with Ginny and the children, although still holding back from church membership. In his own mind he decided this was the church he wanted to join but their stay in each place was so short that somehow he did not get around to it. There was one American church in Buenos Aires. It was Methodist and while he tried to adjust to its preaching, Bruce found himself resisting. Occasionally he and Ginny attended services in the Church of England. Sometimes on trips out of the city with his military associates he accompanied them to Roman Catholic masses where he felt more at ease than in Methodism although uncomfortable in the Latin liturgy.

Bruce and his officers spent much time in Argentine military schools working with their faculties to update instruction on tactics and techniques developed in World War II. They received close attention since the host army fully expected to introduce U.S. arms and armament in the course of the next several years. The Argentinians had felt sympathy for Germany before and during the war. In fact, Nazi influence was rather strong in certain parts of South America. The presence of Bruce's mission undoubtedly fit in with an American policy to try to reestablish properly cordial relations with its hemispheric neighbors. Thus Bruce's team also sought to persuade the Argentinians to abandon German military procedures in favor of American ones; this included the "goose step" in marching formations, which the Argentine army discarded reluctantly and, as it turned out, only temporarily.

The Americans continued to draw pay from the United States while living allowances were paid by the host government. This became a bonanza for Bruce and Ginny who were still paying off those debts incurred in the bankrupt auto business. Bruce received the monthly payments in dollars and converted them to pesos which, under Dictator Peron's rule, were frequently devalued. As a result the rent for their villa cost only fourteen dollars monthly. He finally retired the last of his obligations while Ginny managed to put aside some of his salary in savings. A pleasant surprise came in a letter from the army, he had been selected for brigadier general in the reserves. But since he was now a member of the regular army, nothing came of it.

General Matthew Ridgway, U.S. commander in the Caribbean area, bossed all American military missions in South America. He brought his wife, Penny, to Buenos Aires in 1949. Bruce and Ginny entertained in their honor. Ridgway commanded the 18th Airborne Division of the First Army in France so the two men had much to talk about. Bruce expressed strongly held views about the necessity of modernizing army doctrine in the supply services and found Ridgway in complete agreement. When the visit ended, Ridgway dispatched a letter to Washington urging immediate promotion of Bruce to brigadier general. The recommendation joined other similar letters in his file.

A new war threat in the Far East followed the invasion of South Korea by North Korean forces intent on establishing a Communist state bordering Red China and the Soviet Union. Badly outnumbered, lacking aircraft and tanks, the South Koreans retreated. The invaders had been well equipped by their Red allies. The United Nations appealed to member states on July 27, 1950 to assist the embattled South Koreans. President Harry Truman authorized air and naval forces to support the South and followed up by sending ground troops into the country from Japan.

Bruce reacted immediately. He wired General Ridgway offering his services, but was instructed to stay put since the success of the first army mission in Argentina was of great importance.

General Douglas MacArthur became United Nations commander in Korea. His Eighth Army halted the Communist advance just outside the southern port city of Pusan across the straits from Japan. As his forces grew larger, MacArthur launched a counterattack and drove the North Koreans back. The capital city of Seoul was liberated in late October and UN forces drove northward to the Yalu River, the border of mainland China. By that time the United Nations had taken 100,000 North Korean prisoners.

The character of the war changed overnight—with all the portents of widening conflict—when 300,000 Chinese Communist troops launched an offensive on November 25, forcing the Eighth Army back to the 38th Parallel, inflicting heavy casualties with utter disregard of their own losses. By January 1, 1951 the Chinese had half a million men in Korea against the UN force of 365,000. Lieutenant General Ridgway took over the command of Eighth Army as Chinese legions smashed their way into Seoul. A counterattack forced the Reds back to the 38th Parallel in bitter combat. Trying to head off a general war, Truman fired MacArthur, Ridgway took the top command and Lieutenant General James Van Fleet succeeded as Eighth Army commander. Fighting continued until June 23, 1951 when the Chinese opened peace talks. Battles for position broke out along the uneasy front at heavy cost to both sides.

An attempted coup shook Argentina in September and was squelched by overwhelming forces directed by Peron. Bruce was in his office when shooting broke out in the city. His first impulse was to get his group out of danger. He phoned a store where Ginny was shopping and told her to return home at once. After he was sure the other U.S. officers were safe, he told his chauffeur to take him to the villa in Olivos. Peron's supporters blocked streets leading into the city with parked buses and trucks to cut off reinforcements from the rebel faction. Bruce encountered a roadblock, got out and pointed to the U.S. insignia on the sedan, explained his status in Spanish and asked for passage. The buses were moved aside to let him through. In a few days Peron forces restored order.

Marilyn had married Eugene Stillings, a former army lieutenant with a master's degree in horticulture from Ohio State University, and now lived in Utah. The Medaris family and servants celebrated the news that Bruce had become a grandfather with the arrival of Jeffry Stillings, first child of the marriage, who was born in Salt Lake City where Stillings taught at the University of Utah.

Marta completed high school with honors. For a time her parents thought she was bound to join the Roman Catholic church because of her friendship with a missionary, but Marta decided against it. Since the seasons are reversed south of the Equator, it was the wrong time of year for Marta to continue her studies in the States. Bruce had guessed she would become a secretary while his son would enter the army. For eighteen months she worked and played, growing closer to her father. He taught her photography and golf until she became a tournament player. She made friends easily with young Argentinians.

Young Bruce would finish grammar school shortly and his parents faced a dilemma.

"I want him to attend prep school in Maryland," Bruce told Ginny. "He will get the foundation there which he needs to enter West Point. My old friend Colonel Emil Del Sasse, will look after Bruce so that he will have a home and foster family to join on weekends. If we keep Bruce with us he will lose a full year."

"I hate to send him away at his age," Ginny remarked,

"but he wants an army career so badly . . . let's ask him."

They talked it over with their son who readily accepted the plan. He liked Del Sasse and wanted to return to familiar surroundings, having struggled with Spanish in school. Young Bruce flew home alone, his temporary parents greeted him at the airport and saw him installed at school. He did very well.

While they remained in Buenos Aires, Bruce and Ginny took Marta with them to diplomatic and cultural affairs which his position involved. Their daughter enjoyed the gala social events. Musically inclined like her mother, she heard some of the world's foremost musicians in concert. As she matured Marta became a close companion of Ginny.

Ending the stay in Argentina, they made a leisurely return trip visiting Lima, Peru; Panama, where Bruce soldiered in the 1920s; on to Havana, Cuba, then to Mexico City where he renewed friendships with the officers who worked the TNT deal during World War II. They spent some time in California before flying east, concluding the 12,000-mile journey in Detroit, Michigan where Bruce bought a new car and drove to Washington. The Argentine government conferred the Order of General San Martin in gratitude for his professional assistance.

When Bruce reported to the Pentagon he learned that his next assignment would be Frankford Arsenal, an old-line ordnance installation in Philadelphia. Wondering at this choice, Bruce presented his orders to Colonel Ward Becker, the commander, remembering all too keenly having exchanged hot words with Becker in North Africa when Bruce's order was challenged for new equipment to replace battle losses at Kasserine Pass. Becker cleared up the mystery of his orders to Frankford in a disturbing conversation.

"I have to tell you, Bruce," he began, "that all of the ordnance commanders met in the Pentagon a few weeks ago to look over officers due for new assignments. Your name came up in the process since we knew that you were returning from Argentina soon."

Becker paused, then he went on, "I can tell you that no one, and I mean nobody, offered to take you. You've acquired a reputation as a troublemaker who is hard to handle. You shouldn't be surprised considering how you treated the ordnance people in Africa, Sicily and England while you were with Bradley and Hodges. I finally agreed to take you on as my deputy. That's why you are here and that is the job you will have. How we get along is pretty much up to you. I know that we need some changes, but you've got to remember that I am the boss and you work for me."

Bruce took the news stoically, churning inwardly, and replied, "I'm part of your command, Ward, and I'll follow your orders."

Much to Ginny's dislike, they were assigned a small house within the arsenal compound which was surrounded by an industrial area. It was not the kind of setting she wanted for Marta, but she would make the best of it. Bruce knew something about the entrenched civilian hierarchy that controlled Frankford Arsenal and their ties with the local congressional delegation. He determined to remedy that situation by restoring military control. He anticipated an unpleasant but interesting tour for the normal span of three years.

Bruce set up a task force without delay to study arsenal methods of transacting business, bringing aboard John Dale, a reserve officer who was expert in accounting procedures, as his troubleshooter.

Ginny had barely had time to become acquainted with the other officer wives living on the arsenal when Bruce took a phone call twelve days later. The caller was Lieutenant General Louis Ford, the chief of ordnance.

"Bruce?" Ford inquired.

"Yes sir, this is Medaris," he responded.

"I'm sorry to dislocate you so soon," Ford said, "but you are urgently needed in Washington."

"Can you tell me what's up?" Bruce asked.

"No, I don't want to talk about it on the phone," Ford replied. "We are in a serious jam and I think you are the one man who might find a way out."

"I'll have to inform Ward Becker," Bruce concluded.

"You let me talk to Ward, and be here tomorrow," Ford told him.

Bruce summoned Dale, told him he was leaving and asked him to carry on until Colonel Becker acquired a new deputy. He drove home immediately.

"Ginny, Marta," he called to them, "pack my things. I've got to be in the Pentagon tomorrow morning. And it looks as if our stay here will be cut short by two years, eleven months and fifteen days, more or less."

"I can't believe you're serious," Ginny said.

"Indeed, I am, the chief wants me," he said over his shoulder as he went through his briefcase.

It takes a special kind of woman to keep her sense of humor in situations like this which are all too familiar to military wives. Ginny felt that the army was asking too much of a wife and mother who spent four years out of the country only to learn that she must move again in less than two weeks.

"Do you suppose we will ever manage to settle down some place, some time?" she asked Bruce as she tucked uniforms and shirts into a suitcase.

"Yep," he replied. "The day I retire."

Bruce stopped at Becker's office.

"You've heard from the chief?" he inquired.

"Yes," the commander answered. "I don't know any more

than you about what is going on, but you needn't worry about Ginny. She can remain in the quarters and we'll look after her until you decide on a move."

"Thanks, Ward," Bruce replied. "I want to express my appreciation for your willingness to take me on. I may not have a chance to say this again, but I want you to understand that I did what was necessary in my best judgment to support the army in combat. If I stepped on your toes, or those of my seniors, that is regrettable. But in my opinion, there was no other course. I have no apologies."

Becker nodded. "That's what sets you apart," he said. "You give your allegiance to the combat commander with very little regard to your associates in ordnance."

They shook hands solemnly without another word being spoken.

When he reached the quarters, Ginny had his suitcase packed in readiness. She was smiling nervously.

"Bruce, I hope this doesn't mean a long separation," she greeted him. "You're not going overseas again?"

"I don't think so," he answered slowly. "Louie Ford was pretty close-mouthed. Something is up but I have a feeling that the trouble is in Washington and not overseas."

He said goodbye to Marta and told Ginny that he would call her from Washington as soon as he knew what was happening.

"I hope it won't be too long," Ginny said with a smile. "But we'll be ready for another move whenever you say."

"Let's pray," he said as he kissed her, "that we'll be together wherever I must go next."

# 9

# THE FIREMAN COMETH

As Bruce strode into General Ford's comfortable office, the ordnance chief walked around the desk to shake his hand, closed the door and motioned to a facing chair.

"We're in trouble, Bruce," Ford began. "I need a man free of any vested interests who can dig into a messy situation, keep me informed on what he finds, and tell us what must be done to straighten this out. I know that you are aggressive," Ford smiled and added, "some would say, to a fault. But there's no time left for pussyfooting, so I want you to handle this as my personal representative."

The fighting in Korea, he explained, lasted much longer than Pentagon planners anticipated, and as a result, a critical ammunition shortage developed. The army was under great pressure to speed up deliveries to the front where General Van Fleet complained of dangerously low stocks.

"We've got to find out why these shortages occurred and what can be done to overcome them," General Ford added.

"I can tell you in all honesty that the reputation of the ordnance corps is at stake. Either we deliver or someone will produce another solution and take over."

Ford emphasized that Bruce would speak for him and have full support if it became necessary to knock heads. He would serve as deputy to Brigadier General Merle H. Davis, the ammunition boss, but report directly to Ford when he wished. Davis enjoyed an excellent reputation as a specialist in his field; however, there were management problems in the ammunition system. It was the same kind of problem Bruce talked about in army command schools before the Argentine tour. He would also work directly with Brigadier General Emerson Cummings who supervised ordnance manufacture. Davis and Cummings told him bluntly they did not welcome General Ford's choice of a fireman to extinguish the criticism. Bruce promised that he would perform his mission as fairly as possible while trying to spare ordnance further embarrassment. But he left no doubt that he would do the job.

"I'm not running a popularity contest," he declared.

Expecting to remain in Washington at least three years, Bruce bought a home in Falls Church, Virginia, within easy commuting distance of the Pentagon, and moved Ginny and Marta from Philadelphia. Young Bruce would spend two years in Falls Church high school, then return to his prep school for a year before entering West Point. Marilyn had married Gene Stillings and was living in Ohio.

Their son delighted Bruce and Ginny by announcing that he had joined the Episcopal church while they had remained in Argentina. A square-shouldered, dark-haired teen-ager, he served as usher and acolyte, assisting the priest during services. His independence impressed a father who remembered his boyhood resistance to Methodism.

Since returning from South America, Bruce had felt a

gnawing compulsion to demonstrate his faith. With Ginny he joined an adult class in the Episcopal parish near their home to prepare for confirmation and full membership. Marta joined a young people's group for the same purpose. All three were confirmed by the bishop who laid hands on them as they knelt before the altar, saying: "Defend, O Lord, this thy Child with thy heavenly grace; that he may continue thine for ever; and daily increase in thy Holy Spirit more and more, until he come unto thy everlasting kingdom" (*The Book of Common Prayer*, p. 297). Bruce read the Scriptures before leaving for the office each morning. Prayer had gradually become part of his life style.

It was time for Marta to resume her education. Bruce selected a business school where she could prepare for a secretarial position, one that held no attraction for his daughter who nevertheless understood its value. She obediently enrolled, but inwardly she determined to find another career.

Bruce formed a task force with a hard-working assistant, Colonel John Zierdt, to collect information about the ammunition problems at home and in Korea. They found troubles at every level. The root cause, however, stemmed from a Department of Defense policy carried over from the Truman administration. All Korean planning was based on a war of six months' duration. Since the fighting intensified with the influx of Chinese armies, the six months became a constantly moving period. The war had been in progress three years.

So-called experts who never fought a war ignored the unpleasant fact that ammunition plants, idle since World War II, could not be cranked up within 180 days. The lead time problem was simply ignored. The army could place orders only for ninety days' supply yet it took sixty days to move ammunition across the country and the Pacific Ocean to Japan, sixty days more to unload, store, select and transship to Korea, and thirty days to receive, sort, and move ammunition forward to the guns.

Eighth Army and allied United Nations forces lacked a firm policy to control usage of artillery shells. Estimates of how many shells each gun required were not adjusted when the combat situation changed. The high command failed to understand that by quadrupling the daily ration of shells, they added an entire shipload to the supply line.

The army's chief of staff, General J. Lawton Collins, took Bruce with him to Japan and Korea for a firsthand look. What they found angered both men. None of the senior ordnance officers had combat experience. As fast as ammunition arrived in Korea it was shoved up front. There was no reserve available that could be drawn on to meet Chinese attacks along the fluid battle line. The Reds assaulted only one corps sector at a time, but no one shuttled ammunition stocks from quiet sectors to meet sudden crises.

Such problems could be corrected even if it meant, as it did in some cases, replacing officers who refused to learn from their mistakes. A more sensitive problem involved the Eighth Army commander, General Van Fleet, whose son was killed in the bitter fighting. Van Fleet employed artillery with gusto, burning up shells to save his soldiers. As a consequence, ammunition was consumed at rates far greater than those of World War II. When the general's helicopter appeared at the front, artillery batteries started firing and continued until he left, whether targets were real or imaginary. If one Chinese soldier appeared on a distant hillside it was cause to fire a 155-millimeter cannon until he disappeared. Jittery troops fired small arms at prodigious rates.

Vehicles were scarce because headquarters in Japan insisted that any in need of repair must be shipped back for rebuild in Japanese assembly lines, the forerunners of today's Japanese auto plants. Many could have been restored to service by maintenance troops in Korea, but this was not permitted. To compound the problem, shipping damage was more severe than breakdowns caused by wear on the dirt roads.

Arguments and desk pounding corrected the situation. With General Collins' backing, Bruce forced recalcitrant officers to adopt new methods, leaving behind more people who resented his tough tactics. Returning to Washington, he spent months improving the transportation system and regulating the flow of ammunition to West Coast ports.

He and Ginny faced a small crisis at home. At nineteen years of age, Marta had to undergo a serious operation to remove a golf-ball-sized growth which was endangering her heart. She had finished secretarial training and entered Walter Reed Hospital for surgery while her parents prayed for help. By the time she recovered, Marta had determined to become a nurse.

"Dad," she addressed Bruce quickly, "I'm going to enter nursing."

Bruce thought that she should enter college for degree training, but Marta disagreed. She wanted to enroll in a hospital.

"That's a tough, dirty and painful experience," Bruce argued. "I'd rather you took the professional courses in a university."

"You're not listening," she retorted. "I've made up my mind and mother agrees."

Looking at her, Bruce realized that the daughter of yesterday, his golfing partner, had grown into a young woman almost without his notice. If he recalled a young marine who refused to study law against *his* father's wishes, he didn't admit it to her.

Probing around on her initiative, Marta found that the

District of Columbia General Hospital provided nurses' training under federal subsidy. She took physical and educational tests, passed without difficulty, and enrolled. When Bruce later addressed her class at the traditional capping ceremony, he had only kind words for nurses and nursing. If this was a retreat, Bruce knew how to carry it off gracefully.

Meanwhile alarming stories from Korea made page one news across the country. Headlines reported that American soldiers were said to be disheartened and in dire danger because they lacked ammunition. Congress reacted angrily. The public was already weary of this seemingly endless conflict which killed men, drained resources, interfered with consumer goods production and inflated prices.

The United States Senate ordered a searching investigation by a special committee chaired by Senator Margaret Chase Smith of Maine. Senators Symington, Saltonstall and Byrd served with her. They summoned General Van Fleet from the war front to testify. He asserted that his troops lacked ammunition.

Coming from the Eighth Army commander, this allegation aroused more indignation. Senator Smith gave the army two weeks to reply. General Collins told ordnance that he wanted Bruce Medaris to prepare the defense. His immediate chief, General Ford, gave him unlimited authority to call upon resources of the ordnance corps.

Ginny saw little of Bruce during this hectic period. He worked twenty hours a day with Zierdt, interviewing officers returning from Korea, conducting teletype conferences with sources in Tokyo and Seoul. One assistant lost twenty-eight pounds. Bruce catnapped at his desk more than one night. Zierdt looked on in amazement as Bruce dictated to three secretaries on unrelated topics. As one girl filled a page of shorthand notes he resumed dictating to another.

General Collins called Bruce with a new instruction. "I'm going to complicate your job," he said. "Whatever comes of this, I don't want any criticism of Van Fleet from an army witness. Keep that in mind when you get before the Senate committee."

Praying for strength, Bruce concluded there was but one course to follow. He would present the facts objectively and let the senators make the judgments. Meantime his task force assembled fifteen volumes of evidence, listing all army ammunition contracts.

When the hearings opened with newsmen attending, Bruce had answers ready for every question he could anticipate. If a surprise query arose, he could deliver the reply later that day. As the army unfolded the story, Bruce tactfully reminded the committee that before war broke out in Korea in 1950, the economic policies of Congress forced severe cutbacks in ammunition manufacture. World War II loading plants were shuttered. No money was available to keep them in a state of readiness. He displayed copies of army messages to Congress pleading for money. Attached to each was a record of the exact status of ammunition supplies on that date. The gap between the army's needs and what Congress appropriated became glaringly apparent.

Without naming Van Fleet, Bruce demonstrated with large charts that U.S. divisions consumed more ammunition after the Chinese attack than the entire Pacific Theater required in World War II. The army reduced supplies in the States to dangerously low levels in order to meet Korea's demands. Tons of shells were fired during the Chinese "human wave" attacks. The senators learned that money and time were needed to turn on production lines.

Since hand grenades were supposedly scarce, Bruce took one apart before the committee, calling attention to the number of parts and the precision required in their manufacture and assembly.

"If we let down on our standards to speed production," he warned, "we do so at the peril of our troops who deserve the safest and most effective firepower we can provide."

Van Fleet reportedly told commanders to create so many shell holes that "you can't walk without stepping in one" so as to slow Chinese advances. Bruce argued that that was a professional military judgment which the Senate should not challenge. A fellow officer listening to the proceedings observed that "when Bruce got into this I was spellbound. I lost all track of time. I came away with the conviction that when Medaris said something, the committee believed him."

A letter from Senator Smith's son in Korea was introduced. Senator Byrd commented that it was painful for a mother to read her son's plea for bullets. Bruce asked to see the letter. After reading it he pointed out that young Smith wanted .32-caliber hand gun bullets, never supplied by the army, for target practice. The hearings wound up in a relaxed atmosphere as Bruce proved that the army accomplished the near impossible by providing guns and ammunition to Eighth Army.

General Collins saw enough of Bruce Medaris to make a judgment. He ordered him promoted to brigadier general in April, 1953. Ordnance promptly assigned him as chief of ammunition. Ginny shared his pride and gratitude.

On July 27 United Nations and Communist negotiators met at Panmunjon and agreed upon a truce that divided Korea at the 38th Parallel. The war ended at a cost of 230,000 UN casualties while North Korea and China lost 1,000,000 men.

A happy surprise greeted Bruce and Ginny when Marilyn and her husband came from Ohio with an important announcement. Eugene Stillings decided to leave his career and enter seminary to become an Episcopal priest. They did not ask for Bruce's help, all they wanted was his blessing which was given immediately. Bruce and Ginny attended their son-in-law's ordination in December, 1957.

General Cummings became ordnance chief. Bruce succeeded him as director of industrial operations, supervising fourteen procurement districts including the one in Cincinnati where he served in 1939, and eight manufacturing arsenals. He improved management and installed better methods over the next two years. Visiting installations around the country, he flew into Redstone Arsenal in Huntsville, Alabama where Wernher von Braun and his former Peenemuende associates worked on Army rockets. When he met von Braun, Bruce told him of the near miss when a V-2 rocket landed near his command post.

Wernher shook his blond head. "There were many times," he explained, "when it was safer at the receiving end than at the launch site. We never had time to engineer reliability into the V-2. But I'm glad that you escaped."

The Germans in Huntsville were developing a new rocket for the army called Redstone which was larger than the V-2. There was some dissatisfaction in Washington about the pace of their progress; von Braun blamed it on meager funding. Bruce would have something to do with that soon, but neither man was aware of what was about to happen.

A sorrowing letter came from Marilyn. Her mother died in Bellefontaine and was buried in North Carolina beside her second husband. Bruce prayed for her and their daughter.

Young Bruce completed his prep studies and was admitted to the plebe class at West Point in 1955. General Ridgway became chief of staff. In May, 1955, he compiled a list of officers for promotion and sent it to President Eisenhower for approval. For the first time, Ridgway elected to make the list public. His first choice for major general was John Bruce Medaris who thus became the first reserve officer integrated into the regular army to win a second star. Eisenhower sent the nominations to the Senate where they were promptly confirmed.

Now fifty-three years old, having proved his abilities to the army, Bruce thought of retirement. He and Ginny discussed their future. She had been a faithful army wife, accepting frequent dislocations without complaint and enduring many separations while Bruce put out troublesome brush fires. Marta was doing well in nursing, Bruce was keeping up with his classmates at the academy. Now, Ginny felt, was a good time to enjoy a more settled life. Bruce agreed and said he would follow up an unsolicited and attractive offer. He spoke to General Cummings the following day.

"I'm going to step down, Em," he explained. "Ginny and I believe we ought to have more time together, which would mean leaving the army. I'm grateful for the help you gave and I've enjoyed my service in ordnance. But General Bradley asked me to join him in the Bulova company and I want to accept his offer. As you know, I've had nothing to do with Bulova contracts with the army, so there can be no finger pointing on that score. I don't believe we need to make this decision of mine public now, but I wanted you to have ample notice."

Cummings told Bruce that he would be missed. "I don't know any other officer who has given so freely of his talents and earned retirement so fully," he added.

Arrangements with Bulova were practically completed by October. Ginny prepared for one more move, breaking the news to friends and the family. Her happiness pleased them and her husband.

Bruce was dictating to his secretary one morning, preparing to wind up his affairs, when the phone rang. She took the call, then handed him the instrument.

"General Medaris," he answered.

"Sir, this is Colonel Littlejohn of General Magruder's staff," the caller said. "The general wants to see you at ten A.M. Saturday."

"Saturday?" Bruce asked. "Can't we meet at another time? How about Monday?"

"No, sir," the officer affirmed. "The general must see you Saturday morning."

"All right, I'll be there," Bruce said, instructing his secretary to cancel a planned golf match.

Pondering the meaning of this summons when he retired that night, Bruce prayed earnestly for guidance, believing some important decision hinged on his forthcoming talk with Magruder. Several weeks earlier he and Emerson Cummings proposed forming a ballistic missile agency for the express purpose of developing a long-range missile that could deliver an atomic bomb. The new agency would take over the von Braun team at Redstone Arsenal, push the 200-mile Redstone rocket to completion and build a Jupiter missile with a range of 1,750 miles. No such rocket existed in this country or elsewhere. They allowed only three years to complete the undertaking at a cost of hundreds of millions and planned to involve large segments of American industry. That proposal awaited decisions by Secretary of the Army Wilbur Brucker and the secretary of defense. Bruce was convinced this was behind the Magruder interview.

He knew that the security of Europe and the American forces in NATO might be at stake. Top-secret intelligence data over a period of months confirmed that the Russians successfully tested a powerful rocket that could fly 750 miles. They could launch such a weapon from bases within the Soviet Union and rain destruction on Western Europe. At the very least, the Communists could practice nuclear blackmail. To counter the threat, U.S. military chiefs were considering proposals for rockets able to hit Soviet targets from launching sites well beyond the range of their missile. The air force proposed a 1,750-mile weapon called Thor; the army recommended its Jupiter that would make use of components already tested in the smaller Redstone, while the navy suggested a new missile of this caliber ought to be launched from ships or submarines.

Bruce walked along the quiet Pentagon corridor to Magruder's third floor office, sat down in a chair facing his host and listened attentively.

"We're in a serious bind," Magruder began. "The air force briefed the Joint Chiefs of Staff on their Thor project and put up a strong case that since the long-range rocket may replace manned bombers as a strategic weapon, it belongs to them. The navy, on the other hand, shrewdly threw its weight behind our Jupiter project with the understanding that the army will develop the weapon for use either on land or at sea. That complicates our task but it lined up the senior services against the air force.

"We like that scheme which you and Em Cummings proposed. It promises the kind of aggressive management we must have to meet the timetable. Our problem is that Secretary Brucker has turned down several nominations for the command. He believes each man is a hidebound, ordnance conservative, who can't provide the kind of leadership required."

Bruce surmised what was coming next but kept silent.

"So that brings me to the purpose of this discussion," Magruder continued. "I've talked this out with the other staff officers and we're in complete agreement. The only general officer who can do the job and who will be acceptable to Secretary Brucker and the Defense Department is the man I'm talking to. Will you accept?"

"You've told me the problem and I appreciate that vote of confidence," Bruce responded. "But I also have a problem of a personal nature. Em Cummings knows that I planned to retire soon. Ginny deserves better than she has had from me during our marriage. General Bradley made me an attractive offer to join Bulova which I'm inclined to accept. On the other hand, I don't want to see the army sold down the river. The only sensible approach is the one von Braun put forward. His team is the key. It is a tremendous challenge. Let me talk it over with Ginny and I'll get back to you no later than Monday."

He drove home to confront Ginny with one more disappointment. If he accepted, her dream of a quiet life would be shelved for the next four years.

"I hate to ask this of you," Bruce said, "but my conscience is bothering me. I can't let the army down. It will mean another trying time when I'm bound to be away from home."

Ginny did not hesitate. "Bruce, I'm disappointed and I can't help worrying about the awful pressures this will put on you. But I am your wife, Bruce, and where you go, I go."

He sought guidance again that night. Next day he located General Bradley and explained the problem. Bradley urged him to accept. When Bruce met with Magruder and other senior officers on Monday he knew what must be done. Secretary Brucker eagerly accepted his nomination.

The Defense Department issued the verdict on November 8, 1955. The air force would develop Thor while the army and navy would jointly build Jupiter. The army published orders naming Major General Medaris commander of the new Ballistic Missile Agency effective February 1, 1956. The entire von Braun team of 1,600 scientists and engineers and the facilities they occupied in Alabama were transferred to the

Medaris command. History had come full circle. The men who created the V-2 would now build missiles for the United States against the Communist threat. Bruce would learn at a later time that von Braun, his technical chief, was a God-fearing man who also prayed for guidance and help. Those who found this trait difficult to reconcile with the awesome havoc wrought by German rockets in World War II forgot that the men of Peenemuende tried to defend their homeland against Allied bombings and invasions.

Bruce flew into Redstone Arsenal for searching discussions with its commander, Brigadier General H. N. Toftoy, his military and civilian managers, and von Braun, in order to pave the way for assuming the command in ninety days. He found von Braun anxious to deal on a first name basis and genuinely happy about the new agency. They talked at length about his plans.

"We have a tough schedule, Wernher," Bruce said, "and I intend to see that we meet it. You are going to head up the development organization and I will assemble the finest military talent to make sure that your designs satisfy the military requirements and to keep us in direct contact with army and navy resources."

"You can rely upon us," von Braun replied. "Jupiter is our first crack at a bigger missile and we're eager to show the army and the nation what we can do."

Wernher called in his top colleagues to meet their new boss: Dr. Eberhard Rees, his deputy; Dr. Walter Haeussermann and Fritz Mueller, guidance experts; Dr. Ernst Geissler, specialist in aeroballistics; Hans Maus, fabrication boss; William Mrazek, designer of missile structures; Dr. Helmut Hoelzer, computer expert; Eric Neubert, the reliability watchman; Hans Hueter, designer of missile support equipment; Karl Heimburg, boss of testing, and Dr. Kurt H. Debus, who launched more missiles than any man this side of the Iron Curtain. They would again write history; in time, as they built ever larger rockets, they would make it possible for men to reach the moon.

From their arrival in the United States in 1946 until 1950, the 110 expatriate rocket inventors assembled and launched fifty V-2 rockets from carloads of parts collected in Germany. American scientists built research equipment which was carried in the missiles to learn more about the upper atmosphere and fringes of outer space. Reporters discovered a promising news source when they interviewed von Braun in El Paso, Texas and heard him say it was possible to build a space platform which would hover 5,000 miles from earth where men could assemble expeditions to the moon.

When the supply of V-2 rockets came to an end, the army realized that the White Sands Missile Range in New Mexico was too small an area to fly bigger rockets safely. The Defense Department selected Cape Canaveral in central Florida as a major testing ground in 1949. The army moved the von Braun group to Alabama the following year and assigned them their first big project. They would build a Redstone missile that could carry an atom bomb weighing 6,000 pounds up to 200 miles. Such a weapon did not then exist in the Free World.

Setting up shop in Redstone Arsenal, von Braun's crew assembled a larger team of American-born engineers and mechanics, and undertook the work even though hampered by money shortages. The city of Huntsville, located on the western slopes of the Appalachian mountains, drained by the Tennessee River, was transformed from a cotton production center by the influx of people attracted by this revolutionary industry.

When war began in Korea there was sudden interest in the rocket work. However, von Braun found that he was dealing with people in the Pentagon who had little appreciation of the time, effort and cost involved in perfecting a large missile. There were no easily obtainable parts that could be assembled into such a rocket. No one was interested in the feasibility of exploring outer space. Stymied by military disinterest, von Braun tried to reach the public through a series of articles published in *Collier's Magazine* in 1953 dealing with satellites, space platforms and space ships. He made films with Walt Disney about travel in space. Much of what he predicted would eventually come to pass, but there were no takers at the time.

So the team kept on working and testing early Redstones at Cape Canaveral where the army built a blockhouse and launch pads. The rocket performed well. Its guidance and control system met the army's tough specification—it must place the warhead within 3,000 feet of a target at maximum range of 200 miles. When industry was asked to bid on a contract to produce the Redstone, only three companies responded. Industry could see little future in this exotic field. After some hesitation, the Chrysler Corporation agreed to tackle the job.

When Bruce assumed command, Chrysler assembled the rockets in a Michigan plant having learned the techniques by looking over the shoulders of the Redstone Arsenal team. Reynolds Metals Company shaped the fuselages at Muscle Shoals, Alabama; Ford Instrument Company supplied guidance and control equipment from a Long Island factory, and the Atomic Energy Commission furnished nuclear warheads. Hundreds of suppliers, large and small, contributed to the project.

Before moving to Huntsville, there were important matters to occupy Bruce. He appeared before the President's National Security Council and outlined the Jupiter project as spokesman for the army and navy, pointing out the missile's dimensions were limited by space available for them aboard naval ships. Early in January he faced the first of many disagreements with the air force. Bruce wanted to contract directly with North American Aviation, an air force supplier, for rocket engines. The other service insisted that he must place the orders through their ballistic missiles division. After much wrangling, the air force finally consented to allow the army to deal with the engine maker.

Later that month, a Defense Department scientific advisory committee decided that both the Thor and Jupiter projects should continue. However, they held up nearly $7,000,000 which the army needed to buy ground equipment for Jupiter. According to the Defense Department, that was outside the mission of Bruce's agency. Without supporting gear, Jupiter could not be launched from land. There were ominous overtones in the Defense Department's attitude which would be better understood in the coming months.

General and Mrs. Medaris drove into the arsenal from Washington on January 30, 1956 and were greeted by General Toftoy who arranged a luncheon. At a ceremony the following day Bruce activated his new agency before a crowd representing the 11,000 civilians and 2,000 military personnel engaged in various rocket projects on the arsenal, including antiaircraft missiles, short range battlefield rockets and antitank weapons.

He entered the most rewarding and frustrating phase of his military career. Along the way his agency would achieve notable successes and launch the first American earth satellite.

"With God's help, we'll make it," he told Ginny their first night in Alabama.

*The Medaris home in Springfield, Ohio. Young Bruce and his mother are on the porch.*

*Pop Wagner's Sunday school class at the Springfield Methodist Church. Roy A. Wagner is in the back row, center; Bruce is seated at the left.*

*Looking dour for the photographer at Springfield High School.*

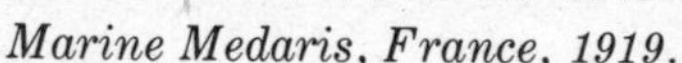

*Marine Medaris, France, 1919.*

*Sporting his physique as a Red Cross swimming instructor at Fort Benning.*

*Captain Medaris and his troop return from a three-day expedition in the Panama Canal Zone, January, 1926.*

*Election Board No. 5 for the American-administered plebiscite to settle the Tacna-Arica border dispute between Chile and Peru. The president of the board, Bruce Medaris, is seated in the middle. (April 2, 1926.)*

*Aboard the* Dorothea Dix *headed for North Africa in 1943. Bruce stands at the left, next to the ship's captain.*

*Standing tall as the First Army's ordnance officer.*

*Lieutenant Generals Omar Bradley (right) and Courtney Hodges (center) listen as Colonel Medaris talks. (March 22, 1945.)*

*General Koeltz of the French army bestows the Legion of Honor, Grade of Chevalier, on Bruce. (April 28, 1945.)*

Photo: U.S. Army Signal Corps.

*New York City welcomed the Argentine Minister of Defense shortly after the close of World War II. The minister waves happily to the crowds as his escort-interpreter, Colonel Medaris, looks on.*

*Major General J. B. Medaris, U.S. Army, Commanding General, Army Ordnance Missile Command, Huntsville, Alabama.*

*Wernher von Braun and his two daughters, Iris and Margrit, pose with General Medaris after the parade in Huntsville celebrating the launch of* Pioneer IV *to the Moon.*

*Bruce and Virginia Medaris together at home in Huntsville, 1957.*

*Bruce and Wernher von Braun at Redstone Arsenal. Behind them are Jupiter, Juno, and Redstone missiles (vertical) and a Zeus (canted).*
Photo: Official U.S. Army Photograph

*A family reunion at Redstone Arsenal (Huntsville) in 1959. Standing (left to right) are Captain Woody (Marta's first husband), West Point Cadet Bruce Medaris II, and the general. Seated are Eugene and Marilyn Stillings, Marta, and Mrs. Medaris—all with various children.*

*T. Keith Glennan (the first NASA administrator), Medaris, von Braun, and General John Barclay pose smilingly around a model of a Saturn rocket in 1959.*

*The first American astronauts visited Bruce in Huntsville late in 1959. Facing the general to his right are (right to left) the late Virgil Grissom, Donald K. Slayton, Walter Schirra, John Glenn, Alan Shepard, and Scott Carpenter. Shepard was the first of them to travel in space in May, 1961.* Photo: Official U.S. Army Photograph.

*General Medaris at the controls of his Aero Commander aircraft in Huntsville, 1958.*

*General Medaris, on the stand, receives the congratulations of his colleague, Major General Donald Yates, U.S. Air Force, who commanded the launch site at Cape Canaveral during the Medaris years. Looking on are Secretary of the Army Wilbur Brucker and Lieutenant General John Hinrichs, the Chief of Ordnance. This picture was taken at the Medaris retirement ceremonies in January, 1960, at the Redstone Arsenal.*

*After his retirement Bruce was an honored guest at the Cape Canaveral blockhouse to observe the launching of a Jupiter rocket in 1960. Kurt Debus is to his left, Eberhard Rees and Albert Zeiler, colleagues of Wernher von Braun, are on his right.*

*Deacon Medaris, newly ordained in 1969, at the Church of the Good Shepherd in Maitland, Florida.*

*Father Bruce with Bishop William Folwell at Bruce's ordination, June 29, 1970.*

*The Reverend Bruce Medaris in the Protestant pulpit at a Pentagon service.* Photo: Military District of Washington, Signal Support Unit, U.S. Army.

*Father Bruce in 1976.*

# 10

# ORDEALS OF MEN AND MISSILES

Bruce Medaris became the first officer in army history entrusted with total responsibility for research, development, production and deployment of a major weapon system. It was a heady and demanding assignment and, to help him fulfill it, Secretary of the Army Wilbur Brucker and the chief of staff, General Maxwell Taylor, gave him extraordinary powers. He could tap officers anywhere, shortcut slow contracting procedures, and, for two years, was immune to inspections and audits.

The significance of these authorities was not lost on the man who wielded them. With characteristic flair, he arranged extra flourishes to impress official visitors and build esprit de corps in his unique organization. There was a special flag, a distinctive shoulder patch worn on uniforms, the insignia of which also appeared on aircraft and other missile agency equipment. Impeccably dressed military police (not less than six feet tall) stood guard by elevators carrying passengers from the first to second floors. He brandished a swagger stick, symbol of his Marine Corps days, whenever he wore the general's cap dressed in gold braid.

Redstone Arsenal had never seen the like. Bruce sometimes drove a Jaguar sports car. Military policemen regaled newcomers with the story about the MP who stopped a speeding car one day, talking roughly to its driver who wore golf clothes.

"Didn't you see that speed limit sign back there?" the MP demanded.

"What did it say?" the driver asked.

"Forty-five miles an hour and you were going sixty," the policeman asserted.

"Do you know who I am?"

"No, I don't," retorted the MP.

"Son, I am General Medaris and the speed limit has just been raised to sixty."

Heads would nod as listeners laughed and said, "That's the Big M!" The fact was that the incident involved a former arsenal commander, General Vincent, but it seemed to fit the Medaris personality. Determined to bring the entire army into the Jupiter program, Bruce obtained officers for his staff from the transportation, signal and engineers corps who could muster the expert assistance of their branches. The Continental Army Command sent Colonel Charles G. Patterson, his crony in the First Army during World War II, to represent the combat arms. Patterson would make sure the missiles met the needs of troops.

The hand-picked staff included Brigadier General John A. Barclay as deputy commander; Captain William Hassler, representing the navy; Colonel John C. Nickerson, field coordinator; Colonel Milton H. Clark, executive officer; Lieutenant Colonels William Durrenberger, financial manager, and James Killough, security chief. Colonel Thurston

Paul was buying a house in Washington when the summons from Alabama stopped the deal. Colonel John Zierdt, top aide in the ammunition probe, was pulled out of class at the Army War College. One officer was driving to a new assignment in California when Illinois highway patrolmen stopped his car and turned him south toward Redstone Arsenal.

Either Lieutenant Horace Tousley or Lieutenant Henry Magill, Bruce's aides, traveled with him wherever he went. One or the other drove to his quarters each morning, reported overnight events at breakfast, and accompanied him to headquarters promptly at eight. Adhering to his custom, Bruce read the Bible on awaking. Ginny furnished the ranch type house on Squirrel Hill near the officers' club. Her piano dominated the living room. She kept up a busy schedule of social events, welcoming wives of arriving officers, and keeping a watchful eye on club activities.

There were many vital decisions and Bruce made them without flinching, telling his aides, "I learned from General Bradley that when you are told to do a job and given the resources you need, you have lost all excuse for failure. The buck stops with you. Once you realize the only place you have to look for an excuse is the mirror, you stop trying to invent one." That was his creed and he expected his subordinates to embrace it as well.

He believed in the direct approach. While showing Secretary Brucker around the place, Bruce said he wanted to fence off the Missile Agency from the rest of the 40,000-acre arsenal. He did not, however, relish the time and paper work necessary to justify fencing. Brucker took out a pen and scribbled on an envelope: "You are authorized to procure and install fencing." Noses were out of joint in other Army offices when they learned that Bruce knew how to beat the system.

Agency recruiters opened offices in New York City, San

Francisco, Dallas and St. Louis. They combed universities in search of young engineers. While the government pay did not match industry, they had a powerful inducement in the chance to work with the von Braun team with the possibility of a stake in space exploration. They would work in a creative environment that encouraged initiative. So they came, at first a trickle and later in steadily increasing numbers until the agency employed more than 5,000 civilians.

Huntsville, first capital of the Confederacy, groaned at the seams. Heavy commuting traffic saturated two-lane roads. Housing was scarce, rents skyrocketed and trailer camps appeared overnight. Some newcomers occupied houseboats on the Tennessee River flowing along the arsenal's southern boundary. Bruce talked to Mayor R. B. Searcy and provided engineers to plan new roads. They agreed that the army should look after housing military personnel while the mayor and council encouraged civilian accommodations. A commission was set up to improve the airport.

At Bruce's suggestion, the city reluctantly agreed to expand its boundaries. Sewage and water systems were extended to obtain federal mortgage loans for thousands of new homes. The city's population increased from 16,000 in 1950 until it passed the 72,000 mark ten years later and doubled again in the next decade.

Lieutenant Tousley recalled the hectic pace of early 1956: "We worked overtime to prepare a formal report covering the 1956-57 period, spending all hours of the day and night six and a half days weekly in the office. We fought hard for everything the agency needed but before the general would move, a lot of blood, sweat and tears were shed. . . . His grasp of detail was astounding. He could leaf through ten pages of typescript and scan a page in thirty seconds. The first time it happened, you thought he didn't care. But if there was a weak point, however small, he pounced on it, asked one question and you knew that he had you nailed. And he could quote figures weeks later. Because of his comprehension and ability to get things done, he enjoyed the respect of von Braun and the staff."

Two weeks after his arrival, Bruce established the test firing schedule for Jupiter at Cape Canaveral. The first launch over the maximum range of 1,750 miles would occur May 1, 1957; meanwhile, modified versions of the smaller Redstone would carry Jupiter components in early tests. A fully operational missile would be ready by the end of 1958. Secretary of Defense Charles Wilson approved the basic design accepted by the army and navy, Jupiter would measure 58 feet in length and 105 inches in diameter. Secretary Brucker passed along secret instructions from Defense, after which Bruce summoned von Braun.

"Wernher, we have another tall order," he began. "The president is concerned about Soviet intentions. If we can show that a missile can fly 2,000 miles or more, so as to hit enemy targets from bases beyond their retaliatory power, it will help allay some real fears. Can we do it?"

"I think we can but it will take some months to prepare," von Braun assured him. "You know that we tried to sell the idea two years ago of putting up a small satellite and got nowhere. But we put aside two Redstone missiles at the time and they are still available."

With the assistance of the Jet Propulsion Laboratory in Pasadena, California, working under Army contracts, von Braun's designers planned to install a spinning tub on top of a Redstone. Small rockets in the tub would fire in sequence at the proper altitude above earth and propel a twenty-pound satellite to a speed of 17,000 miles per hour, which was the minimum velocity to maintain orbit as it fell around earth. The combination of big and little rockets could perform another mission related to the secret conversation with

Secretary Brucker. A Jupiter missile weighing 100,000 pounds would develop a speed of 15,000 feet per second in less than three minutes. Its warhead would slam back into the atmosphere at 10,000 miles an hour. Atmospheric friction built up 3,000 degrees of heat, enough to melt steel. How to shield the nuclear warhead from that fierce heating posed a major challenge to missile development. More was involved than protecting a deadly explosive, because the solution would also make it possible to hurl men into space and return them to earth.

The army team explored more than fifty approaches, testing many kinds of materials, until time was running out and funds dwindled. A choice had to be made and tested by constructing a model-size nose cone. Bruce, von Braun and the others concerned with the investigation understood they must make the right choice or lose out. Faced with this challenge, Bruce sought guidance in prayer. He chose an ablation concept, coating the metal shell with material that would melt like ice in sunshine and dissipate the heat. Small nose cones could be carried on the multi-stage rocket for the acid test. Bruce instructed von Braun to prepare a rocket for launch in September, hoping it would hurl the radio-equipped tip 3,000 miles across the Atlantic Ocean.

About eight weeks after taking command, Bruce sat down at his desk to examine reports of a Redstone launch that carried some components of the new Jupiter. Things were moving along very well, but he needed relief from an annoying sinus problem. He called the army hospital a few miles from his office.

"Hello, Dr. Salna speaking."

"This is General Medaris," he said. "I have a small problem with a sinus condition, been fighting it for years, and want some antihistamines. Will you send some over?"

"Yes, General, I'll be glad to provide medication. But if

you will pardon my insistence, I think we ought to do more. Your health is important to us and the army, so we ought to become acquainted. Why don't you come over for examination?"

Bruce chuckled. He had received a complete physical examination, including the usual prostate checkup, in October before leaving Washington. But the young physician had a point, he owed him the courtesy, so he told Louise Parker, his secretary, to fit the hospital visit into his schedule.

Jonas Salna was an interesting conversationalist. Bruce chatted amiably while the doctor went about the examination and commented favorably on his eyesight, hearing and general condition. He finished with a prostatic scrutiny. Bruce's good humor chilled as Dr. Salna said: "There is something here I don't like. I don't know what it is, but it shouldn't be there. It feels small and might just be a minor infection."

As Bruce sat up, regarding him intently, Salna added, "I want you to fly over to Fort Benning where there is a topflight urologist and let him take a look."

"I'd appreciate your discretion," Bruce said as he dressed. "I don't want to alarm Mrs. Medaris unnecessarily or shake up my staff."

"Of course, General," Salna responded. "There may be no reason for alarm."

Intuitively, Bruce knew he had prostate cancer although the physician did not mention the word. He kept this to himself, telling Ginny only that he would fly down to Benning for a day. Dr. Salna went along to introduce him to the urologist. The examination confirmed the presence of a tumor; however, a biopsy would determine if it was malignant. Bruce put off the test, wanting time to think over the situation, and returned to the arsenal.

As he walked into his office Miss Parker announced a call coming in from Colonel Jack Schwartz, chief of urology at Walter Reed Hospital in Washington. Bruce listened as Schwartz good-naturedly said, "I want you to get your tail up here as quickly as you can." The arsenal's medical officer, informed of the finding by Dr. Salna, had called Schwartz. Bruce pleaded a busy schedule, but his caller interrupted, "Do you want me to get an order from the chief of staff?" Bruce stopped arguing and promised to report in two days. He informed General Barclay and his aides, asking them to keep quiet about his trip until the facts were known.

He talked with Ginny. "I've got to fly up to Walter Reed," he explained. "Jack Schwartz wants to do a biopsy just as a precaution. He'll probably find out this is wasting his time and mine, but I'll go along to humor him."

Trying to conceal her fear, Ginny said, "I'm going, too."

They flew to Washington as the words of St. Luke ran through his mind, "The power of the Lord was present to heal." Bruce stopped at the small chapel to pray as they drove into the hospital grounds. Ginny arranged to live close by and take her meals with her husband. Marta left her nursing classes to be with her parents.

More tests followed. Lieutenant Colonel Van Buskirk, the surgeon assigned to the case, explained the procedure to Ginny and Bruce. They would prepare for surgery, administering a partial spinal anesthetic in the operating room, then a sample would be excised and sent to the pathology laboratory. If no malignancy existed, Bruce would return to his room for other treatment. If there was malignancy, Van Buskirk would proceed with a radical prostatectomy.

Dimly aware of activity as he lay on the operating table, Bruce heard Van Buskirk talking to the laboratory by phone. "You sure of that?" the surgeon asked. "Yes," came the reply. "Let's go!" Van Buskirk ordered and Bruce heard no more. He awakened later in severe pain. The surgeon inserted a catheter because Bruce lost control of his bladder.

As Van Buskirk described the operation to Bruce and Ginny, he assured them that all traces of the cancer were gone. There was one chance in 10,000, he added, that a patient could eventually regain all normal functions. Unless this occurred, Bruce would be forever impotent.

"Do you know what you've done?" Ginny cried out in protest.

Time proved that Bruce was not the exception. The surgeon's knife had brought an end to conjugal intimacy for him and Ginny. The emotional impact of that harsh reality would linger long after the physical wound had healed. But they found that their love could transcend even the absence of its most characteristic expression. Bruce became more tender towards Ginny. He found comfort in the belief that the Almighty spared him for the missile program. "The Lord was good to me," he acknowledged to close friends. "There was no other explanation for that unscheduled physical examination. Apart from young Salna's concern, the cancer would have done its lethal work."

Privately Bruce concluded that the loss of sexual power might have been a Divine judgment. He accepted it.

Ginny remarked to Marta that "Bruce is a very complex person as we both know, but he has taken this in stride without any of the angry repercussions that I might have expected from any other man."

After two days of bed rest, he insisted upon picking up his duties even though Ginny objected that it was much too soon. Bruce arranged with Van Buskirk that his aide, Lieutenant Magill, could visit the hospital daily to report events occurring in the Pentagon and Huntsville of interest to Bruce. Briefers from the National Science Foundation and the army brought him up-to-date on scientific and technical developments that might apply to missile projects.

He rigged up a clothes hanger to support the catheter device with its flexible tube and receptacle so that he could walk from his room to the lounge where he spent five hours daily talking with visitors or reading until a watchful nurse ordered him to bed. Van Buskirk checked his progress with obvious satisfaction. Bruce asked him why a gifted surgeon chose military service instead of a lucrative civilian practice.

"Anyone who comes in here gets what he needs without regard to his pocketbook," Van answered. "That is more important to me than money."

Bruce and Ginny flew back to Alabama ten days after the operation. Defying the surgeon's order to rest for a month, he resumed his schedule wearing a "motorman's friend," a device he learned about working on the Springfield trolley cars. It was a tube concealed in his trousers that ran into a small sack strapped on his ankle. Meticulous in dress, Bruce was embarrassed at the prospect of going through life with an uncontrollable bladder. Finally he sought the advice of a doctor who told him "get rid of that tube or you will never regain control." He followed this dictum and the problem disappeared.

Having completed her training, Marta found nursing positions readily available in Washington. But she was concerned about her father's health and her mother's anxiety over the pace he kept up. Marta called their quarters in Alabama.

"Dad," she told Bruce, "I'm coming home. I want to be closer to you and mother."

Happy at the prospect, Bruce called Ginny to the phone, telling Marta "Come on, we want you and we love you."

She found a job quickly in the arsenal hospital. Her presence helped Ginny who now had Marta to share her evenings when Bruce traveled as he shuttled to and from Washington, the Cape and the West Coast.

General Bradley had become chief of the Veterans' Administration. He had heard of Bruce's operation and invited him to participate in a research project. His scientists had developed a technique of blood testing which promised to detect cancer at an early stage. Thereafter Bruce underwent tests at six-month intervals with negative results while he remained in the army.

On his fifty-fourth birthday he took Ginny to a dance at the officers club. Watching the festivities, he remarked, "Ginny, the doctor says I shouldn't dance, but I can't sit here and listen to that music. Let's try it." They did, to her delight and the applause of their friends.

The Eisenhower administration had announced Project Vanguard, which was supposed to produce America's first earth satellite, the previous year. The competing army proposal, shaped by Wernher von Braun, had been rejected. Now the Defense Department committee that had made the decision asked Huntsville for a new proposal.

In 1956 Bruce and von Braun had proposed to launch seven rockets that would carry small satellites between January 1957 and December 1958 at a cost of $18 million. A month passed, then Bruce received curt orders forbidding him to use any part of Redstone or Jupiter missile programs to launch satellites. He secretly told von Braun to hide two rockets because he firmly believed they would be needed later.

When he told the story to Congress months later, under far different circumstances, Bruce remarked "there continued to be such opposition to army participation in the space program that it was imprudent to admit we had retained those rockets."

Some of the officers and civilian managers closest to Bruce noted a gradual change taking place after the cancer attack.

When an important decision was needed he would listen to arguments pro and con, then get up and walk over to a window, apparently weighing the merits, before returning with a verdict. They did not know he was actually praying about it, asking God to guide his decisions.

His crowded schedule left little time to deal with community affairs so Bruce instructed General Toftoy to continue as the army contact with Huntsville. The city saw little of Bruce except when he attended services at the Church of the Nativity, the pre-Civil War edifice close to Court House Square.

Driving for better air service, he made the new army control tower at the arsenal landing field available to serve the city's airport. Thus equipped by proxy, Huntsville succeeded in obtaining additional commercial flights to the East Coast and South for the benefit of thousands of visitors to the missile agency. Later in the year Bruce qualified for the silver wings of an army pilot. From then on he flew his light plane to Washington, the West Coast and other business appointments.

Still concerned about the housing situation, he prodded engineers to complete several hundred units for military personnel on the arsenal grounds. At the same time he furnished data to Senator John Sparkman, a resident of Huntsville, and Congressman Bob Jones who sponsored legislation that directed the Federal Housing Administration to release mortgage money that would encourage civilian housing in the city.

As the months went by, the von Braun team was still preparing for that long range rocket flight, in secrecy. If the Jupiter C vehicle performed as expected, the instruments mounted on its nose would be hurled three thousand miles before splashing into the Atlantic Ocean off the African coast. Sand filled part of the rocket; if a smaller rocket were installed in its place, the instrument package would become an earth satellite. That, the Pentagon ruled, must not occur.

Bruce relayed instructions to von Braun and Kurt Debus at Cape Canaveral that "our success in missile firings appears to be in inverse ratio to the number of distinguished guests present, so there will be none for this launch."

Ginny and Marta wondered why Bruce appeared tense and withdrawn. He could not explain his concern. It was one of the penalties of the secrecy order.

A rehearsal September 17 went off smoothly and Debus started the launch countdown at noon next day only to stop when severe thunderstorms occurred in the area. The launch crew tried again September 19. Jupiter C roared away into a dark sky at 1:47 A.M. September 20.

The small package atop flashed signals to tracking stations on islands stretching from the Bahamas southeast across the Atlantic. It reached a peak altitude of 682 miles and traveled 3,350 miles in 1,560 seconds, by far the longest flight achieved by the United States. Debus transmitted a report of the successful mission to Alabama, telling Bruce that "orbital flight could have been readily obtained if the last stage was fired." Secretaries Brucker and Wilson got their three thousand-mile flight as Bruce had promised months before. The launch and performance data were kept secret, Defense telling the agency that "no information in part or in full" would be made public. But a trade magazine carried a description of the flight in October, touching off a furious but futile search for the person who released the information.

The wave of optimism that spread through the agency after this demonstration soon disappeared, however. The navy talked of withdrawing from the Jupiter program, intending to develop a new submarine-mounted rocket called Polaris. Bruce learned of this in Washington shortly before he addressed an army convention about a radical plan to deliver troops and supplies behind enemy lines by carrying them in large missiles. *Life* magazine published pictures of the proposed troop carrier to the discomfiture of the Defense Department and the air force. The press considered the proposal newsworthy, but few understood its significance. Bruce was trying to get across the real meaning, that a suitably shielded nose cone which could protect a nuclear warhead could also protect an astronaut returning from space. But it would be five years before Alan Shepard rode a Redstone rocket as the first American space pilot.

The army and its missile agency suffered a severe blow in November when Secretary of Defense Wilson published a "roles and mission" order carving up the ballistic missile projects of the army, navy and air force. Wilson ruled that the air force would operate intercontinental missiles like Atlas, then in development, and its successors, Titan and Minuteman, capable of transporting the A-bomb from 5,000 to 10,000 miles. The navy decided to go ahead with a solid propellant missile, the Polaris, assisted by Bruce's agency. But otherwise they quit the ship-based Jupiter program. The air force would also control the land-based 1,750-mile missiles, like Thor and Jupiter. As for the army, Wilson determined the oldest of the services could have missiles limited to 200 miles which happened to be the range of the Redstone vehicle. While both Thor and Jupiter would continue to compete until a choice could be made later, the army lost its right to possess bigger rockets. With the air force in complete control it seemed unlikely that the Jupiter, coming as it did from von Braun's team, would have much chance of winning that competition.

Morale plummeted at Redstone Arsenal. Huntsville feared its prized industry would disappear. Bruce tried to quell the fears of his team with a brief statement: "Army has authorized me to state that any existing missile program

(Jupiter) has not been affected. The decision on operational responsibilities does not involve the termination of any missile."

These were reassuring words, but how much stock could anyone put in the future? Congress reacted angrily. How could the Secretary of Defense rule against the only team that demonstrated success in actual missile flights?

Senator Richard Russell of Georgia, chairman of the Armed Services Committee, told newsman that "too much money has been invested at Redstone Arsenal to throw it away. We of the committee have offered the army a forum to protest Secretary Wilson's 200-mile limitation. Wilson has been too restrictive on the Army. It cannot safely be deprived of atomic weapons with more than 200 miles range if a potential enemy is not going to abide by those limits." On the other hand, Senator Russell considered the decision a step in the direction of unified weapons policy which, he said, "has been as nebulous as a dancing sunbeam."

Bruce had good reason to believe in Jupiter's future, but he could not say why. Only his closest associates, including von Braun, knew what had happened. Weeks before, Bruce had met the Defense missile czar, William Holaday, and his air force counterpart, General Bernard Schriever for a no-holds-barred, closed door debate on the merits of Thor versus Jupiter. It soon became evident that Bruce knew more about the status of the Thor missile than Schriever. He expressed reservations about the ability of the Thor team to meet the December, 1958, deployment date which was also Jupiter's deadline. Surprised at some of his information, defense executives asked if he could document his statements. He did so in a secret report. Holaday found it impossible to cancel Jupiter and so advised Secretary Wilson. Both men felt that work on the two missiles must continue to ensure that at least one would be ready in time.

Other, less momentous problems also faced Bruce. The Congress said that for a given quantity of dollars, the military must buy a fixed minimum of floor space. So Bruce contracted for prefabricated houses, a novel solution which had to be implemented without the help of the Corps of Engineers, who looked down on ready built structures. The housing, which can accommodate 170 families, is still in use at this writing.

Private industry was hiring some of the best civilian engineers by offering $25,000 salaries and fringe benefits the government could not match. Bruce called in the offending firms who agreed not to proselyte in return for his promise that the army would not steal their people. One thousand more telephone circuits were installed connecting the Pentagon, Cape Canaveral, the air force missile headquarters in California, White Sands Missile Range, and the Chrysler plant in Michigan. So many salesmen jammed missile agency corridors that a new rule was instituted. Before a salesman could enter, the company must furnish written information about its product or services. If the agency had an interest, the salesman would be allowed inside the gate.

The agency commenced a cooperative program with the University of Alabama, Mississippi State College, the University of Tennessee, Auburn and Georgia Tech. A student engineer could hold a government job in the agency, spending part of the year in school, and earn a degree in five years while earning wages.

After a year's experience in the missile business, Bruce concluded that more of the army's resources essential to this unique enterprise ought to come under a single manager. There was too much duplication of effort and dissipation of talent among the half dozen organizations working on related projects. So he appointed General Toftoy chairman of a small, select and tight-lipped group that prepared a study for army and Defense consideration at a later time. The objective was an Army Ordnance Missile Command to oversee all ballistic missiles, air defense and tactical rockets.

As Christmas approached, Bruce looked back with deserved satisfaction on a year of sustained progress despite occasional reverses. Chrysler won the competition as prime contractor to build Jupiters in Michigan, in the same plant where Redstones were assembled. Flight tests at the Cape proved successful. He had recovered from cancer surgery. Cheering holiday messages arrived from top army officials who expressed their pleasure at the notable record of Jupiter's first year.

Of momentous significance for the future, that September flight of a three thousand-mile missile foreshadowed events that would catapult the team into worldwide fame. He and Ginny planned the commander's reception on New Year's Day with light hearts.

# 11

# A TRIAL OF FAITH

Ginny and Bruce's happiness was, however, short-lived. Bitter controversy engulfed the missile agency as the new year arrived, damaging Bruce Medaris, testing his faith and the army's faith in him.

The agonizing dilemma was triggered by Secretary Wilson's decision to place control of all long-range missiles, except those later developed by the navy, with the air force and denying them to the army. A senior staff officer, Colonel John C. Nickerson, a West Point graduate, touched off a clash with civilian authority in the Defense Department. Defying Bruce clandestinely, he tried to reverse the Wilson verdict. Suddenly the agency commander found his integrity in question for the first time in his career as he strove to preserve the von Braun team and keep the Jupiter project alive.

Nickerson was a former artillery officer who had distinguished himself in World War II combat in Europe. He filled a unique Pentagon job in 1954 and 1955 which kept him in close touch with Redstone Arsenal and the missile team. In this capacity he assisted in presenting von Braun's early satellite proposals, none of which won acceptance, to the department. He enjoyed the confidence of the Redstone Arsenal group.

Many army officers shared his resentment over the Wilson decision, and Bruce himself considered it a mistake, but, unlike his colleagues, Nickerson undertook to fight against his commander's orders. Thus he set in motion a chain of events that almost ruined his career, stained the missile agency's reputation, and might have killed the Jupiter program.

General Emerson Cummings persuaded Bruce to take Nickerson as a staff officer despite his reputation for stubbornness and independence. He ran a field coordination office which sent representatives to the air force missiles organization in Los Angeles, the navy in Washington, the army and Defense committees in the Pentagon, and major companies at work on Jupiter contracts. The purpose was to keep information flowing between the agency and these interested groups.

When the Wilson judgment became known Bruce explained its implications to his staff, reminding them that when the Jupiter project began there was no decision as to which branch of the service would eventually control the weapon. "Since Jupiter was given to the army for development without such a decision," he pointed out, "it is illogical to assume that assignment of operational responsibility to the air force changes what we are doing. Neither Thor nor Jupiter has yet proved itself and I do not expect any change until one has demonstrated that it will succeed.

"This was a hard decision for the secretary to make. I'm

sure he was subjected to great pressures. There is one thing we must not do under any circumstances and that is to attack his decision. The last time to harass a man is when he has made a tough judgment. Any such attack would only make him furious and could easily get us thrown out. Our problem is to show who can do the best job for the nation. The ordnance corps has a long history of making weapons for other services and we can use that fact to reinforce our right to be considered on an even basis."

After Bruce spoke this instruction, Nickerson wanted to talk with him about the situation and brought along Lieutenant Colonel Glenn Crane, the agency's representative with the air force in California. Bruce again told the two of his decision not to question the Wilson judgment.

"People who want to help sustain our development assignments should have the essential facts about the competence of the von Braun team and our right to continue," he said, "but we must not be drawn into a fight over control of the weapons. That issue is not our business."

A few days later Nickerson interrupted Bruce by walking into his office unannounced. In angry tones he declared, "We must not let that decision stand. We've got to reverse it so that the army controls the missiles!"

Bruce pointed a warning finger as he said, "Nickerson, I've given you and the staff direct orders. You must not attack Wilson in or out of this agency. Now get out of here!"

In Nickerson's opinion, ballistic missiles were no more than longer range guns, and, since artillery belonged historically to the army, his service should control them. The air force, on the other hand, regarded missiles as strategic weapons that could replace bombers. Nickerson wanted to muster political and industrial support in order to force the secretary of defense to assign missiles to ground forces.

These were matters, however, within the province of army headquarters, not an ordnance command engaged in rocket development.

Bruce determined to preserve the missile team at all costs, sure that its competence would eventually bring just recognition. He would fight for his projects but never entertained any notion of engaging in open political war with the civilian who ran the Defense Department. Mistakenly, as it turned out, he assumed that Nickerson, as a senior staff member, would abide by his decision. He told no one of the brief, angry encounter with his subordinate.

Quietly and stealthily Nickerson brought together a small group of officers and civilians who feared for the agency's future. With their assistance he wrote a document titled "Considerations on the Wilson Memorandum." It contained highly sensitive and secret information known only to a handful of top-level officials. It also criticized Secretary Wilson, air force policy and management, the prime air force contractors on Thor, Douglas Aircraft and the AC Spark Plug division of General Motors Corporation, which worked on Thor's guidance system.

Copies of the document were delivered by Nickerson's assistants to U.S. Senators Lister Hill and John Sparkman of Alabama, Congressmen Bob Jones and George Huddleston, also of Alabama, and executives of several army contractors. One copy was hand carried to Drew Pearson, the muckraking Washington newspaper columnist, and another was mailed to Erik Bergaust, editor of *Missiles and Rockets*, the magazine that published an account of the three thousand-mile flight of Jupiter C.

Nickerson visited Pentagon offices in December, seeking to arouse support for his cause, and somehow wangled an audience with Secretary Brucker. These harangues came to the attention of army officials who ordered Bruce to stop all

Washington visits from his agency unless he personally approved them. This was his first inkling that Nickerson was continuing to argue the case against his order, but so far as he knew at the time, the colonel was doing his talking in military circles.

A Pearson assistant promptly took the "Considerations" paper, which was unsigned, to Major General Kinney, the air force information chief, and left it with him to obtain his comments. That exposure proved to be Nickerson's undoing. When he saw its contents, Kinney delivered the paper to Air Force Secretary Donald Quarles who immediately turned it over to Secretary Wilson. By that time it bore "Secret" stamps supplied by the air force.

Wilson summoned Secretary Brucker on December 28, 1956, and demanded an accounting for this disclosure of secret data which, he concluded, must come from an army source. Brucker was furious when he read the charges. He visited Congress and retrieved copies from the Alabama members, warning them that the document contained data of great value to an enemy power, such as the date when the United States planned to site missiles of 1,750-mile range in Europe aimed at the Soviet Union. Brucker then directed the army's inspector general, Lieutenant General David Ogden, to find the author. Because of its contents it was assumed the paper must have been prepared in the ballistic missile agency.

Ogden and Colonel Richard Conran, an investigator, arrived at Redstone Arsenal on New Year's Day. They asked to see Bruce as soon as the traditional commander's reception for his officers and their wives concluded. He met them that evening. Having introduced himself, Ogden handed Bruce the "Considerations" paper.

"Are you familiar with this?" he asked.

Bruce leafed through the pages quickly.

"No, I've never seen it before," he replied.

Ogden told him of the circumstances that led him to Alabama in search of the culprit. Bruce sensed that the investigators suspected he might be involved. From what little he read, he realized that this attack could well destroy the confidence of Defense and the air force in his team.

"I'll support your investigation in any way possible," he assured Ogden. "I fully appreciate the problem this has created."

Asked if he had any knowledge of possible authorship, Bruce mentioned Colonel Nickerson's strong beliefs and his verbal attacks upon the Defense decision during his recent Washington trip. Seared by the realization that someone in his agency had disobeyed him and bared secret data, Bruce instructed his executive officer and security chief to assist General Ogden.

Within twenty-four hours the essential facts were clear. Investigators found records in the arsenal printing shop of four orders signed by Nickerson employees for sixty-five copies of the document. They found another's signature on a postal receipt for registered mail sent to Bergaust. A security officer reported that he saw black smoke emerging from the chimney of Nickerson's house as if someone were burning paper in the fireplace. The house was searched. Secret papers were discovered in the colonel's briefcase and in the attic. Ogden questioned Nickerson who denied knowledge of the document. Later, when the trail of evidence pointed unmistakably to his office, Nickerson confessed. His security clearance was lifted and he was relieved of duty January 8, 1957, continuing to live in arsenal quarters with his wife and four children.

Ogden prepared to return to Washington, having completed the probe. Bruce asked him to tell Secretary Brucker that he would resign at once if his usefulness was impaired or if Brucker had lost confidence in him. The secretary replied that he had complete faith in his leadership.

The agency buzzed with gossip about mysterious happenings concerning Colonel Nickerson. Only a few key officials knew the story until the case became public knowledge in March. Meanwhile Bruce requested that the case be taken out of his hands so there would be no question of prejudice. The Third Army commander in Atlanta, Georgia, Lieutenant General Thomas F. Hickey, was assigned responsibility for the inevitable court martial.

Nickerson asked to see Bruce. The general's aide, Lieutenant Henry Magill, was present for the brief meeting.

"I guess that I pulled a boner," Nickerson began, "and I'm sorry for the trouble I've caused you."

"You certainly did," Bruce answered. "You know that you went directly against my policy and instructions."

"You're right," Nickerson admitted.

Bruce looked at him. "I will support and defend anyone who makes an honest mistake in trying to carry out my policies," he said, "but I cannot support or defend anyone who intentionally opposes them as you have done."

Only the three men knew of the conversation.

When Bruce told Ginny of the situation, understanding that garrison wives would talk about it, he explained, "I cannot tell the whole story, Ginny, without giving away the secrets which Nickerson disclosed. His disobedience and arbitrary misuse of highly classified details have got him in serious trouble. Whatever his motivation, he has placed this agency and the Jupiter program in jeopardy."

"I'm sorry for his wife and children," Ginny responded. "This must be a terrible ordeal for them. But you're also under suspicion by inference, Bruce, and I don't believe Nickerson and his friends are doing anything to correct the notion that he did these things with your tacit approval. I hate to see you suffer for his mischief."

Ginny knew that Bruce received angry phone calls and

letters from officers distant from the scene who blamed him for failing to support Nickerson, unaware that the colonel disobeyed orders. These attacks hurt both Bruce and Ginny.

Seemingly oblivious to the turmoil, the development team launched the first Jupiter missile sucessfully from Cape Canaveral. The rocket sped toward the heavens for seventy-four seconds and broke up. Jet flames from the engine billowed up into the hollow tail and destroyed control circuits. The team quickly designed a flame resistant shield and installed this protection around engines of later missiles. The short flight occurred just thirteen months after the agency undertook the project. Two days later Bruce and von Braun appeared on a national television program, "Wide, Wide World," and described their progress in rocketry.

The second Jupiter became unstable after ninety-three seconds of flight. The team pinpointed the cause within forty-eight hours. Jupiter's tanks carried more liquid kerosene and oxygen than any previous missile. The propellants sloshed about and shifted the rocket as it pitched into its course, overcoming the control system. Cans fashioned of wire mesh were floated in the tanks thereafter to stabilize the liquid. On May 11, 1957, the third Jupiter traveled over 1,400 miles to the Atlantic Ocean target area. There was renewed confidence that Jupiter would achieve all its objectives. Bruce's agency had registered an important victory in just nineteen action-packed months. He seized the opportunity to present another satellite package to the Pentagon, offering to launch six rockets and seventeen-pound payloads for $18 million. Once more the Defense Department said "no."

As the program forged ahead, Colonel Nickerson solicited help and contributions in Huntsville, among army contractors, West Point classmates and other officers. He retained Robert Bell of Huntsville and Ray Jenkins of Knoxville,

Tennessee, as his attorneys. Jenkins had won press attention earlier as the army's counsel during hearings in which U.S. Senator Joseph McCarthy tried to prove that communists had infiltrated the army. The hearings ended in censure of McCarthy by the Senate. Nickerson also talked to the press about the Wilson decision and repeated his charges on a national television program. He argued that the army was best equipped to use big missiles.

Alabama newspapers blasted the Pentagon and took up Nickerson's case, treating him as a martyr, ignoring his quarrel with the air force and instead telling the public that the colonel was trying to save the missile agency. Bruce refused to talk to the press. As a consequence only the Nickerson version became known. Some assumed that he shouldered the blame for actions encouraged by his commander.

The army placed formal charges against Nickerson ranging from perjury to espionage. His supporters promised sensational disclosures when the court martial convened.

While the local press hailed him as defender of the von Braun group, national publications treated the story differently as their headlines suggested: "Tenacious Colonel," *Newsweek*, "After 31 years, is history repeating air power story?" *U.S. News and World Report*; "Inter-Service Dispute," *Commonweal;* "Air Force Denied Entry at Redstone," *Aviation Week*. The latter magazine reported "there is no doubt Nickerson is getting moral and factual support from some of his superior officers including General Medaris." *Time* pointed out that Nickerson shared the growing fear of army officers that they were being pushed aside by Defense. "Nickerson," *Time* added, "was bent on getting Army slap bang into the Air Force business of long range strategic attack."

The *Saturday Evening Post* saw Nickerson as an officer

who believed the army was being relegated to a caretaker role. "Those who knew him felt he deliberately sought to expose the situation as a Missile Age Billy Mitchell," the *Post* said. Noting that Redstone Arsenal's scientists backed the colonel, the *Post* concluded that "if this pool of genius is dispersed it will cause an appalling loss of a critical national asset." But, the *Post* added, "the colonel was a frustrated scientist, a carper who led himself into deep trouble." *Business Week* viewed the situation as a "nasty brawl between Army and Air Force for control of the 1,750-mile missile."

Grim and tight-lipped, Bruce walked a lonely road during these months. He sought God's comfort in prayer, deeply wounded by the suspicions directed at him, sickened by Nickerson's disregard of his judgment and authority. It was a private Gethsemane which he never expected. He had carefully built a high-spirited organization on the basis of freedom of discussion until he made a decision. Once the judgment was known, his staff gave him complete loyalty, understanding that he alone had the final responsibility. Nickerson had violated that basic obligation.

In late June Colonel Nickerson underwent court martial in a wooden building on the grounds of Redstone Arsenal. Major General Crump Garvin presided over the court of two brigadier generals and five colonels. Seventy-one newsmen attended the open sessions in the one-story structure. A small anteroom was reserved for hearing secret testimony. Contrary to defense hints of juicy revelations, the press learned that the military had dropped the more serious charges in return for Nickerson's plea of guilty to the lesser ones. Reporters concluded that a deal had been made by the Pentagon to prevent possibly embarrassing disclosures. General Garvin announced the court would hear testimony only in mitigation of Nickerson's offenses.

A parade of defense witnesses, including von Braun and

Dr. Ernst Stuhlinger of the missile team, testified in Nickerson's behalf and supported his contention that Jupiter was a superior missile. They described him as an efficient officer who tried to help them. High ranking army officers backed his contention that missiles were long range artillery.

Speaking in defense of his actions, Nickerson read a statement, furnishing copies to the press with the court's approval, in which he reviewed the army's need of long range rockets. Under questioning by the prosecution he admitted passing secret papers to Erik Bergaust who later returned them. He also admitted having burned documents, explaining they were copies of the "Considerations" paper. He told of removing *secret* labels from Defense memoranda, adding "I would never do it again."

The *Huntsville Times* headlined, "Nickerson Flays Aircraft Industry, Tried to Scuttle Army Missile Role."

Nickerson said nothing that inferred he acted with the knowledge or approval of his commander. Both sides rested on June 28, after which the court announced it would call General Medaris next day. Bruce was in Fort Monmouth, New Jersey, attending the wedding of an aide, Lieutenant Horace Tousley, since the court had failed to list him as a witness. He flew back to Redstone Arsenal next morning and drove to the court room, knowing little of what had taken place there. The court did not allow him to make a statement. Instead he could only answer shrewd questions posed by Jenkins, the chief defense attorney who tried to imply that he was somehow involved, or questions asked by the army counsel.

What the court thought Bruce might say will forever remain a mystery. But the press heard an unexpected bombshell. Bruce repeated what others had testified about his order to avoid any challenge of the Wilson decision. Angered by the court's restrictions, he conceded that Nickerson's purpose, not his methods, might be good and labeled the Defense decision against the army "a terrific blow." Then he bluntly declared, "I do not think Nickerson has future potential value to the army and would not want him in my command." What the colonel did, Bruce went on, was "absolutely and diametrically opposed to my orders." As the responsible commander, he could accept no excuse for refusal to obey orders and revealing secret information.

Having built a martyr image for Nickerson, Alabama newspapers next day reported the missile agency employees were "stunned" by the commander's denunciation, a colorful report which lacked foundation in fact. One paper said "Medaris Sinks Nickerson Hopes for Career in Rockets." Jenkins told newsmen that "we had been forewarned that General Medaris assumed an attitude of hostility and animosity towards the colonel but we knew the court would take into consideration his demeanor, attitude and interest or disinterest in the case."

The court was lenient, apparently judging that however misguided, Nickerson fought for the army. He forfeited $100 of his monthly pay for fifteen months, lost privileges of rank and was suspended in rank for one year and reprimanded. The colonel remarked, "I was guilty and properly punished." His lawyers called the sentence "a great victory for Colonel Nickerson and the army." The press described the sentence as a "wrist slap."

Bruce's position received total support from General Hickey, the Third Army commander, who administered the reprimand. He rebuked Nickerson for "unlawful and reprehensible conduct," adding that "you brought discredit upon the army and disrespect for yourself. You have so destroyed confidence in your integrity and judgment as to render you unfit for many assignments. Only by extreme and extraordinary future service can you hope to atone." Nickerson was sent to the Panama Canal Zone for three years as a facilities inspector.

Bruce's faith was justified within a year as Defense removed the constraint on army missiles and authorized the team to develop the longer range Pershing rocket as successor to the Redstone. And the team earned a permanent place in history by launching the Explorer satellite. These and other events affecting the group occurred before Nickerson returned from Panama for an assignment at Fort Bliss, Texas. He visited Huntsville and Redstone Arsenal in February, 1961, after Bruce had retired from the army. Three years later Colonel and Mrs. Nickerson were killed in an automobile accident near Alamagordo, New Mexico. Their two sons and a friend survived the crash. The air force still controls the 1,750-mile missile; however, both Thor and Jupiter became obsolete.

Bruce welcomed a diversion from the strain of events when he and Ginny attended the wedding of their daughter, Marta, to Captain Kenyon Woody in the new Redstone Arsenal chapel as its first ceremony. Cadet John B. Medaris came home from West Point to witness his sister's marriage.

But family matters often took a back seat to the affairs of state and space. Defense Department officials, more than ever conscious of Bruce and his agency, were increasingly sensitive of published reports that the army was interested in satellites. When news stories quoted an unnamed spokesman as saying the agency could put up a satellite, a ranking general descended upon Bruce asking where money came from to build these forbidden devices. Bruce reported that he had not misused funds. He did have Jupiter C rockets which could test model nose cones, an essential part of the Jupiter project. By this time, it was early August, 1957, the Vanguard satellite project authorized by President Eisenhower had cost more than $65 million and the slender rocket had not yet flown.

The army team successfully tested a 300-pound nose cone which was picked up from the ocean by the navy and returned to Cape Canaveral. Kurt Debus, the launch director, surprised Bruce with an unusual gift. It was a letter hidden in the cone, the first rocket mail, which traveled 1,700 miles in less than twenty minutes. Bruce later placed the cone and letter in the Smithsonian Institution's air and space museum in Washington.

Secretary Brucker had another surprise for Bruce as he completed a round of talks in the Pentagon that resulted in a decision to continue both Thor and Jupiter. Mrs. Medaris and Mrs. von Braun flew to Washington without Bruce's knowledge and met him at Fort McNair where Brucker pinned a Legion of Merit medal on his uniform. The secretary praised his work in the missile programs.

A new and alarming factor was about to intrude upon the international scene that would not only resolve the Thor-Jupiter competition, but also exert profound influence on U.S. policy. The Soviet Union scored a resounding triumph October 4, 1957, by launching earth's first artificial satellite, *Sputnik*, its monotonous "beep beep" signal audible to radio listeners as it crossed the northern hemisphere regularly. Chagrined and startled by this exhibition of Soviet technology, the press and Congress sharply criticized the Eisenhower administration and pointed to the comparatively slow progress of U.S. missiles. White House and Defense officials tried to quell the rising storm. Secretary Wilson assured a doubting public that *Sputnik* did not constitute a threat. One spokesman called the Russian satellite a "silly bauble."

President Eisenhower appeared on television in an effort

to reassure the people, displaying with pride a nose cone recovered after a flight through space. He did not tell listeners that the object had been flown on an army rocket by the missile agency and that the army had been the first to solve the reentry heating problem that made possible the cone's recovery. Bruce and the team could not understand this blatant refusal to recognize their achievement.

While the administration tried to talk down the Soviet accomplishment, behind closed doors in the Pentagon there was genuine alarm. Men who understood the potential of satellites knew the Russians could use them to spy on military installations, observe fleets in port or at sea, and perhaps equip them with bombs to be released against any target on earth at the Kremlin's pleasure.

Bruce received a hurried and secret call. Could we destroy a hostile satellite soaring through the skies above America?

"We have no defense against it," he replied.

# 12

# AT THE PINNACLE

*Sputnik* was the best thing that ever happened to the Army Ballistic Missile Agency. It achieved what pleading, proposals, political infighting and even Colonel Nickerson's forlorn hope had failed to do. But it accomplished much more. It catapulted Bruce Medaris and Wernher von Braun into international prominence as the pioneers of American space exploration. Overnight they became heroes.

Late in August, 1957, Dr. Ernst Stuhlinger, a friend and associate of Wernher von Braun, walked into missile agency headquarters in Huntsville and asked to see General Medaris. But Bruce was in North Carolina to visit a missile plant, so an aide asked the scientist to explain his visit. Stuhlinger brought forth a *New York Times* clipping which reported that the Soviets were planning to launch a space satellite. "General Medaris must help the people in

Washington understand the impact a Soviet satellite will make on the uncommitted nations."

The aide was impressed and got Bruce on the phone. "Tell Ernst," he said, "that I've already gone the last mile pleading for an opportunity to launch a satellite. Every door has been closed to me. I agree with his assessment, but there is nothing more I can do."

Six weeks later another of those remarkable coincidences which shaped Bruce's career brought the new Secretary of Defense, Neil McElroy, to the missile agency on a get acquainted visit. That evening, as McElroy dined with Bruce and von Braun, the *Times* of London called to report the launch of *Sputnik* and requested comments from von Braun. When the news reached the trio, Wernher urged McElroy to authorize a satellite. "We can do it in sixty days!" he pleaded. "Make it ninety days," Bruce interjected. They pressed their offer again the next morning. But McElroy left at noon, commenting, "I know when I'm being pressured," promising only to keep the matter in mind. Newsmen camped at arsenal gates waiting to question Bruce and von Braun left empty-handed. McElroy's assistant, Murray Snyder, refused to allow any comments on the Soviet achievement.

Bruce prayed fervently that night, humiliated by the spectacle of Communist superiority, frustrated by the adamant refusal of Defense officials to heed earlier pleas for money and permission to launch satellites. Secretary Brucker picked up the cudgels, appealing to Defense that "unless countered, *Sputnik* can be used to weaken our international position. Its effect on our allies and our citizens is disheartening at least." The surest way to offset the Russian coup, Brucker said, was to authorize the army to launch a satellite. President Eisenhower, who had failed to gauge world reaction to the Soviet feat, secretly ordered Defense to have the army prepare a backup satellite rocket. Bruce received instructions to assemble a vehicle for launch in 1958, but with the stipulation that it would fly only if Vanguard failed.

Overnight the Pentagon became acutely aware of satellites. Suspicions and investigations which hampered the missile agency vanished as *Sputnik's* ominous signals reverberated through Congressional corridors. Defense wanted to know if the army rocket could carry the radio equipment designed for Vanguard and tuned to the earth tracking stations. Bruce assured that the Jet Propulsion Laboratory could satisfy the requirement; an army satellite could also carry an experiment to measure cosmic rays designed by Dr. James Van Allen. He recommended a second try in March, 1958. That would make good Eisenhower's promise to have an American satellite in orbit by that date.

Now the same Defense committee that picked Vanguard over the army proposal in 1954 approved a missile agency plan to launch four satellites for $16 million. Dr. Stuhlinger, von Braun's representative to the scientific community, visited Barcelona, Spain, while these negotiations were still going on. There he talked with Professor Leonid Sedov of the Soviet Union and dispatched a secret report to Bruce.

"We gave our satellite project the highest priority," Sedov said. "Soon we will send rockets to the moon and follow eventually with manned satellites." The Russian scientist could not understand why the American government chose a new and untried rocket to launch Vanguard and passed up the army's proposal. As for *Sputnik*, Sedov dismissed any fears of a military threat. The satellite was only designed for optical and radio tracking, he told Stuhlinger.

As he talked of the Soviet program, Sedov added, "We have plenty of scientists and engineers. It is obvious that the average American cares only for his car, house and electric refrigerator. He has no sense of national purpose nor is he receptive to great ideas which do not pay off immediately. The Russian people accept them."

Pressing their advantage, the Soviets launched *Sputnik II* on November 3. This satellite weighed twelve hundred pounds and carried a dog, Laika, as passenger. Press reaction in the United States reached hysterical levels. Pentagon reporters told their readers the nation lacked a rocket that could handle a satellite of equal size, which was true. Politicians expressed fear that the Soviets might use their satellites to blackmail the Free World.

Troubled by the delaying tactics in Washington, Bruce read with mounting disbelief another secret message: "You are authorized to proceed with necessary preparations to attempt two satellite launches by March, 1958." Secretary Brucker suggested January 30 for the first and March 6 for the second.

Defense issued a press statement on November 8:

"The Secretary of Defense today directed the army to proceed with launching an earth satellite using a modified Jupiter C. This program will supplement the Vanguard project to place an earth satellite in orbit. All test firings of Vanguard have met with success and there is every reason to believe Vanguard will meet its schedule to launch later this year a fully instrumented scientific satellite, which will carry radio equipment compatible with Minitrack ground stations and scientific instruments selected by the National Academy of Sciences."

The statement was incredibly dishonest but the missile agency could not openly attack it. Vanguard's test program had not been an unqualified success. More to the point, Medaris was not authorized to launch anything. Instead Bruce was to "prepare" to launch. If Vanguard put up its small satellite in December, army could return the Jupiter C rocket to cold storage.

"I'm not going to accept this," Bruce told von Braun. "They are playing with national security and trying to delude Congress and the public into believing that we are cranking up a launch. We are not taking a back seat at this stage of the game!"

He dispatched angry wires to the Pentagon refusing to accept the constraint and demanding clear and unequivocal authority to launch two satellites. Bruce was ready to quit, so was von Braun.

Even in this pressure-tight situation the army entertained concerns about its political position. General Lyman Lemnitzer called Bruce to congratulate him on the satellite mission. He professed surprise when told of the restrictions. Lemnitzer mentioned concern in high places about recent press statements attributed to von Braun who declared the nation ought to get on with satellites. President Eisenhower, Lemnitzer said, maintained that the United States was not in a space race with the Soviet Union. Bruce explained that although he himself refused to talk with the press, he would not censor civilian scientists in his command.

In a personal talk with William Holaday, the Defense missiles controller, Bruce finally got the assurance he wanted. He could launch a satellite January 29, 1958, and another in March regardless of Vanguard.

*Sputnik's* echoes were heard again when Secretary McElroy told a Senate committee chaired by Lyndon B. Johnson that both Thor and Jupiter would go into production so that 1,750-mile missiles might be deployed in England, Italy and Turkey as part of NATO's defense shield over Europe. This verdict won loud acclaim in the missile agency.

The Vanguard project, under mounting pressure because

of the Russian satellites, attempted its first launch December 6, at Cape Canaveral near the army's launch pads for Redstone and Jupiter. Several hundred newspaper, radio and television reporters entered the Cape for the first time to report the event. Vanguard lifted off slowly, climbed several feet, settled back and collapsed in a blazing inferno. The disaster sent a chill wind through Washington and left the White House in an untenable position. The prestige of the presidency was staked on a Vanguard success. *The New York Times* called the failure "a blow to national prestige." Senator Johnson termed it "most humiliating." Now it was the army's turn.

Two days before Christmas a Juno rocket left Redstone Arsenal by cargo plane for Cape Canaveral. The Jet Propulsion Laboratory packaged a satellite with the rocket's fourth stage and delivered them to the Cape on January 6. Bruce wired instructions to Kurt Debus, the launch manager:

"Do not admit the presence of the vehicle. Shroud upper stages with canvas and move to the pad not later than 6:30 A.M. Identify the vehicle as a Redstone. I will presumably take leave and happen to be in your area on January 29. Great care should be taken concerning the movements of key personnel from the agency in your vicinity. They will be flown directly to Patrick Air Force Base by special plane. Any violation of this decoy plan will be dealt with severely."

He determined to avoid the kind of advance publicity that surrounded Vanguard preparations in an effort to relieve tension among the launch crew and to spare the nation embarrassment in the event of failure. Before leaving for Florida, Bruce testified before the Lyndon Johnson committee about the Jupiter program. The Senators asked if he had permission to launch a satellite.

"I now have a directive in words of one syllable to go ahead and launch," he replied. "It delights my soul." When newsmen pressed for a launch date, Bruce answered "Soon."

As work proceeded at the Cape, the air force organized its first strategic missile squadron to deploy Jupiter in Italy. More air force representatives occupied offices at the missile agency to master details of the missile system. Chrysler tooled up the production line in Michigan. Meanwhile the army and Defense Department undertook a new ballistic missile project, the Pershing, and chose the Martin Company as prime contractor.

Elated by this quick succession of victories, Bruce informed Ginny of his projected visit to the Cape, asking her not to discuss his movements until the launch occurred. He knew that other wives had learned of the imminent satellite attempt, but wanted to keep the information out of headlines.

"This is our biggest challenge," he added. "We've waited a long while for recognition and now we must make good on our promises. I know that Wernher and his people are pushing themselves to the limit but in all honesty, Ginny, this is such a complex operation that the failure of one little part could defeat us. I'm praying for help."

Ginny helped him pack. As she folded shirts she said, "I just hope you find an hour or two to relax, you're stretching yourself too much. . . . And I'll be praying for you and the others."

Jet Propulsion Laboratory engineers joined in the Cape preparations, checking out high speed upper stages and the cylindrical satellite designed by Josef Boehm of the von Braun team. It measured eighty inches in length, six inches in diameter and weighed 30.8 pounds. Two radio transmitters carried within the device would relay scientific data to earth stations.

Draped in canvas, the rocket was hauled to the launch pad and erected in the vertical firing position at nightfall January

24, without the use of searchlights that might betray its shape. A red service tower was rolled into place beside the seventy-foot tall rocket that weighed thirty-two tons at launch. Bruce flew in from Alabama while von Braun left reluctantly for Washington to await launch with Dr. Van Allen and Dr. William Pickering of the Jet Propulsion Laboratory.

Kurt Debus, the launch boss, planned to remove shrouds hiding the missile before pumping fuel into rocket tanks. As fueling was about to commence January 29, an air force weather officer, Lieutenant John L. Meisenheimer, reported a hazardous situation aloft. The jet stream blowing west to east across the country unexpectedly moved south over Florida. Balloons flown from the Cape encountered wind velocities exceeding 150 knots at 36,000 feet. The shear force was too severe for the tall, slender rocket, so Debus postponed the launch.

Newspapers carried brief items about an imminent satellite mission as two hundred reporters gathered on the scene. Buses would shuttle them to an observation site two miles from the rocket shortly before launch. Major General Donald Yates, air force commander of the Atlantic Missile Range, struck a bargain with the local press corps. He agreed to give them advance information concerning launches if they delayed publication until the missile lifted off or blew up. Then they could report what they saw.

Bruce's agency prepared an information kit for reporters that described the Juno rocket and satellite experiments. The Jet Propulsion Laboratory produced a similar packet and a motion picture describing the project for release after launch. The satellite remained nameless. Secretary Brucker told Bruce that he and General Maxwell Taylor would announce the name only if the attempt succeeded.

Weather observers released more balloons the morning of

January 30. Again the wind readings exceeded the rocket's structural strength. Bruce played golf that day. Vanguard planned a second launch February 3. Scientists warned they could not handle two satellites in orbit unless their launches occurred at least three days apart. Friday, January 31, thus became army's deadline. Later in the morning weather reports seemed more favorable. The jet stream slowly retreated northward. Conferring with Debus, Bruce decided to start the countdown at noon anticipating a launch at 10:30 P.M. January 30.

By 9:20 P.M. thunderstorms threatened the Cape area. Further, the wind conditions were marginal. Once again Debus postponed. En route to the Trade Winds Hotel in Indialantic, twenty-five miles south of the Cape, Bruce remarked, "I know Secretary Brucker and a lot of other people are disappointed. But I still have a missile on the pad."

More balloons ascended early on January 31. Having sought guidance in prayer before retiring, Bruce awakened with the certain knowledge that the launch would occur. He phoned Ginny that he would be delayed at least one more day. She reminded him that preparations were speeding up for the agency's birthday party February 1.

"It would be wonderful if we had another success to celebrate," Ginny teased.

"You're pushing me," Bruce laughed. "But I promise to make the party tomorrow."

Lieutenant Meisenheimer predicted high altitude winds would drop to one hundred knots by nightfall. Debus picked up the countdown at 1:30 P.M., expecting to launch at 10:30 P.M. Bruce drove to the blockhouse with his aide, Lieutenant Magill, watched preparations on the launch pad and chatted with General Yates about a more favorable weather forecast. A food truck arrived and Bruce ate a thick ham and egg sandwich. Robert Moser, a young engineer trained by Debus, called out the count. His voice could be heard plainly in the small firing room. Dr. Jack Froelich of the Jet Propulsion Laboratory hovered near Bruce and Debus. At 9:30 P.M. the red service tower rolled back and the Juno rocket stood alone gleaming white in the searchlights' glare. Newsmen occupied the press site as blockhouse doors were sealed against toxic gases generated by rocket ignition.

Five miles away in a Cape hangar Dr. Stuhlinger and Dr. Walter Haeussermann waited to calculate the exact instant when a radio signal would ignite second stage rocket motors. They would have three minutes to determine when the Juno reached apex. If they signalled too soon, the rocket would disappear into deep space; too late, the rocket would turn earthward and burn up. The motors must fire when Juno was exactly horizontal to earth's surface. As tension built up among newsmen, launch crew and observers, darkness seemed to settle like a blanket over the Cape.

A thousand miles away in a Pentagon communications room Secretary Brucker, General Lemnitzer, von Braun, Pickering and Van Allen watched a screen displaying teletype messages from the Cape. Pickering estimated that it would require 106 minutes for the satellite to make its first trip around earth. Not until West Coast tracking stations picked up a signal would the team know if it achieved orbit.

Crowded with fifty-four men, the blockhouse quieted and tension rose as the count inexorably approached the zero mark. Seconds before, Moser called out, "We have a jet vane deflection, shall I hold?" Debus turned to Bruce who gave him a "thumbs up" signal. The next words were Moser's sharp cry, "Firing command!"

The engine roared to life. Seconds passed while the thrust increased and then *Juno I* rose into the black sky. Rolling thunder filled the blockhouse. Observers saw the rocket move smoothly into the planned course. It vanished from sight to shouts of "Go, baby, go!" Many who watched prayed silently—aware that the nation's prestige rode with the rocket. Four hundred seconds would elapse before the second stage ignited.

Bruce, Debus and others watched intently as recording instruments displayed critical measurements. The first stage engine shut down as planned. The velocity was correct. *Juno* was on course and on time. When they saw the signal indicating second stage ignition, Bruce and Debus climbed into waiting sedans and sped off to a building in the Cape industrial area to await word from tracking stations.

Radio and television networks reported the launch and within minutes millions knew the United States was trying again to orbit a satellite. Secretary Brucker wired Bruce: "I'm out of coffee and running low on cigarets. What do I do now?" Bruce replied, "Send out for more and sweat it out with us." He, too, was anxious but shored up by the conviction born of prayer that success was at hand. After ninety minutes, Pickering could wait no longer. He asked Pasadena if they heard the signal, keeping the line open and watching a wall clock tick off seconds. Suddenly he asked, "You say Earthquake has it?" The Pentagon audience tensed. Pickering nodded, speaking loudly so they could hear. "Yes, Earthquake Valley has the signal, so have Temple City and San Diego. It is in orbit."

Brucker grabbed the phone from von Braun to congratulate Bruce adding that "General Taylor and I named the satellite *Explorer*." President Eisenhower heard the news in Georgia. The official announcement came at 1:30 A.M. Eastern time February 1, 1958.

A wild and impromptu celebration broke out in Huntsville. Police cars and fire trucks drove through the streets with screaming sirens, telling residents to drive to Court House Square. Thousands gathered to cheer, cry and pound the backs of missile agency workers. They hung an effigy of former Defense Secretary Charles Wilson. It was the greatest display of emotion since Yankee cavalry entered the city during the Civil War.

Bruce and key members of the team drove to Patrick Air Force Base fifteen miles south of the Cape to meet the press. En route Froelich and Bruce toasted the victory with Scotch thoughtfully provided by the general's aide. As they walked into the packed theater the press rose and applauded, a rare tribute by newsmen, many of whom had seen the Vanguard fail. General Yates shook hands with Bruce as flash bulbs popped. *Life* magazine published a picture of Bruce as he read from a slip of paper, "Goldstone (the Earthquake Valley tracking station in California) has the bird!"

*Explorer* circled earth at intervals of 114.78 minutes reaching 1,594 miles into space. Now the press kits were distributed. The quiet demeanor and confidence of the missile men only served to heighten press interest in them and their achievements. *Explorer* made page one news in Berlin and Tokyo, Paris and London, Rome, Madrid and in cities and towns west of the Iron Curtain. There seemed to be a universal feeling of relief that the United States had matched the Russians. The fact that *Explorer* was pitifully small compared to the *Sputniks* was glossed over. It had taken the army team eighty-four days to meet the challenge.

As Bruce drove the lonely miles along the ocean to his hotel with two aides, he said in a soft voice, "The Lord was on our side." *Time* magazine reporters trailed the car and talked with him briefly before he got to bed at 3:30 A.M. He fell asleep thanking God. At 5:00 A.M. he got up to fly home to Ginny and an enthusiastic greeting at the missile agency's birthday party which was attended by twenty-thousand happy people.

Kurt Debus dutifully transmitted the postfiring report to

Bruce: "At approximately 2246 hours (10:46 P.M.) Eastern Standard Time on 31 January 1958 the four-stage modified Redstone missile Nr. 29 (*Juno*) was launched from Pad 26-A at Cape Canaveral, Florida. The primary mission was to place in orbit a payload weighing 18.13 pounds at an injection altitude of 322 nautical miles. Mission accomplished." The *secret* label was removed from the wire eight years later.

Bruce spoke to the Huntsville Rotary Club soon afterward, giving credit for *Explorer's* success to his team. He took occasion to remark, "In my travels up and down the country in contact with other communities and other problems, I have never ceased to be grateful for the intelligence, frankness and cooperation that marked the approach of your city to the solution of growth problems. It has been outstanding in the history of the nation in terms of military-community relations."

Congress expressed its relief and satisfaction. Bruce again testified before the Lyndon Johnson committee. Senator Johnson recalled the comment of a California scientist who said, "There are too many people in government who have the right to say no; too few who have authority to say yes, and even less who dare to do so."

Bruce nodded, "That has been my experience."

"That's what is wrong with the entire program," Johnson concluded.

Vanguard tried again in March and placed a three and one-half pound sphere in orbit. Two more *Vanguards* succeeded, another failed under management of the National Aeronautics and Space Administration. NASA's official history of the Vanguard project called it a rousing success, dismissed Bruce as "partisan" and said von Braun oversold the army satellite plan. NASA ignored the army's role in launching the first U.S. satellite.

More *Explorers* followed in March and July, 1958, and

October, 1959. Only the first counted in public and political importance. The second flew over the Russian land mass and measured radioactivity created by the explosion of A-bombs launched on Redstone missiles from Johnston Island in the Pacific Ocean. For the von Braun team *Explorer* fulfilled a fifteen-year-old dream. Dr. Vannevar Bush, who directed U.S. scientific research during World War II, commented that "*Sputnik* was one of the finest things Russia ever did for the United States. It waked up this country."

Ginny modestly accepted congratulations pouring into their home from friends in the States and overseas. Honors and fame showered on four men, the dashing army commander, Bruce Medaris; the visionary rocket builder, Wernher von Braun; the scientist-manager, William Pickering and Dr. Van Allen of the State University of Iowa, whose instruments discovered belts of intense radioactivity above earth which bear his name.

Requests for personal appearances by Bruce and von Braun came from all manner of organizations. Army publicists were intoxicated, they had two star performers and a veritable feast of opportunities until Bruce pulled them up short with a brusque reminder that he and Wernher had work to do. Some invitations could not be rejected. Bruce appeared on NBC's "Meet the Press," von Braun on CBS's "Face the Nation." "Wide, Wide World" returned for a live telecast from the arsenal. "Person to Person" pictured Bruce and Ginny at home. The late Edward Murrow and Fred Friendly filmed an authentic documentary, "Biography of a Missile," in the arsenal and at Cape Canaveral. CBS aired it nationwide and BBC broadcast it in the British Isles as well.

Dr. von Braun was a reluctant hero. He fought against social engagements, preferring to spend what little time he could with his wife, Maria, and their children. But, Bruce gently prodded him, "There's more to this business than the technical side." He wanted the public to know von Braun for what he was, a warm-hearted genius and prophet who had uncanny ability to inspire hard-headed engineers to achieve great deeds.

Colleges and universities conferred honorary degrees on both men. They addressed scientific, engineering and industrial audiences from coast to coast, advocating a strong national space program. They emphasized the need of more powerful rockets to overtake the Soviet lead and they predicted men would travel to the moon and elsewhere in space. Some religious people demurred that space exploration was a presumptuous act of which God would not approve. Bruce argued that "if God did not want us to explore His kingdom, He would have stopped us on the launch pad."

Despite the multiple demands on his time, Bruce showed concern for seemingly trivial matters. His secretary heard the pitiful story of a former employee dismissed because of drinking. Having broken the habit he wanted desperately to return. Bruce listened as Miss Parker described the case and said, "I'll have to pray about that." She arranged a thirty-minute appointment. While staff officers fretted, Bruce spent three hours with the man and ordered him reinstated. "He suffered long enough," he told his secretary.

Now Defense established the Army Ordnance Missile Command which Bruce would direct. His new organization included the missile agency, Jet Propulsion Laboratory, White Sands Missile Range, Redstone Arsenal, the Army Rocket and Guided Missile Agency, and test units at Point Mugu, Fort Churchill, China Lake, Kwajalein Island in mid-Pacific and an office in Paris that dealt with NATO. The command employed eighteen thousand civilians, five thousand military personnel, and had a $2 billion budget. In a rare departure, the army gave AOMC the responsibility for training army and air force crews to operate Redstone and Jupiter missiles. Bruce appointed von Braun chairman of a top level committee to plan future space projects. The former newsboy from Springfield, Ohio, supervised all of the army's rocket and space undertakings.

# 13

# IN AND OUT OF SPACE

Tasting the sweet fruits of notable achievements, Bruce Medaris believed that his team stood first in the budding space program. Jupiter neared completion. Air force accepted the weapon system and installed the squat, powerful rockets in Turkey as well as Italy. More satellites flew in orbit. The Martin Company progressed steadily with the Pershing rocket except for its guidance and control systems which the von Braun group would provide. So the team could take on any space assignment.

Bruce was very wrong. He would unwittingly play a starring role in an incredible drama growing out of power plays staged by interests determined to control the multi-billion dollar space program whose first objective was the elimination of the army. Only the missile agency in Alabama could design, fabricate, test and launch big missiles. To the aerospace industry this was dangerous and embarrassing competition. What's more, the work of the team provided hard data with which to compare industry costs.

The Defense Department created a new agency that would parcel out space missions to the military services, making use of their rockets to orbit satellites. Several exciting projects were handed to the army including a small probe to the moon and the launch of heavier satellites. Congress debated about the nation's missiles and space ventures while those ambitious Russians continued to fly bigger satellites. President Eisenhower approved the new Defense agency but added cautionary language: "If and when a civilian space agency is created, these projects will be subject to review to determine which should remain under cognizance of the Department of Defense and which under cognizance of the new agency."

Battle lines were drawn. The military wanted to continue their control, only the army and air force possessed the kind of rockets that could place satellites in orbit. The Lyndon Johnson committee of the Senate leaned toward civilian management. Nelson Rockefeller examined the alternatives for Eisenhower and recommended separating civilian from military space projects. The president urged Congress to support a new civil agency fervently supported by the National Advisory Committee for Aeronautics which wanted a piece of the action.

With fierce intellectual honesty, Bruce disagreed with the president in the heated discussions within the defense establishment. Splitting up this juicy pie, he insisted, would be an "attempt to divide the indivisible." In his opinion the army, air force and navy jointly possessed all the human talents and physical resources to execute a broad space program primarily oriented to national security. Artificial separation would mean duplication, increased costs, and unwieldy competition.

While the debate continued, all three services vied with

one another for a "man in space" project. The air force advanced one plan, the navy another and the missile agency still another called Project Adam. The army's proposal would install a man in a sealed capsule, protected by the same material employed for Jupiter warheads, and launch him atop a Redstone missile to an altitude of 150 miles before the space pilot splashed in the Atlantic Ocean off Cape Canaveral. The plan died in Defense files two years before Alan Shepard rode into space on a Redstone rocket, but under the aegis of a civilian agency, not the army.

Undaunted by repeated turndowns, the von Braun group came up with more proposals, communications satellites, lunar exploration, even a more powerful booster rocket which could be fashioned by clustering existing rocket engines. Defense accepted the latter and authorized a modest test. Fortunately Redstone Arsenal possessed an immense test stand that could restrain a booster with ten times the power of Jupiter. Bruce had persuaded army and Defense to build that tower when no one dared talk openly about heavy rockets. Eventually they would carry satellites measured in tons and astronauts riding in Apollo spacecraft.

The die was cast when Congress passed the National Space Act which was signed by President Eisenhower July 29, 1958. The law embodied the policy urged by Eisenhower and shaped by Lyndon Johnson. Defense would continue to exercise control of military space ventures while a new organization, the National Aeronautics and Space Administration, explored space for peaceful purposes under civilian management. Its sponsors overlooked the fact that the Defense Department provided civilian management of the military. Bruce swallowed his misgivings for a time; at least, it appeared the nation would have some kind of space program.

The law transferred to NASA the National Advisory

Committee on Aeronautics and $350 million worth of facilities at Langely, Virginia; Cleveland, Ohio; Moffet Field and Edwards Air Force Base, California and a small rocket launch site at Wallops Island, Virginia, along with eight thousand employees. NASA built its management structure around the NACA managers.

Dr. T. Keith Glennan, the first NASA administrator, dispatched teams to appraise Defense Department installations with the objective of taking those of value to his organization. Glennan made his bid two weeks after NASA opened for business. He wanted the von Braun team and the facilities they occupied as well as the Jet Propulsion Laboratory in Pasadena, the vital creative divisions of Bruce's command.

Secretary Brucker professed shock. The army had spent fifteen years building the teams NASA wanted, numbering forty-five hundred people and including $154 million worth of plants and equipment. Unable to register his protest with the president, Brucker talked over the dilemma with Bruce. They understood that Defense supported the takeover, the attitude was "let's get that Huntsville bunch out of our hair." The solution pleased the aerospace contractors who were eager to eliminate military competition. NASA's official history observed that "in fighting the proposed transfer, Army marshalled its friends in Congress and among the public by going outside of official channels and leaking the story to the *Baltimore Sun.*"

Bruce did just that. He saw no way to stop NASA short of taking direct action. There was nothing secret about the matter, but those involved were keeping it quiet to avoid any criticism. So Bruce met with an old friend, Mark Watson of the *Sun*, and told him what was afoot. The *Sun* broke the story next morning. A flurry of protests resulted. Congress warned the White House that Glennan's demands would tamper with national defense resources. Other newspapers picked up the report and carried editorials protesting the division of the army's team. "Army missiles have the best record of success," the *Detroit Free Press* commented, "and there is nothing like inter-service jealousy to stir up Pentagon conniving."

The uproar forced the White House to back off. A compromise resulted. NASA would get the Jet Propulsion Laboratory which would finish up work in progress for the army. The von Braun team would remain with Medaris's missile agency to perform assigned tasks for NASA. Eisenhower told the press that he alone would decide the future of the von Braun group.

Bruce reassured his people that "analysis of all the factors will not result in actions detrimental to our people and the nation. We will continue to advance military and scientific programs assigned to us." The press demanded a statement from von Braun. "The missile team organized under the army's sponsorship and direction has won recognition as a national asset," he said. "The only question which should be asked is 'How can this team best serve the nation?' It would be less than prudent to risk the dissolution of such an asset at a time when national security and prestige demand a unified effort to achieve supremacy in rocket and space technologies."

Bruce issued a thoughtful Christmas message to his command while harboring serious doubts about the future. Some in the von Braun team believed that he was mistaken in his firm stand. Space exploration prospects appeared more exciting and rewarding than the grim business of developing weapons. The new Pied Piper, Dr. Glennan, played a tune pleasing to their ears. They hoped their general would work out something that included the best of two worlds—security in their army jobs but more work in space. The latter beckoned and they responded.

Heartsick at the gloomy prospect, Bruce shared his worries with Ginny. "We've won a temporary truce and that's all," he said. "NASA won't stop. They have powerful allies in Congress. They want von Braun and his people. I can't look for much help from the army, since there are debates now as to the amount we invested in rockets versus tanks and guns. We still have too many officers who don't understand and therefore distrust the new weapons. Defense would gladly give away the store. . . ."

"And the storekeeper," she murmured.

"Yes," he agreed, "they'd like to get this troublemaker out of sight and hearing. I hope that Wernher isn't hurt in this squabble."

"Bruce, you've got to remember your position," Ginny declared firmly. "People will think you put yourself above the president and that will not work. Don't fight the inevitable. Why don't you call quits and get out? This is tearing you apart."

Grimly determined, he tried to shake off her warning. On Christmas he attended communion service in the Church of the Nativity, singing familiar carols with enthusiasm. Other worshippers could not guess at the problems racing through his mind as he prayed for strength to carry on.

The new year opened with arsenal shops full of big missiles, Jupiters for overseas destinations, Junos for Defense and NASA space missions. An observer would discount any hint of underlying difficulties, but they were all too real. The civilian agency looked askance at a list of research projects suggested by von Braun and sliced the $20 million price tag to $1 million. A NASA official informed Defense his agency would pay only for work performed by the von Braun group.

NASA refused to give them money for work conducted by contractors. Bruce concluded this represented a deliberate attempt to starve his team into submission. Called to testify in Congress, Dr. Glennan said he would use the von Braun team but this arrangement was not as satisfactory as if NASA managed them. All the money his agency provided in 1959 represented only five percent of the team's $400 million budget.

Despite these ominous portents, the army forged ahead. The team registered another space feat in March, flying a *Pioneer* space probe within 37,000 miles of the moon. The fourteen-pound device transmitted signals to earth stations until batteries failed at a range of 407,000 miles. Three air force attempts failed to reach the moon. Two monkeys were recovered alive after a flight of 1,800 miles in a Jupiter nose cone, indicating the strong probability that man could survive similar exposure in space flight.

But relations with NASA reached low ebb when the agency dropped two scheduled Jupiter launches from Project Mercury, its man-in-space project. As NASA's history admitted, "having cancelled the Jupiter series rather precipitously, the Space Task Group unceremoniously relegated the four thousand members of von Braun's division almost to task element status."

Bruce put nagging problems aside temporarily to address the Alabama legislature, urging establishment of a state university in Huntsville to meet the needs of a growing industrial center. The legislature subsequently authorized the school which houses ten thousand students.

NASA's plan to launch Americans into space prompted the Associated Press to ask Bruce and von Braun the same question, "Will the intoxication of man's first flight in space cast doubt on the existence of God?" Their answers appeared in newspapers July 8, 1959:

"The ten commandments have guided men and safely brought them through upheavals of the past," Bruce declared. "They should be the rock of man's decisions today and tomorrow. I am convinced that our scientific advances were made possible by the grace of God. Leading figures of all major faiths including Pius XII saw no defiance of Divinity in our initial ventures in space. The door would have closed in our faces if what we are attempting contravenes God's will. Our first steps have reemphasized the beauty and order of creation and verified natural laws which govern all existence. As he ponders these things man must come to believe anew, as once he did before false intellectualism, bigotry and superstition turned him away from truth."

Dr. von Braun said that science and religion are not incompatible. "Only with God reinstated in men's hearts will He furnish mankind the ethical guidance through dangers and pitfalls of the technological revolution."

Mercury astronauts training for space flights visited the missile command. Alan Shepard, Virgil Grissom, John Glenn, Scott Carpenter, Gordon Cooper, Walter Schirra and Donald Slayton talked with Bruce about the army rockets that would launch manned capsules. Shepard would fly the first May 5, 1961. They toured laboratories and shops with von Braun.

A new threat came from Defense aimed at killing off the clustered Saturn rocket, on the ground that it lacked potential users. The air force didn't want the big booster; NASA showed little interest. Instead, the air force proposed a Titan III vehicle and eventually won approval for another man-in-space project called Dynosaur. After investing millions, Defense later killed the project.

At this desperate juncture, Army made a final bid for Project Horizon, jointly planned by its technical services that would establish a military outpost on the moon using a Saturn rocket. Commencing in 1965 and continuing two years, 149 Saturns would transport 500,000 pounds of equipment and materials to the lunar surface. The plan envisaged permanent housing, production of life-sustaining oxygen and water, and growing food by hydroponic culture for teams of explorers who would remain for months. Defense stamped the documents top secret and locked them up. President John F. Kennedy never heard of Horizon when he initiated the Apollo Moon program in 1961 conducted by NASA.

Visibly tiring and emotionally drained by stunning victories followed by crushing setbacks, Bruce enjoyed a visit from the Reverend Eugene Stillings, rector of an Episcopal church in Indiana; his wife, Marilyn, and their children. Ginny encouraged them to come to Alabama, hoping it would lift Bruce out of depression. His aides overheard animated talks about theology between Bruce and his son-in-law, expressing amazement about their commander's knowledge of the subject. Marilyn's happiness in her marriage and her commitment to her faith delighted Bruce and Ginny.

But the clouds gathered. Defense split up the space pie, giving some projects to NASA. The air force would thereafter control all military space rockets which immediately doomed Redstone and Jupiter to short lifetimes. The navy could establish a navigation satellite for its fleet. The army won the right to launch a communications satellite but management of this project was not assigned to Bruce. NASA decided to undertake development of a monster rocket known as Nova, apparently dooming Saturn.

"I'm worn out, Ginny," Bruce remarked after dinner on a fall evening. "I see no future for Wernher and the team in the army. Jupiter is practically finished. They have only a limited role in Pershing and no takers for Saturn. Defense and NASA shot all of our proposals down. In the near future there will be no major project to occupy von Braun and his people. He's aware of the situation. The cards are stacked against us. Maybe I ought to think pretty hard about retiring."

She immediately embraced the idea and planted a kiss on his cheek. "I'm with you, Bruce," she answered. "For your sake and mine, let's get out and enjoy what time we have left."

"All right, I'll do it," he promised. "But until some things are cleared up, let's keep it our secret."

Lieutenant General J. H. Hinrichs, the ordnance chief, discussed the outlook with Bruce. There were two choices left, either give the von Braun team to NASA, or to the air force. Bruce promised to consider the alternatives and give Hinrichs an early reply.

Before doing so he made a last proposal to Dr. Glennan. Bruce suggested that NASA ought to plan and manage the space projects while allowing the military services to do the work. Glennan refused. He wanted NASA to have its own installations and assurance that NASA would not be pushed aside for military priorities. He knew that the army could not support the von Braun team much longer.

Bruce talked privately with von Braun and a few close associates, asking each which course he favored. Several liked the air force better because of its experience in managing large projects with an ample budget. Others favored NASA, fearing that if the air force moved into Redstone Arsenal the army would eventually be forced out of the installation. Weighing the conflicting opinions, Bruce turned to prayer. He knew the answer next morning. He telephoned General Hinrichs and Secretary Brucker, recommending that NASA should acquire the team. He would not oppose transfer.

Even as these developments took place, Secretary of Defense McElroy approached NASA to find out if there was still interest in acquiring the army team. Lacking a capability to design and build large rockets, NASA replied affirmatively but insisted on guarantees that there would be no repetition of the political hassle Glennan walked into the previous year. The transfer plan was discussed in the White House October 20, and negotiations were completed to hand over the organization and the Saturn program to NASA. Dr. Glennan got what he wanted on his terms.

Assured that President Eisenhower accepted the plan, Bruce announced his decision to retire October 21. He would leave the army January 31, 1960. An offer of a third star and a post in Washington failed to dissuade him.

When the news broke, letters, telegrams and phone calls poured into his office, expressing regret, urging him to stay on, praising his service to the country. A Richmond, Virginia, boy spoke for many when he sent a moving appeal not to resign and to continue. Touched by the letter, Bruce replied, "I am not resigning, I am retiring. With my great love and respect for the army I could not resign nor will I cease to support everything it stands for. Taking off the uniform for the last time will evoke deep emotion but it would have been just as difficult when the law required me to retire for age." He was fifty-seven.

Eisenhower announced the von Braun transfer and praised the team's accomplishments in the army. He ordered the Saturn project stepped up and authorized $100 million for the booster, the same one Defense tried to kill and for which NASA expressed little interest previously. Dr. von Braun told the press, "We look forward to continuing our efforts in a progressive space program."

Huntsville hailed the president's decision as proof that the city would gain a major NASA investment while holding on to its army installation. Reaction at the arsenal reflected personal hopes, the military people were disappointed, civilians happy over the prospects of more and better jobs.

Newsmen caught up with Bruce in New York City where he had a speaking engagement. He expressed pride in having organized and supported the von Braun team during its greatest growth. Reporters thought he was unhappy and asked if he retired in protest. "No," he answered, "I am very tired after years of unending stress." When one asked if he would enter the ministry, Bruce dismissed the idea. He might enter private industry, he said, "to make some money for my grandchildren."

The Associated Press published an interview in which Bruce asked, "Are we or are we not going to compete with the Russians in outer space? There must be a positive decision to undertake a solid and well-financed space program. We have straddled the issue."

His words irked the White House. General Lemnitzer informed Bruce that the President discouraged talk of competition with the Soviet Union. Bruce heard the same argument months before. He was not persuaded.

Dr. Glennan returned to Huntsville where Bruce pledged to do everything possible to assure a smooth transition. The NASA administrator announced that von Braun would direct all launch and space vehicle activities. Bruce saw the NASA-Defense agreement a few days afterward. NASA acquired Saturn, facilities at Redstone Arsenal and Cape Canaveral, and 4,230 employees. Army retained 850 people engaged in Redstone, Jupiter and Pershing projects. The transfer would take place July 1, 1960, when von Braun became director of the new George C. Marshall Space Flight Center on Redstone Arsenal.

Looking forward to the more leisurely life which he and Ginny wanted so keenly, but determined to do nothing that might reflect unfavorably upon the army or his command, Bruce summoned Frank Buckley, the chief counsel.

"Buck, when we first met in 1956, I gave you a special

responsibility," he began. "You were to review every pending contract wherein I might exercise those special powers delegated by Secretary Brucker to expedite the process and put your stamp of approval on the paper prior to any decision I might make. You've done a thorough job and you have my thanks. Now it's time to ask you for a complete list of all the companies doing business with us for whom I cut through the paper train."

"Of course, General," Buckley answered. "May I ask why?"

"I want to know the names of all, Buck," he replied. "There may be job offers coming to me in retirement and I will not accept employment with any firm on that list. Otherwise, there might be suspicion in some quarters of a special favor deal. I don't want to open the door even slightly to any such possibility in the interests of the army and my successor."

Several days passed before Buckley returned. Handing his commander four typewritten pages, he remarked, "There it is, General Medaris, it is really a 'Who's Who of American Industry' because every company in the aerospace and electronics fields is listed plus many others in other types of industry. Good luck to you!"

Lawrence Spivak induced the retiring general to return for a second "Meet the Press" television program. Bruce spoke of the urgent need to strengthen the space program. Huntsville civic clubs tendered a farewell luncheon while officer wives honored Ginny. His Christmas message contained a farewell to his command: "You handed me the one indispensable weapon, the greatest any leader can receive, in victories and accomplishments, one after the other in endless succession. You were sober in victory, fearless in crisis, steadfast against threats of defeat and always magnificent. As we observe Christmas, let us remember the Man who told us that if we but follow in His footsteps, there need never be goodbye."

Huntsville celebrated "Big M Day" January 15, with a parade witnessed by ten thousand followed by a reception and dinner in honor of General and Mrs. Medaris. The desk and chair he occupied as commander were presented by the city who bought exact duplicates for the army. Bruce reviewed the troops with Secretary Brucker on the arsenal parade ground, taking the salute for the last time. Threatening skies and intermittent rain marred the occasion.

Brucker pinned a distinguished service medal on Bruce saying "a lot of people said four years ago that it couldn't be done but you did it. You have earned the highest tribute of a grateful nation for superb leadership." A rare tribute came from the air force which conferred a medal on the officer who induced them to accept the Jupiter missile. Bruce and the airmen who voted the honor knew that Jupiter's superior guidance system and warhead yield placed it far ahead of the rival Thor missile.

Bruce summoned thirty of his military and civilian colleagues to his conference room and presented awards in gratitude for their help. "It wasn't I who made our success possible," he told them. "It was the challenge and the freedom which you and Wernher von Braun were given that inspired you to do great things."

Joyfully Ginny packed for a sojourn in Florida. Bruce arranged to lease a furnished house on Melbourne Beach not far from the Cape where he would dictate a book. Happy that her husband was at long last escaping the pressures he willingly endured in the time of great achievements, she looked forward eagerly to quiet retirement.

For Secretary Brucker, his staunch ally in the quarrels with the air force, the Defense Department and NASA, Bruce penned a personal account of the problems and accomplishments of the four years in Alabama.

"The army was given a job to do and one way or another, it got the job done," he wrote. "When the political adversities which beset us are taken into account, the accomplishments take on phenomenal significance. Adversities seemed to increase in direct ratio to our successes.

"We received support from every element of the army, technical services, combat arms and the top staff. It was one place where we became solidly united. The political situation was such that Jupiter was always on the verge of extinction for no reason except a calculated desire on the part of the opposition to stifle competition. Even the most valid technical competence and zeal can be seriously diluted by the effects of unwarranted pressures from various economic, political and vested interests. Public recognition of army achievements, while substantial, was often adulterated by irresponsible claims from other sources."

He reported that every program assigned to his command had been completed successfully or was then on schedule at minimum cost. "Since we are now removed from playing the game, our satisfaction comes from contributions made to our nation. . . ."

Now Wernher von Braun and his team would perform the same missions under a new manager. He summed up the record of four fruitful years:

—Redstone became the first U.S. ballistic missile with inertial guidance

—First demonstration of satellite capability in the September, 1956, flight of Jupiter C over 3,000 miles

—First launch of the 1,750-mile missile in May, 1957

—First object recovered from space, the nose cone of August, 1957

—First U.S. satellite, *Explorer 1*, January 31, 1958

—First U.S. probe to the moon, *Pioneer IV*, March, 1959

—First primates recovered after space flight, May 1959

He signed his last official document January 31, 1960. It notified the Army Ballistic Missile Committee of the first Pershing launch. He wore a business suit next day, visiting the chapel alone to give thanks to God for bringing him through so many trials and tribulations to this conclusion.

# 14

# ANOTHER BEGINNING

Kurt Debus presented an unusual but fitting gift to his former commander three days after Bruce retired by launching the twenty-ninth Jupiter missile, bringing to an end its development phase. Dressed in a sports jacket and slacks, looking very much a man of leisure, Bruce watched the fiery spectacle in the Cape Canaveral blockhouse. It was the eighty-fifth launch since he had assumed command of the missile agency in 1956. Only five of them had failed.

He had flown to Florida to undertake a self-imposed task. He wanted to make public his concerns about national defense management by writing a book. Ginny accompanied him to Melbourne Beach where he dictated the manuscript in their beach home.

While the launch team cleaned up, Bruce shook hands with Debus. They enjoyed an unusual relationship during his four years in Alabama because he gave Kurt full responsibility for each launch. Once the rocket arrived at the Cape,

Debus alone called the signals regardless of the opinions of other members of the von Braun organization.

A quiet and unassuming engineer, Debus stood alone in his unique profession as a master of launch technology based upon his work at Peenemuende, White Sands and the Cape.

"You've done an outstanding job, Kurt," Bruce told him. "Much of our success was due to your meticulous preparation. I wish you and Wernher the best in your NASA careers. Maybe the new boys on the block can get you the money and projects we could not muster."

"It's kind of you to say that, General," Debus replied. "We'll miss you."

What would Bruce do? First he would write the book. After that he looked forward to joining one or more firms as consultant or director. He did not relish the idea of a full-time position, planning to spend more time with Ginny and their growing family. Huntsville made an offer that touched him. The city's leaders wanted Bruce to remain and lead a campaign to bring more industry to the area, expecting diversification to strengthen the local economy. Much as he loved the city and its people, Bruce did not accept, knowing that it would be painful to watch the dissolution of the missile organization he created. His fears were soon justified. Two major divisions vanished in two years.

Even before he left, efforts were afoot in the Pentagon to strip away those special authorities entrusted to him by Secretary Brucker and General Taylor. For every friend he made in exercising that authority he counted ten more enemies among the Pentagon's clusters of lawyers and administrators. The army never gave another commander comparable powers.

Bruce understood that leaving Huntsville would be difficult for Ginny, too. They had made lasting friendships. They repeated their marriage vows on the twenty-fifth anniversary in the old chapel. Marta was married in the new chapel which Bruce had built. The arsenal had grown mightily under his supervision, six hundred more military homes, twenty-two thousand people on the payroll of $137 million a year. Huntsville erected signs along main routes to greet visitors: "Space Capital of the USA."

For a short time Bruce believed that he might accept a full-time appointment which interested him greatly. He expected to join the $6 million Joseph P. Kennedy, Jr. Foundation for mentally retarded children. The family established the institution in memory of a son killed in action during World War II. Robert F. Kennedy was its president; Eunice Kennedy Shriver, vice president, and her husband served as executive director. Bruce met Joseph Kennedy, head of the clan, in late 1959. The two men got along well and Kennedy asked him to run the foundation. The offer was especially pleasing because of its high purpose and complete separation from government.

Bruce signed a $90,000 contract to buy an airplane for his use and that of other Kennedy interests. He expected the elder Kennedy to announce his selection February 1, the day after he took off the uniform. But there was another meeting at which Kennedy talked of his son's likely nomination for president and asked Bruce to become an advisor to John F. Kennedy. He wrote the father a detailed letter, reviewing the terms of their verbal understandings, and then addressed the relationship with Senator Kennedy:

"I will not lay myself open to any charge or insinuation that through official actions in the army, I laid the groundwork for a favored position with a commercial organization. My accumulated judgment and any advice I might give would not under any circumstance be slanted for political reasons but in all cases must simply be my best judgment."

That frank statement broke off the negotiations. He received a warm letter from the senior Kennedy thanking him for his interest and terminating the correspondence. The plane contract was cancelled. Bruce had not considered any other position because he had been sure of the appointment.

With that episode behind him, he worked hard on the book manuscript and completed his draft in six weeks. Arthur Gordon, a well-known writer, edited and polished the text for publication. When *Countdown for Decision* appeared late that year it pleased friends in the army, Congress and industry, and antagonized others in the Defense Department, the air force and NASA. Later the book was translated and published in Germany also, because of lively interest there in Wernher von Braun and other Germans who had served at Huntsville.

There were more honors. He enjoyed a visit to Columbus, Ohio, where he attended the unversity forty years earlier, to accept the Governor's award for service to state and country. The Freedom Foundation presented an award at Valley Forge, Pennsylvania. House and Senate committees called him to Washington for more praise and to hear his views on space and defense. Job offers came unsolicited. Mississippi State University considered him as a candidate for its presidency. The University of Florida invited him to head its aeronautical engineering department. McCann Erickson, a large New York advertising agency, wanted him full time. Rockefeller and Armour Research Foundations extended feelers. His friends, Ed Murrow and Fred Friendly of the Columbia Broadcasting System, wanted to try a weekly series in which he would discuss space progress. Army Intelligence asked him to become a consultant, a request he could not refuse.

Meantime a distant relative, John E. Medaris, sought to interest him in joining the Electronic Teaching Laboratories of Washington. The firm produced sound equipment and educational tape recordings for use in schools and colleges. A new teaching tool, the concept was finding acceptance among educators and the military who employed the equipment to teach foreign languages. Bruce agreed to become board chairman in a part-time capacity.

They leased a house in Arlington, Virginia, convenient to Washington, and installed Ginny's grand piano and the desk given to him by the people of Huntsville. When a retired general's wife asked Ginny how retirement compared with her previous life, she laughed heartily. "While we lived at the arsenal," she explained, "Bruce had two secretaries, two aides and a houseboy. Now I'm all of them!" She wanted her restless and energetic husband to get out of business entanglements. Both enjoyed North Carolina's mountain country and Ginny flew to Greensboro to find a suitable property on which to build a home Bruce would design.

But the demands continued and he was unwilling to refuse people anxious to hear his views. He addressed a manufacturers' convention in Florida, the AFL-CIO Conference on World Affairs in New York, Chicago's real estate board, a tool engineers' meeting in Detroit, the Air War College in Alabama and other audiences. Golf and leisure time were not enough, he wanted some commitment that would occupy his mind and afford outlet for that burning desire to excel.

At this critical period an attractive offer came from the Lionel Corporation of New York, best known as an old-line manufacturing company which produced toy trains at a well-equipped plant in Irvington, New Jersey. The factory had produced precision components of army ammunition during the Korean War but was not involved in current space and missiles projects. Lionel's directors wanted to expand into electronics and create a broader production base for other types of manufactured goods. The opportunity to manage a reputable firm with growth potential at a salary that would provide him and Ginny with more income than he ever received in military service struck a responsive chord. Roy Cohen whose family held controlling interest in the corporation urged Bruce to become Lionel's president.

He knew of Cohen as counsel for the late Senator Joseph McCarthy of Wisconsin who launched a much publicized but abortive investigation of alleged Communist infiltration in the army. The Senate censured McCarthy when the investigation failed to substantiate his charges.

Close friends cautioned Bruce about accepting, arguing that Lionel wanted to repair its public image and perhaps attract military business. He consulted a New York attorney, Walter Scheyer, who drew up a proposed contract for a five-year period calling for an annual salary of $50,000, a chauffeur-driven sedan, and rental of a hotel suite for business use. Lionel's operating officials and those representing subsidiaries would report to Bruce. He would be the sole spokesman for operating divisions on the board of directors. Cohen accepted the terms.

When he met with directors Bruce outlined his plans and stressed that he meant every word of the contract with respect to exercising sole authority. The board ratified the agreement and raised his salary to $60,000. Bruce located a pleasant home in Essex Fells, New Jersey, a short drive from the Irvington plant and his office in downtown New York.

Ginny put aside hopes of retirement and moved again.

"I hope this isn't forever," she jokingly reminded Bruce. "Some day we will retire, won't we?"

"You know I can't be happy unless I'm busy," he said. "We can stand another five years because it will build up our reserves and allow us to enjoy some things we might not otherwise afford."

They transferred their church affiliation to the Essex Fells Episcopal parish. Bruce immersed himself in his new management responsibilities, building up contacts in the financial community, making public appearances on behalf of Lionel, entertaining clients and investigating smaller firms which the corporation might acquire. He spoke to civic and military groups in New York and New Jersey. The retirement of Major General John Barclay prompted him to return to Alabama in mid-1961 and he persuaded Barclay to join Lionel. Investors showed more interest in the company as Lionel's stock increased in price.

In time the corporation absorbed an electronics firm and another company equipped to fabricate large metal assemblies. Bruce looked ahead to building a balanced organization that might take on major projects in military or space related fields. *Time*, *Newsweek* and other leading periodicals commented on his book, *Countdown for Decision*, and his vigorous views about the quality of management in government.

Television networks called upon Bruce to comment on new Soviet space feats and the early U.S. manned flights of Alan Shepard and Virgil Grissom who were launched on army-developed Redstone missiles.

At his next meeting with newsmen in New York, Bruce gave an "iffy" reply to questions about a sweeping reorganization initiated by the new Secretary of Defense, Robert McNamara, with the support of President Kennedy. Army's technical services, traditional storehouses of specialized knowledge and supreme within their realms, were virtually gutted. The chiefs of ordnance, signal, chemical, quartermaster and transportation corps disappeared. An Army Materiel Command sprang up in their place. For the first time officers of combat arms would manage such technical installations as ordnance arsenals, like those familiar to

Bruce. Only the engineers chief, whose Congressional favor is one of the awesome facts of life in Washington, escaped the wipeout.

Defense moved to consolidate common supplies under a single manager. Previously the army, navy and air force had each bought its own. A jointly staffed Defense Supply Agency would thereafter buy, store and distribute to the services their food, clothing, medical and general supplies, construction materials and petroleum products. Lieutenant General Andrew T. McNamara, Bruce's close friend in Africa and Europe, the First Army quartermaster, became director.

Bruce wrote his son, now an army lieutenant:

"Dear Bruce . . . while I detested the parochialism that infected the tech services in my time, they kept alive knowledge of incalculable value in time of war. Under this new deal, I fear the army will lose the know-how in ammunition and communications essential in combat."

He had more personal worries in 1962, as he realized that his control of Lionel was slipping. Key officials dealt with Roy Cohen, their former boss, and bypassed the president's office. Unable to straighten out the situation, Bruce called for a showdown with the directors.

"Gentlemen, we have a serious problem," he stated. "For reasons beyond my understanding, responsible men in this company prefer to seek counsel from Roy instead of me. I cannot discharge my responsibilities if it is allowed to continue. We discussed the significance of my contract at our first meeting. I said then that it stated my conditions. Either you want Bruce Medaris to run Lionel or you do not."

Listening to hurried assurances of understanding and support, Bruce remained skeptical but hoped things would change for the better. They didn't. He consulted Scheyer who formally notified Cohen and the directors that they would be held accountable for the contract. Later Bruce and the attorney breakfasted with Cohen and warned that a breach of contract suit would be initiated. Cohen promised to pay Bruce in full for the remaining three years. In turn, Bruce resigned the presidency but agreed to serve another year on the board of directors.

As a consequence of a merger with another company Cohen lost management control. The new Lionel firm wanted to cut Bruce off. Scheyer promptly filed suit and a New York court ordered Lionel to pay in full.

Ginny was disappointed but relieved that Bruce had extricated himself. She hoped they might at last establish a home in North Carolina.

Jack Barclay remained for a while, then he also resigned and went back to Huntsville where he joined the Northrop Corporation as resident manager. Bruce and Ginny sailed to Europe where they relished a happy reunion with their son-in-law and daughter, Major and Mrs. Woody, in Wiesbaden, Germany, and their son, Bruce, who had completed a tour in Viet Nam and was stationed on the border of Czechoslovakia. On Bruce's sixtieth birthday his children and friends staged a party in Wiesbaden. They remained a month while Bruce revisited some of the cities fought over in World War II.

When they returned Bruce sold the New Jersey house. They decided to move to Orlando in central Florida where many retired officers, including some of his ordnance associates, made their homes. He was still in demand as a public speaker filling such invitations as he could, including an address to the convention of the Episcopal Diocese of Chicago where he spoke of God's help in recovering from the cancer attack and during his strenuous years in Alabama.

Bruce rented a house near the Orlando Country Club, a haven for retired couples in a quiet, residential section. Here he and Ginny could golf year round. Bruce prayed that the warm climate would help Ginny whose health was not as good as they might wish. Within hours of their arrival they were in contact with old friends, including the same Colonel Luce, now retired, who helped Bruce fight that ammunition fire in Normandy until he had been struck by shrapnel. His World War II and Redstone Arsenal colleague, Colonel Charles G. Patterson, maintained an extensive garden at his nearby home in Maitland.

Bruce's name and reputation interested businesses of all kinds including the All States Development Corporation which acquired a large tract of land east of Orlando and midway to Cape Canaveral for a housing development. With much fanfare and conspicuous display of the general's name in national advertising, the promoter began selling lots in "Rocket City," as he named the project. As Bruce learned more about the company, in which he had made a substantial investment, he disliked the high-pressure sales tactics and expressed his fears to other investors. They banded together and gave the developer a choice, either sell his interest to them or repay their investments. He chose the latter course. Unfortunately, the name of Medaris had been so cleverly intertwined with "Rocket City" that the break in relations failed to achieve its purpose. When the venture collapsed, people who bought property mistakenly believed that Bruce profited from their misfortune. The stigma was not easily removed.

Coming on the heels of the disappointing experience with Lionel, the bitter lesson convinced Bruce that he must avoid ventures he could not control. An uneasy thought ran through his mind; perhaps these misadventures were not entirely the fault of himself or others. Perhaps they occurred because he had not listened for that guidance which served so well in the past. He had again substituted his own will for God's.

"No more," he promised Ginny. "I've let myself be talked into the last mess by other people. Maybe I thought that I was smarter than I am. The thing that hurts most is the fact that other people who believed in me wound up by getting hurt. I won't risk hurting any others."

He established a management consultant firm with Colonel Patterson. Soon they built up an imposing clientele including the General Electric Company. GE employed 1,700 people in a Daytona Beach plant fifty miles east where automatic test equipment was assembled for Apollo moon ships. GE installed these devices at the Kennedy Space Center, the Johnson Space Center in Texas, and at contractor plants in Long Island and California. Bruce's former team in Huntsville under von Braun managed the construction of immense Saturn rockets that would make flight to the moon possible. GE provided services to the Alabama installation and its offshoot, a large testing installation in Mississippi where big rockets underwent static firing before delivery to Cape Canaveral for launch.

Bruce picked out a spacious lot on Lake Maitland and drafted plans for a new home, the kind of house which he and Ginny dreamed of for thirty years. It would have a spacious living room that could easily accommodate her grand piano, and a paneled study overlooking the lake for his big desk and correspondence files.

They became active in community affairs. Having attended All Saints Church in Winter Park for a time, Bruce and Ginny were drawn to the smaller mission of the Good Shepherd in Maitland. Services were conducted in the little white chapel built by Bishop Whipple in 1884 and used sporadically over the years until it became a mission supported by the Central Florida diocese. At the time the congregation was barely large enough to finance its changed status to that of a parish church. Bruce soon came to know the rector, Reverend Alfred Durrance, as a friend. Soon that chapel and Al Durrance would assume much greater importance in his life.

Construction proceeded on the new house. The summer heat had enveloped the Orlando area when Bruce and Ginny moved into the home in June, 1964. Floor to ceiling glass panels across the rear opened on a wide St. Augustine grass lawn which ran down to the lake shore. A boathouse sheltered a fiberglass runabout because Bruce planned to resume bass fishing, a sport he had enjoyed years before in Ohio and Canada. Ginny gave much of her time to scheming a landscape plan, selecting the kind of shrubs and plants suited to the subtropical climate. She continued to visit physicians, having problems with breathing, while Bruce seemed to thrive on the abundant sunshine. He golfed regularly with business friends and other retired officers, seemingly in excellent health.

Eight years had passed since the cancer operation performed at Walter Reed Hospital. Except for a minor cold his physical condition remained uniformly good. The results of blood sampling at six month intervals while in Alabama were negative. When he retired in 1960 the doctors at Walter Reed examined him over a period of three days. They found no indication of cancer and no disability. Officially, the army said he was cured. A year later the Lionel company bought a $100,000 life insurance policy on him. After checking his medical records the underwriter issued the policy without extra premium. While living in New Jersey in 1961 and 1962 Bruce underwent similar blood testing at the army hospital in Fort Monmouth and came through with flying colors. As these assurances built up he simply put all thought of cancer from his mind.

Bruce had skipped physical examination since 1962, having concluded that any health problem that might appear would not be malignant. So he was unpleasantly surprised on a sultry July night when intense pain wakened him.

"What's the trouble, Bruce?" Ginny asked as she heard him moving about.

"I just don't know," he said. "I seem to have severe pain and can't pin down where it comes from. It keeps moving about."

Ginny gave him a mild sedative and he tried to rest. The pain intensified and he spent the remainder of the night walking about aimlessly, asking himself what could possibly explain this sudden attack. The discomfort became so severe that he realized there must be a major problem. In the morning he and Ginny drove to the military hospital at Orlando's air force base. Physicians examined him carefully and concluded as a preliminary diagnosis that it must be an attack of neuralgia. They gave him pills which proved of little help. The pain became worse.

He continued to suffer agony for a week until Ginny took over and insisted that he must see Dr. Duncan McEwen, a friend whom they had met while living near the country club. Dr. McEwen located what seemed to be the central pain source and administered cortisone. The pain continued. McEwen then referred Bruce to an orthopedic surgeon who took x-rays of his midsection and, after examining the films, sent him to Dr. Miles Thomley for urological assessment. At that point and before any further diagnosis Bruce knew—as he had in Dr. Salna's office eight years before—that he had cancer. He was neither surprised nor frightened when Dr. Thomley diagnosed his ailment as osteosarcoma or bone cancer. He showed Bruce x-rays which revealed lesions, some as large as a fifty-cent piece, on pelvic bones, hip and thigh, and smaller lesions on his ribs. Obviously, the urologist concluded, the disease had been spreading for some time.

As Bruce walked out his first thought was of Ginny. He could not hide the truth from her. Driving home, surrounded by the sight and sound of teeming life, children at play in a schoolyard, it was difficult to realize that he faced death.

"Sit down beside me, Ginny," Bruce asked as he entered the Florida room of their home.

Looking at his face, she surmised the news was unfavorable. "What did Dr. Thomley say?" she asked.

"It's bone cancer," Bruce replied. "The x-rays made it very clear. There can be no mistake. I want you to understand what will happen. Thomley arranged for my admission to the hospital. There is a fairly simple surgical procedure which will cut off glands that secrete male hormones. That may reduce or even eliminate the pain. So that's a first step. Then he will begin administering female hormones which I must take daily. That won't cure anything but it will control the pain."

He paused as Ginny sobbed quietly. Reaching out to her hand, Bruce pleaded, "Now, don't cry. You must bear up."

"You haven't said a word about getting better," she said.

"Let's not talk about that part of the problem until we know more," Bruce went on. "I've got some things to do that won't wait."

After the surgery the pain ceased. Dr. Thomley explained the regimen Bruce must follow including the hormone treatment. "You must take those daily doses for the rest of your life," his physician said.

Bruce remembered a fellow officer stricken by bone

cancer after World War II. He had died eighteen months after diagnosis.

"Am I a terminal patient?" he asked.

The doctor nodded. "Bruce," he added, "there is no known cure."

"How long do I have?"

"I would suggest that you clear up anything important as soon as possible," the doctor replied. "You may have a year, but not more than eighteen months."

He told Bruce to return at ninety-day intervals for check-ups on the progress of the disease.

Ginny was perilously close to collapse when Bruce relayed the physician's words. Having survived one cancer ordeal, she cried out against the sentence of death hanging over them.

"We've got to tell the children," she pointed out. Bruce agreed. "You tell Marta and Bruce," he said. "Marilyn and Eugene are vacationing and I don't want to upset them, so I'll write her."

Driving to his office next day, he told Patterson of his uncertain future. His associate tried to comfort him.

"Pat, let it alone," Bruce cut him off. "I'd appreciate your help in looking after the business for a while. You can understand there are a number of things I must take care of for Ginny's sake—bank accounts, investments, the real estate, pension—I want to be sure these are all in good shape when the time comes."

"By all means," Patterson replied. "Don't worry about the business. How is Ginny taking this?"

"That's my first concern," Bruce answered. "She is so dependent upon me that I don't like to think of leaving her alone. Marta and young Bruce are devoted to their mother, as they should be, but Marta has her family to think about and I don't need to tell you that Bruce goes where the army wants him to."

He busied himself with personal affairs. As one unmistakable evidence of cancerous activity his body filled with fluid regularly. His legs swelled to twice their normal size so that walking became a hardship. Tapping and drugs offered only temporary relief. Despite the discomfort and the nagging questions in his mind, Bruce carried on in his customary fashion, even choosing as pall bearers men who were close to him over the years . His studied calm disarmed others, but had little effect on Ginny.

# 15

# TRIAL AND TRIUMPH

A man who had achieved greatness by dint of will power, endurance and brilliant intellect, approached the day of reckoning with little hope. A mind honed by technical logic and military tradition reluctantly accepted a professional judgment. Bruce Medaris understood all too well that death awaited.

That so many friends wrote, called, or came in person when they learned of this second cancer attack, to comfort Bruce and Ginny, salved his ego but did little to seriously allay the consequences of what lay before them. He could sit by and toll off the remaining months, weeks and days in a relentless countdown, meanwhile deriving some measure of satisfaction from his memories. What else remained?

Ginny's desperate messages brought the children: Marilyn, Marta and Bruce with their families to see grandfather for, perhaps, the last time. The Reverend Stillings, their son-in-law, dropped in to talk with Al Durrance. He told Durrance what had happened and to call on Bruce and Ginny, commenting that "they are not taking it easily. Please watch over them so they don't become unstrung when the time comes."

Durrance promised to visit. He drove to the new lake shore home somewhat in awe of Bruce because of his remarkable career. Like other Good Shepherd people, the rector addressed him as "General." Relating the situation to a brother cleric, Durrance said he found the couple subdued but pleased by his visit.

"I knew that Bruce underwent a serious operation some time earlier, but I had no idea of its nature," Durrance related. "He described the first cancer attack, which had rather unusual long-term consequences, but otherwise he made complete recovery. I guess that it must have been the Holy Spirit who prompted me to take along a copy of John Large's book, *God Is Able.* I liked the title while having mixed emotions about the contents and felt I ought to leave something with them. Bruce accepted my suggestion that he do something in the spiritual realm, as well as in the medical, in order to meet his Maker. As we talked, I began to believe that he might have the faith to be healed."

Bruce put the book aside when Durrance left, but Ginny read it with quickening hope. That night, alone in his study, Bruce picked up the volume and leafed through its opening pages. As he did, he was suddenly aware of facing a reality which he never before experienced. He laid the book down and dropped to his knees weeping.

"My God, take this worthless body and do with it as You will," he pleaded. "I've run my course and now I surrender to You body, mind and soul. From now on what happens will be in Your hands and I willingly accept Your judgment."

A peace which he never before experienced calmed his

body and mind. When he rose, he believed that his spirit was being healed, for he felt such immense relief from fear.

At Durrance's invitation Bruce attended healing services conducted Monday evenings in Good Shepherd chapel. People came to these meetings, some from the parish, others from nearby communities seeking help for themselves, relatives or friends. The simple ritual followed that of the Order of St. Luke, an interdenominational fellowship of physicians and clergymen who believe in God's power to heal. As the service concluded, the sick walked forward and knelt at the rail where the minister placed his hands on their heads and prayed, "O Lord, look down from Heaven, behold, visit, and relieve this thy servant. Look upon him with the eyes of thy mercy, give him comfort and sure confidence in thee, defend him in all danger, and keep him in perpetual peace and safety; through Jesus Christ our Lord."

Bruce was humbly grateful as these people, many of them strangers, prayed for his recovery. After the service they gathered in the parish hall for fellowship. He found these occasions refreshing as he sought to help those who helped him. Ginny joined a prayer group which met at the home of Jimmie and Betty Ezelle, their neighbors who were active in the charismatic life of Good Shepherd.

Weeks passed uneventfully. Bruce only knew he felt peaceful and that he had a growing sense that God was doing something different in his life.

Then, one day, Father Durrance took Bruce aside and told him that Virginia Lively would be visiting the parish in the near future.

"The Lord selects his own instruments," Durrance said. "Virginia is one of them. Some years ago she almost lost her father, Roy Wolff, who was ill with tuberculosis. The doctors said there was no hope for recovery. She was a member of our church and prayed diligently for her father. In time a close friend insisted there was more to faith than reciting prayers. Virginia fought the problem for quite a while, trying futilely to prove her faith. Then she happened to read a book by C. S. Lewis that confirmed what her friend told her, that it was possible to have an all-encompassing experience with the Lord. At that instant she gave herself to God."

Bruce nodded, "What happened?"

"Jesus Christ appeared to her in a vision not once, but again and again over a period of months," Durrance went on. "She saw him as the perfect Healer. In one vision she saw a scarred, cavity-filled lung and then a healthy lung. She was convinced that her father would recover. And he did. He subsequently became a devout churchman and teacher. Virginia had some problems in her church associations. As she read more and more of the Bible and found many assurances of the Lord's power to heal the sick, she became angered because the church seemingly did not preach or pursue this ministry. She wanted to help people, understanding somehow that the Lord had chosen her as one of his instruments.

"I was fresh out of seminary, working in a small parish in South Florida, when I heard of this woman and thought her personal experience might inspire others. So I asked her to come and talk to some of my people. That was the beginning of her unique ministry which has reached out beyond Florida to congregations and individuals elsewhere in the South. There have been many instances of healings following her wherever she goes. I'd like to have you meet her."

Bruce agreed, but a longstanding commitment prevented him from attending the healing service which Mrs. Lively conducted. Two nights later wind and rain buffeted Maitland when she visited a prayer group at the home of Bucky and Eleanor Kendricks who lived near Bruce and Ginny. Jimmie Ezelle phoned, "I know you wanted to meet Virginia.

Why don't you and Ginny come over to the Kendricks', with Betty and me?"

"All right, we'll come for a little while," Bruce replied.

He told Ginny of the invitation. He had been favorably impressed by Al Durrance's story of Mrs. Lively's ministry, but both he and Ginny were uneasy about charismatic activity which was a new and troubling phenomenon in old-line denominations although long familiar in the Pentecostal churches. Good Shepherd parishioners like Episcopalians elsewhere entertained sharply divergent opinions about the charismatic movement. Much the same doubt raged among Methodists, Roman Catholics, Baptists and other church groups. The idea that the Holy Spirit might empower lay people in all walks of life had frightening aspects. But Bruce and Ginny liked and respected the Ezelles and Kendricks as neighbors.

Bruce and Ginny walked through driving rain to the Kendricks home. When they entered Bruce took a chair in the kitchen where some of the men were drinking coffee. He admired Mrs. Lively's devotion and voluntary work, but the prospect of sharing what he considered an entirely private experience with other people bothered him. Finally he moved his chair into the doorway so that he could observe and listen to Mrs. Lively. She was a woman of average height with a faint touch of gray in dark brown hair, speaking quietly but with unmistakable authority. Other people in the room told of their experiences with God's healing power as she listened. During this time, Mrs. Lively became aware of the stranger watching her. She knew nothing about Bruce Medaris, his background or his illness. She only noticed that he paid close heed, leaning back in the chair and stroking his chin slowly.

Following her custom, Virginia asked if anyone wanted

her to pray for them. A young couple responded. As they went back to their chairs, Bruce jumped to his feet and asked for prayer without understanding why. Mrs. Lively said later, "I had no knowledge of him or his problem, but I knew immediately that he would be healed. He sat down in a large chair and I stood behind, placing my hands on his head and praying for the Lord's intervention. When he got up he grasped my hands and said he felt an electric-like surge of power race through his body. I did not feel it, but the conviction of his healing remained very strong. After Bruce and his wife left, the Kendricks told me of his remarkable career and the bone cancer."

Bruce went to sleep that night with a lighter heart. He woke feeling stronger and picked up his Bible searching for vaguely remembered words in Mark's gospel. He found them, "They shall lay hands on the sick and they shall recover." His heart thrilled.

Ginny happily told their children of his experiences with the John Large book and Virginia Lively. "I believe sincerely that Bruce has been redeemed by our Saviour," she said. "We are very much heartened by the assurance that the Lord is helping him."

Father Durrance noted the change in Bruce's attitude and inquired about his apparent happiness. Bruce described his prayer of surrender—which he regarded as a conversion—and his vivid encounter with Virginia Lively.

"You are receiving from God what God received from you—your life," the minister observed.

Bruce returned to Dr. Thomley for blood tests and more x-rays at Christmas time. The doctor phoned three days later and reported, "We've had a good look at the pictures. I'm pleased to say that you are not getting any worse. The cancer is not progressing as rapidly as expected."

"Am I being healed?" Bruce asked pointedly.

"I don't want you to have any false notions," the physician replied, "but you may have more time than we thought."

His patient responded with a chuckle. "Yes, I am being healed! Have a happy New Year."

When Virginia Lively next visited Good Shepherd to conduct healing services she dined with the Ezelles in their home. While they were eating they heard the front door open and an excited voice calling, "Where is she? Where is she?" Bruce bounded into the dining room, grasped Virginia in a tight embrace and cried, "I am healing! God is removing the cancer!" When he quieted, Virginia softly told him, "I never had any doubt. I knew when we met that the Lord would remove your problem, whatever it was."

Wernher von Braun called his former boss from Huntsville in early spring. "I hope you won't feel that I am butting in," Wernher said, "but we've heard of your problem. I have a friend who has done unusual work with cancer and I'd like you to meet him. He is Dr. J. R. Maxfield of Dallas, Texas, who operates a clinic with his brother, Dr. Jack."

Bruce welcomed the suggestion. The rocket builder arranged for him to talk with Dr. Maxfield at the Kennedy Space Center, an hour's drive from Maitland, where a regional nuclear commission was in session. The group included representatives of state governments, industrialists, scientists and the medical profession interested in nuclear energy. They saw two Gemini astronauts begin their mission in space.

Maxfield described to Bruce the techniques employed in the Dallas clinic. They used radioactive isotopes to detect cancer cells. Bruce agreed to visit Dallas with his x-ray films.

"Wernher's recommendation and my talk with Jim Maxfield have convinced me that I ought to fly out there," he told Ginny. "If nothing more, we will at least know what the cancer is doing."

"I'll be praying for the best," she answered.

Dr. Maxfield demonstrated his equipment. An electronic scanning device traced radioactive particles as they circulated in the patient's blood stream. Where cancer cells existed the scanner pinpointed their location within the body. The technique is now in common use; in 1965, the Maxfields were among the pioneers.

An isotope of strontium was implanted in Bruce, after which he dined with Maxfield. Next morning the scanner conducted a skeletal survey of his entire body. Bruce heard the familiar clicking of a Geiger counter during the procedure. From his familiarity with nuclear technology, he knew that all he heard was background radiation, not the excited signals that betrayed cancerous "hot spots." Dr. Maxfield gave him a thorough physical examination and took blood samples. When he finished the physician informed Bruce that he found a stable situation. The cancer was not spreading.

"So we are not going to try any treatment," Maxfield added. "We will keep the big weapon in reserve." He referred to radioactive potassium. Bruce met an Arkansas farmer in the clinic who received the potassium treatment some years before and looked hale and hearty. When he boarded the plane for Florida, Bruce knew that he still carried the menace but that God had checked its growth.

After that some of his business acquaintances persuaded him to seek election to the Maitland City Council, something he would have dismissed as impossible five months earlier. He won the election on March 2, 1965, becoming public works director of the city of 8,000 residents.

Bruce could not forget Al Durrance's comment about receiving from God what he had given Him. He became more active in the church as usher and vestryman. The vestry was divided on the issue of whether to build a larger sanctuary for worship or a parish hall. Bruce contended they must first serve the spiritual needs of the growing congregation; if they did, the hall would follow in God's time. That was the vestry's decision.

He was still uncertain, however, about his relationship with the Lord. On a warm April night he realized that he could not communicate. Ginny shared his profound despair which led him to call the Ezelles, forced by agony to rely upon a fellow human. Betty Ezelle explained that Jimmie was not home and offered to help. Bruce asked her to join him. They went into his study, surrounded by the wall displays of his military career, where he poured out his heart.

"I've tried but I can't believe my prayers are being heard," he told Betty. "My depression is so acute that I don't know where to turn. What could I have done to bring this about?"

Betty began to pray softly and, in time, his grief eased a little. Bruce thanked her and insisted on escorting her to the nearby house. As they approached he saw Jimmie's parked car and entered with Betty who quickly explained his problem.

Husband and wife placed their hands on him and prayed. They continued until early morning when, as Bruce explained later, "the dam suddenly burst. I cried as a baby would, not in pain, but in joy. The Lord was where He belonged and I turned to see Him. I was anointed by the Holy Spirit and received the gift of tongues."

Sharing his happiness, the Ezelles prayed, laughed, drank coffee and gave thanks until dawn. A new Bruce Medaris, humble and contrite, emerged from that ordeal.

Six months after his first visit to Dallas he returned for

another examination. Again Dr. Maxfield concluded that no treatment was indicated. "I'm willing to say that you appear to be recovering," he told an elated patient. Christmas, 1965, became an especially memorable season for a man who was supposed to be at death's door. When he next saw Maxfield at midyear the physician said, "Bruce, there is no longer any evidence of bone cancer. The x-rays showed no lesions. You may as well quit taking those female hormones."

Bruce left Texas jubilantly praising God. He looked about the jet aircraft, seeing his fellow passengers not as strangers, but as witnesses sharing his rebirth. As he strode through the Orlando air terminal later, head erect and smiling, he ran into Andy McNamara waiting for a plane to Washington. A retired lieutenant general, McNamara was a close friend from the World War II days.

They shook hands warmly and Bruce explained what had transpired in the last six months, the body fluid slowly disappearing, his strength returning, and now undisputed medical evidence of complete healing. Tears came to his eyes as he exclaimed, "Andy, it seems like a miracle! I am well!"

McNamara grasped his arm. "God has been good to you, Bruce," he said. "I'm very happy for you and Ginny."

His wife cried with joy when he reported Dr. Maxfield's verdict. "Thank God, Bruce, you've come back to me," she said fervently. They telephoned the children, sharing their contagious joy.

Dr. Thomley congratulated Bruce, remarking that this was the first time he stopped prescribing hormones to a bone cancer victim.

As the news spread, the delight of friends clashed with doubts of others who considered his recovery incredible. The man's background and those achievements that brought him fame added zest and weight to the story. By letters and telephone calls, people trying to help the sick appealed to Bruce for advice. To each he repeated, "I did nothing except surrender to God. It was the power of the Holy Spirit that healed me, nothing less and no one else."

He wanted to say more—to introduce people more directly to the Lord Jesus—but he was not prepared for such a task, in spite of his long experience as a commander and manager. Thus he began to plunge ever more deeply into the life of the Good Shepherd parish. He was especially drawn to help Father Durrance. In so doing they became much closer. Julie Durrance, Al's wife, adopted Bruce as a foster father and they too drew closer.

The third member of the Durrance family, four-year-old John Paul, was slower to accept him. When Bruce asked him one day to get him a book, he responded by kicking Bruce's shin. The retired general promptly returned the kick and the pair glared like little children.

"I'm ready to be your friend, John Paul," Bruce said as he grinned.

"O.K.," the boy replied. "Now I'll get you the book."

Encouraged by Durrance, Bruce formed a prayer group of business and professional men that met weekly at his home before going to work. They shared problems and prayed together. Father Durrance remarked that "we came to know one another and confessed our shortcomings, sure that God would extend a helping hand. We talked, prayed and watched Ginny's pet gallinule as he stalked about the yard. Bruce met with men of all walks of life without consciousness of his former stature. No one was aware of rank or privilege, only of our common needs. We prayed, loved one another, and came together as our Lord willed. One could see the grace of God operating among his people."

Bruce could not escape his past. Prominent Republicans asked him to run for governor of Florida. Honored by their trust, he refused on the grounds that he was a novice in politics. He agreed to serve as state chairman for U.S. Senator Barry Goldwater, who lost the presidency to Lyndon B. Johnson in the fall election.

In constant demand as a public speaker Bruce returned to the platform, but with a different urgency in his message. He addressed the graduating class of Embry Riddle Aeronautical Institute, observing that "the more you learn in life, the more you must accept the fact that this world is an instrument of God." He told a technical society, "The divine dimension of the human race is the ability to project, imagine, invent and plan." He flew to Huntsville to address a men's group and to Dallas where he spoke to the Council on World Affairs, assuring both audiences that "the Lord helped me as the Psalm promised."

But he also began to receive invitations to speak to religious groups. At the Holy Spirit Teaching Mission in Fort Lauderdale he met Dennis Bennett of Seattle, the Episcopal priest who figured prominently in the charismatic movement and whose story had become widely known through his book, *Nine O'Clock in the Morning*. At a Miami gathering Bruce declared "there is no new knowledge, only revealed knowledge which is neither good nor bad of itself but only as men use it."

And he grew bolder in addressing nonreligious audiences. To a university group this retired officer who led one of the foremost scientific teams of modern times commented that "our precise scientific knowledge of God's universe is about equal to one speck of dust in this room when measured against its totality." To industrial engineers in St. Petersburg he pointed out that man intercepted radio messages over vast distances, like those flashed to earth by the army moon probe over a gulf of 400,000 miles. "We know how to tune in those signals," he commented. "But can we say the same about our communications with God?"

Strangely, as he plunged more and more into the spiritual, his management business prospered even though he devoted less time to it than he had in the past. Watching his activities, perceiving the focus of his interest, Durrance encouraged Bruce to take on new responsibilities.

"I'd like to have you serve as a lay reader, Bruce," the minister said. "That would give you a sense of participation in the service I think you'll enjoy."

Bruce enrolled in a course taught by the Reverend Larry D. Lossing at St. Luke's Cathedral in Orlando. There he began to grasp the underlying relationship between Old and New Testaments for the first time. He completed his studies and received a certificate that qualified him as a lay reader in late fall 1966. In this capacity he read from the Scriptures during the church service. He could recite the offices of morning and evening prayer omitting only the confession and absolution which the Episcopal church reserves to bishops and priests.

When Ginny and Bruce drove up to their summer home in Highlands, North Carolina, Bruce told the Reverend Gale D. Webbe, rector of the Church of the Incarnation, of his new status. He soon received authority from Bishop Matthew G. Henry of western Carolina to perform these functions in the Highlands church. Bishop Henry went further, granting him license to preach.

A timely reminder of past glory arrived from the Huntsville, Alabama, *Times*. The newspaper asked Bruce to furnish a statement for a special issue commemorating the tenth anniversary of *Explorer 1*, America's first satellite. He seized the opportunity to sound a familiar warning.

"The army satellite project began in an atmosphere of

suspicion and bitter competition fraught with artificial restrictions, grudging approvals and meager financing," he wrote. "So powerful were the hatreds that even the president refrained from acknowledging the small but determined band of dedicated people who restored national prestige after the unnecessary and degrading shellacking by the Russians when they launched *Sputniks 1* and *2*.

"The clock is still ticking. Time and history overrun the community and nation that cannot keep vision fixed on the future and maintain momentum by making sound decisions before reaching a fork in the road. We planned further along the way than NASA aims. We advanced Project Horizon which was never acknowledged and officially smothered. Yet it would have given the country a productive lunar colony and pointed the way beyond. Who today will raise his head above the crowd and dare to challenge the nation to press on as a loving God has opened the way?"

He flew to Washington for the anniversary dinner January 31, 1968, meeting old friends like Senator John Sparkman, the host; Dr. William Pickering of the Jet Propulsion Laboratory; Thomas Morrow of Chrysler; Dr. James Van Allen and Werner von Braun. Former President Dwight Eisenhower sent a message in which he called the satellite "one of our brightest technical achievements."

Early in the new year another cancer attack came upon him suddenly. Bruce had been a heavy smoker. His mouth became painfully sore, and x-rays indicated that he suffered from leukoplakia. Ginny's fears mounted—cancer, for the third time!

"Is it possible, Bruce?" she pleaded. "Could there be some mistake?"

"No, Ginny, I'm afraid my old enemy has returned in another place at another time," he said. "I'm going to make an appointment to see Jim Maxfield in Dallas and find out what he can do."

Dr. Maxfield confirmed the findings. They visited a mechanical dentist who, working under Maxfield's direction, fashioned a plate thin enough to slip under Bruce's tongue. As the plate was built up in very thin layers, like an onion, Dr. Maxfield inserted tiny cobalt seeds following a predetermined pattern, measuring the level of radioactivity as the work progressed. A lead shield of extreme thinness topped off the plate. Bruce must wear it six hours daily in two evenly divided periods.

Bruce returned home and wore the plate ten days when he called Maxfield and reported more soreness. The physician prescribed an anesthetic solution. Ten days later he called Dallas again and reported, "My mouth is burning up!" Dr. Maxfield chuckled. "Okay," he said, "now return the plate to me." Three months later a checkup confirmed the cancer was gone and new skin had replaced damaged tissue. The problem never returned.

As the months passed, the conviction grew stronger in Bruce that God must have some further purpose for his life, having preserved it through three attacks of cancer. After he sought answer in prayer, he mentioned this to Ginny who asked, "What more can you possibly do?"

"I'm not sure yet," he replied, "but I've got to talk this over with Al Durrance and Larry Lossing. It's almost as if I am being pushed."

Father Durrance had something to tell Bruce. "I've decided to accept a call to the Ocala parish," he said. "So I will leave Good Shepherd soon. It won't mean an end to our friendship, Bruce, I promise you."

"I'm real sorry that we will lose you, Al," Bruce replied, "but I know all our people will pray for your success in your new charge. There is a matter I wanted to discuss, it has to do with my work in the church. The lay reader activity has given me a welcome outlet, but somehow it hasn't satisfied my total need. Al, I must help to bring God's message to His children. He gave my life back to me and I want others to understand that if they will only surrender their wills to Him, they will find the kind of peace He brought to me."

"I've guessed at your problem," Durrance said calmly. "You can't be content with halfway measures. Bruce, you must seek guidance. I'll pray for you, too, because I really believe the Lord wants you as His servant. You should seriously consider studying for the diaconate which would admit you to holy orders."

Father Lossing seconded this advice. Bruce prayed as they suggested. He received direction so clear and forceful that there could be no question of its source.

"I'm going to talk to the bishop," he informed Ginny. "If he will let me try, I want to prepare for ordination as a deacon."

"I'm worried about you, Bruce," she said. "You have put stress on your mind and body again and again. You survived three cancer attacks with God's help but how much more can you honestly expect of Him?"

"If the bishop says no, I'll accept the verdict," he promised.

Bruce went alone to consult the Right Reverend Henry I. Louttit, the bishop of south Florida. Explaining the purpose of his visit, Bruce added, "I want you to know that I'm not here of my own choice. There have been several occasions in my life when the Almighty carried me through real problems. Now I sincerely believe He wants me to do this, but I will be sixty-six in May. If you think that age or any other factor stands in my way, I'll bow to your judgment."

"I don't make these judgments, Bruce," Bishop Louttit replied with a smile. "I also take orders from the same Power that brought you here. You have my blessing to stand for the examination."

Following the customary procedure, Bruce appeared before the diocesan standing committee and asked permission to undertake preparations which would qualify him as a permanent deacon. The committee accepted his candidacy.

At this juncture his collaborator in *Countdown for Decision*, the book he had written in retirement, got in touch with Bruce. Arthur Gordon was now a roving editor for *Guideposts*, the nationally circulated pocket-size magazine that publishes personal accounts of religious experiences. At Gordon's request, Bruce typed out this account:

"Many of us through ignorance, arrogance or stupidity keep running from God's love as fast as we can. My own flight began when I was a child. As a Methodist I went to Sunday School. But I was forced to. There might be a Supreme Being, I conceded, but religion was not for me. I was sure that I was more intelligent, more energetic, and more competitive than anyone around. I could paddle my own canoe. For the next few decades I did just that. It was really amazing how anyone with such a high opinion of himself could make such a mess of things in the area of life that really counted . . . I was impatient, hard-driving, self-centered. I felt that I constantly had to prove my superiority and didn't care how I did it. As a career soldier I was a success. As a human being, well, I don't enjoy thinking about it.

"All this time I was aware that something, luck or fate or chance, was favoring me. I came through three wars without a scratch. The thought sometimes crossed my mind that perhaps this power, whatever it was, was keeping me intact because there was some important job I was destined to do. Sometimes I would say, half jokingly, that the Lord must have His eyes on me. I was perfectly willing to let the Lord be president of the company, so long as I was chairman of the board.

"Now and then there would be a faint stirring of something indefinable, a gentle pressure, an inner urging, a faint yearning that was almost like homesickness."

He mentioned his experience in Bristol Cathedral in 1943 and his admission to the Episcopal Church when the family returned from Argentina. After this came a brief account of the missile agency and his recovery from prostate cancer. He believed that it was the missile program for which he was spared.

"I began to be strongly aware," he continued, "that when problems were thrust upon me, problems too complex for any one man to handle, all I had to do was ask for help and listen—and I would get it. My staff became aware of this. They would watch me go to the window, stand there for a few moments, then come back and say, 'Let's not go down that road right now . . . the alarm bells are ringing.'

"Sometimes the guidance was affirmative. Then we would go down that road whatever it was. And in a proportion far higher than any mortal man could hope to achieve alone, those decisions proved right."

He described the second cancer attack and his introduction to the John Large book which persuaded him that God can do anything He wills.

"The result of this sudden, almost blinding flash of insight was that I stopped being doubtful about the power of prayer and began to ask urgently for help." Describing his meeting with Virginia Lively, he said, "I let go that night of the last tattered shreds of ego and surrendered to God.

"To me," Bruce concluded, "this means that God's unbelievably patient, tolerant and understanding love will pursue a man, even one as full of the sin of self as I was, until it catches up with him. Perhaps the real reason my life had been spared was so that I could tell the story of my personal encounter with my Lord, an encounter that has left me filled with abiding joy."

His priestly advisors, Fathers Lossing and Durrance, mapped a course of study which he undertook immediately. He spent six weeks in Highlands studying religious works for the canonical examinations, having first passed a suitability test. Marta spent some time with her parents in North Carolina, keenly interested in Bruce's objective. A strong believer in the charismatic movement, Marta played an active role in her Albuquerque, New Mexico, parish.

Bruce returned to Florida in June to undergo examination by a committee of priests along with two other candidates for the diaconate and six seminary graduates who would enter the priesthood. The examiners were satisfied after three days of searching discussions, probing his knowledge of the church, the Bible, parish administration and kindred subjects.

"Are you sure this is what you want?" Ginny asked when he returned to Maitland. "You understand that this will probably mean the eventual closing of your business?"

"It's no longer a question of what I want," he gently assured her. "This must be done because the Lord has set me on this path."

The newly completed Church of the Good Shepherd was filled June 19,1969, a warm and sunny day, for the admission of John Bruce Medaris to sacred orders. Ginny and her son, Major Bruce Medaris, greeted friends at the door. The little family occupied the first pew as the clergy slowly approached the altar.

Canon Paul Reeves preached the sermon. Bruce's confessor, Al Durrance, read the Prayer Book charge. David Suellau, the new rector, presented the ordinand to Bishop Louttit. Bruce's son-in-law, Father Stillings, led the congregation in reciting the litany and suffrages for ordinations. Canon William H. Folwell read the epistle from Acts, chapter six.

Then Bishop Louttit conducted the solemn examination of the candidate before the people. He placed hands upon Bruce who knelt before him: "Take thou authority to execute the office of a Deacon in the Church of God. . . ."

Deacon Bruce Medaris stood to read the words of St. Luke: "Let your loins be girded about, and your lights burning; and ye yourselves like unto men that wait for their Lord, when he will return from the wedding; that when he cometh and knocketh, they may open unto him immediately. Blessed are those servants, whom the Lord when he cometh shall find watching; verily I say unto you that he shall gird himself, and make them to sit down to meat, and will come forth and serve them. And if he shall come in the second watch, or in the third watch, and find them so, blessed are those servants."

Bishop Louttit celebrated communion. A reception followed in the parish hall where the clergy and friends congratulated Bruce and Ginny. The former general had received a new command in a new army.

# 16

# THY WILL BE DONE

Bruce's ordination evoked a variety of responses within the army and his community. Officers exposed to the forceful commander during his military years could not understand this metamorphosis. Neither could they explain his healing. Business associates wondered how they should deal with this changed personality who was both humbler and yet visibly proud of his new status. The sick and desolate sought him out for help.

From her Wisconsin home, sensing the mixed reaction, Marilyn expressed her thoughts to Ginny in a thoughtful letter:

"I can believe that you and dad must run into doubters, as I have, among some who knew the Bruce Medaris of my childhood. Dad's life offers two important proofs of God's grace: first, that He can change human nature even in a person as strong-willed as he was, and, second, that God uses personality to His purpose, He does not destroy all of its characteristics. Too many of us suffer from the delusion that to become a committed Christian, we must change drastically. But the change follows the commitment."

How to address Bruce troubled some people. Was he still General Medaris? Or the Reverend Bruce Medaris? He responded to either without a fuss. The Episcopal church encompasses a broad spectrum of Christian experience. The low church tradition emphasizes the Bible and the preaching, while the high church tradition lays greater emphasis on the church and the sacraments. Charismatics can be found in both high and low church parishes. Sometimes they are embraced by local rectors and vestries, sometimes ignored or shunned. Bruce is an Anglo-Catholic with strong charismatic beliefs. He knew the Holy Spirit's power firsthand.

An army friend came to Florida on a golfing vacation and played a match with Bruce. When they finished he said, "I had to come and see for myself because I couldn't believe the stories about you. I remember a Bruce Medaris who cursed his way around the golf course. But you didn't swear once during this game!"

Bruce laughed heartily. "You're right," he admitted. "But I didn't do it by myself. The Holy Spirit cleansed my tongue."

Ginny was increasingly concerned about the strain on his health. He was spending more time in the church while keeping up his business obligations. Bruce decided to sell the Lake Maitland home because of the expense, and to extricate himself gradually from his enterprises. Ginny located a waterfront apartment in Winter Park nearer Good Shepherd Church and within walking distance of shops. Bruce told Colonel Patterson that he would withdraw from active participation.

"I can't do what the Lord intends and hold up my responsibilities in the office," he explained. "So I want you to think it over and decide what you wish to do. Medaris Management will phase out in the near future."

Patterson willingly agreed to carry on for a while and to relieve Bruce of his business commitments as much as possible.

Bruce wore clerical garb when engaged in religious duties which included visits to other parishes where he was in frequent demand as a speaker. Ginny discovered that she, too, joined the ministerial life. Distressed people seeking help called at all hours. She counseled them and promised that Bruce would contact them.

"I feel awfully inadequate," she told her husband. "I have no training to act as a counsellor and, Bruce, I can't stop thinking of all the troubles these unfortunate people describe to me."

"I know, Ginny," he replied. "Be patient with them. Sometimes you do more good than you realize simply by listening to their problems. They have nowhere else to turn."

The mail brought more appeals as word of the healing and conversion spread into other states. A priest in Virginia confessed that he was in despair because he lost contact with God. Urging him to keep his faith, Bruce replied that "before I was picked up in the merciful arms of our Lord and felt his love, I had not cried since childhood. Now, I find myself entirely free and tears come easily. There are no lost souls, only those who have temporarily lost touch with our Lord's love. His arms are always open."

A cancer victim in Georgia asked the inevitable question, why had God healed Bruce and not him? "God heals in many ways," Bruce wrote, "and not always as we in our ignorance would like. Whenever we pray in faith God will heal the spirit so that we attain the joy that passes understanding and will join Him gladly."

Bruce cautioned all correspondents that "the person who lays on hands is not the healing power, but only the channel by which it comes from the Lord." Their names were added to Good Shepherd's prayer list.

Bruce took Father Suellau with him on a flight to West Virginia where another Episcopal minister sought help to renew his faith. The two men prayed with him until he regained his trust in God. It was a vital experience for Bruce who gradually recognized the truth—God wanted more of him than he was giving.

Bruce soon found himself speaking to congregations in Florida, Texas and North Carolina. His testimony held special appeal to the legions of retired people living in central and south Florida who saw in his conversion and healing reason for hope in their personal difficulties. He explained to all of these groups that "I used to lecture and made a fair amount of money in that way, but when the Holy Spirit got hold of me He no longer permitted me to make money. Now I go where He tells me, and if I try to go where He doesn't want me, I fall over more stones and logs than you can imagine. . . . What you hear is more important than what I say. You will hear what the Lord intends if your ears and heart are open."

To an audience in Delray Beach he said grimly, "We are being cheated. Somewhere along the line the church forgot that our Lord promised a great many things right now. People become so hipped on preparing for the hereafter that they are cheated out of the Now. I've heard this called the 'Holy Now' and that is the right name. Most Christians are torn between the temptations and requirements of today in order to have some fun and reward out of life, and what they believe they must do to reach eternal life."

To his listeners in Delray Beach and in Dallas and elsewhere, Bruce voiced a challenge: "You don't have the nerve to try. You can't go up and say, 'Lord, you promised, now deliver! I'm giving to you, you give to me.' No, we're afraid that He can't do as good a job with our lives as we can. Sometimes we want to turn over our lives. We do that every time we get in trouble. Then we say, 'I've made a mess, so You take my life and straighten it out.' When everything is all right we want it back. We profess to surrender but in the back of our minds we say, 'I'm giving it to You, but if You don't toe the line, Lord, I'll be right there to put the veto on You. You tell me something I don't want to hear and oh, boy, I'm going to say no!' "

He paused and shook his head. "That won't work. Let me share a little background which explains why I can be so positive about my statements.

"I haven't any business to be here by any standard other than the Lord's. Five and a half years ago I was told flat out by good doctors that I wouldn't live eighteen months. Well, here I am! I feel younger every day. Some of my friends don't understand, but I do. Because what came to me is the ability to trust the Lord. There is a great gap between faith and trust. The whole reversal in my life came when the Lord informed me directly and positively that I was all right. How I don't know but suddenly I knew it and knew that no matter what happened, alive or dead, sick or well, hurt or no hurt, I was all right."

His face radiant with joy, Bruce continued, "That is a tremendous discovery and it came to me that way. I walked out in total happiness even though I had no idea that I would be around more than a year. That was five months after I was confirmed as a terminal case of bone cancer. I was loaded with it. And yet, not having the slightest idea that I would be healed, I was suddenly at peace. I had more than faith, I trusted the Lord."

He preached a special message to the retired, explaining

that "I want to qualify myself because I sometimes fool people. My oldest grandchild is married and I'm expecting a great-grandchild. These white hairs are more indicative than my face. There are people all over Florida who retired when I left the army. But they said, 'I'm going to retire' and meant it as they climbed into a rocking chair. It breaks my heart to see what happened to them. I'll meet one I haven't seen in a year, of my age and as healthy as I was at retirement, but he looks five years older. The Lord didn't build mankind for idleness. This marvellous body the Lord gave us is supposed to be busy and active. But more than the body, the spirit has to be active. More than that, you must believe there is reason to be alive tomorrow. When you do, you don't grow older, you become younger. I'll witness to the fact because I have never been healthier in my life, not even at twenty.

"The Lord not only healed me. He is healing people all the time, people who are sick, people who think they are sick, and I'm not always able to tell the difference. People who are healed have learned to trust the Lord and that is the route to obedience. Only through obedience can one expect the Lord to make good on His promise, not in the future, but now."

Bruce dared a men's group in Palm Beach to test their faith. "Think of people around you and pick out the one you like the least," he suggested. "If there is one you just cannot stand, he is the one for this experiment. Then spend enough time praying and meditating about it and get to the point where you can deliberately seek him out with affection and understanding, and say 'Hi, how are you? The Lord loves you and so do I.' Watch what happens. I've dared a lot of people to do this. Try it! Nine times out of ten that person will, within a week, turn out to be the person you like most. Others reflect what you think of them. What you think comes back to you. So when you give the love which the Lord tells you, that is what is coming back."

There was a new note in his talks to businessmen. "Seek first the kingdom of God and He will take care of other things," he quoted from Scripture. "I got carried away and started letting business go to pot. All of a sudden I found that my material things were doing better than ever. I wanted to do the Lord's work, so I wouldn't seek any more business. Know what happened? In the next six months more business walked in than I had dredged up in two years. This isn't accidental, it didn't happen just once. I run into the same story time and again."

At Christmas season Bruce visited his dentist, Dr. Jack Wilkins, who also treated Bishop Louttit. Wilkins asked when Bruce would become a priest. Shaking his head he replied, "Not at my age." "Don't say that," the dentist retorted. "Bishop Louttit is looking for you."

Disturbed by this unexpected news, he returned to the small office assigned him at Good Shepherd and prayed earnestly for guidance, mindful of age and keenly aware of the significance of the priesthood. He asked his wife what she thought and felt.

"I'm deeply troubled, Ginny," he said. "I think the bishop expects me to seek admission to the priesthood. The Lord knows how much I love and trust Him, but I'm concerned whether He considers me fit. You know how much our lives have been affected by my ordination. As a priest, I must belong wholly to my God and my church. What remains of my business would have to go, of course. I would not accept any stipend which means we must get by on our annuities. What do you think I should do?"

Ginny sighed as she replied gently, "I can't tell you what God wants you to do. Only He can tell you that. I gave up any idea of life in retirement when you became a deacon. You will go on, Bruce, doing what you are impelled to do. I've seen the effect your sermons and talks have on people. I know how many of them want and need your help to find health and peace. The Lord spared you for something. I think you should see the bishop."

Bishop Louttit greeted Bruce warmly. "The Lord told me you were coming," he said. "I wondered why you hesitated."

"He didn't tell me," Bruce replied, "until Jack Wilkins mentioned you were expecting me. I have prayed for guidance and I believe I should apply for ordination to the priesthood."

The bishop nodded approvingly.

"We will need an endorsement from the vestry of Good Shepherd Church, Bruce. You've done well in the examinations for the diaconate, now the clergy will want to test your knowledge of our church and Holy Scriptures in more depth. They will report their findings to me."

During the weeks that followed Bruce spent long hours in study and prayer. There was a disturbing development. Bishop Louttit retired because of ill health. Bruce looked to him as his spiritual mentor and grieved at his departure from the diocesan leadership. Canon William H. Folwell was elected his successor. In June, 1970, Bruce appeared before the committee of priests and passed the examinations. He was sixty-eight years old.

Bruce wrote each of his children: Marilyn, whose husband was rector of St. James Church in Milwaukee, Wisconsin; Marta, now the wife of Charles Smith, a musician, of Albuquerque, New Mexico; and Major Bruce Medaris, who had survived two Viet Nam tours. He told them of his convictions and devotion, and asked that, if possible, they might attend the second ordination.

Marta arrived in late June and talked at length with her

dad, who had always been larger than life to her. She saw a marked change, commenting later to Ginny, "Mother, it seems I've known three personalities in dad: the arrogant and hot tempered man of my childhood, then the more mature, less violent and brilliant man of the Huntsville years, and now a humble, introspective and loving person who brings his perception and wisdom to his Lord as an obedient servant."

"Yes," Ginny agreed, "this is a new Bruce. His values have changed, and mine, too. He is no longer fighting to prove his superiority, that left him when the cancer disappeared. Now he lives to serve people."

Marilyn came, warming her father with the news that she had become an associate of the Community of St. Mary which committed her to a daily prayer regimen. Bruce and his son retired to the study for talks about changes in the army, some of which the former general did not relish.

Bishop Folwell scheduled the ordination for June 29. Good Shepherd filled for the service. His counselors, Al Durrance and Larry Lossing, took part in the solemn rites. Marta's husband, Charles G. Smith, Jr., came from Albuquerque to play the organ. As the congregation sang the processional hymn, "I bind unto myself the strong name of the Trinity," the robed choir, priests, deacons, Bishop Folwell and the ordinand processed to the altar.

The Reverend A. Robert Rizner delivered the preface following Father Lossing's sermon. Next the people sang "God of the prophets bless the prophets' sons." Good Shepherd's rector, David Suellau, began the ordination by addressing the bishop: "Reverend Father in God, I present unto you this person present to be admitted to the Order of the Priesthood." The bishop rose and addressed the people, "Good people, this is he whom we purpose, God willing, to receive this day unto the holy Office of priest; for, after due examination, we find not to the contrary, but that he is lawfully called to his Function and Ministry, and that he is a person meet for the same. But yet, if there be any of you who knoweth any Impediment or notable Crime, for the which he ought not to be received into this holy Ministry, let him come forth in the Name of God and show what the Crime or Impediment is" (*BCP*,p. 536).

The Reverend Donis D. Patterson read the Litany with the congregation. Father James G. Radebaugh read the Epistle and Father Durrance the Gospel.

Bruce knelt before the Bishop who read the charge and examined him: "Do you think in your heart, that you are truly called, according to the will of our Lord Jesus Christ, and according to the Canons of this Church, to the Order and Ministry of Priesthood?" Bruce replied firmly, "I think it" (*BCP*, p. 541).

The people rose as Bishop Folwell said, "Almighty God, who hath given you this will to do all these things; Grant also unto you strength and power to perform the same, that he may accomplish his work which he hath begun in you; through Jesus Christ our Lord" (p. 543).

The congregation sang "Come Holy Ghost our souls inspire, and lighten with celestial fire" as the ceremony reached its climax. Bruce knelt as the bishop anointed his palms with oil saying, "Receive the Holy Ghost for the Office and Work of a Priest in the Church of God, now committed unto thee by the Imposition of our hands. Whose sins thou dost forgive, they are forgiven; and whose sins thou dost retain, they are retained. And be thou a faithful Dispenser of the Word of God, and of his holy Sacraments; in the Name of the Father, and of the Son, and of the Holy Ghost." He gave Bruce the holy vessels containing bread and wine. Handing him a Bible, the bishop said: "Take thou Authority to preach the Word of God, and to minister the holy Sacraments in the

Congregation, where thou shall be lawfully appointed thereunto."

When the service began, Bruce wore deacon's vestments, the white alb and amice, cincture and stole over one shoulder and fixed to his side. The apparel traces back to the Roman Empire: the alb was then a toga, the amice a cloth covering the head as protection against the elements, the stole a sign of magisterial authority while the cincture secured the garments about the waist. Vestments worn only by priests were draped on the altar rail. He put them on after receiving the bishop's blessing: the chasuble, a long white garment which protected travelers from the cold; a maniple, worn on the left arm, symbolic of the towel used by Christ when he washed the apostles' feet at the last supper. Now the stole draped over both shoulders, across his chest and secured by the cincture.

Bishop Folwell celebrated the Eucharist. Father Bruce administered the wafers, representing the bread which Jesus gave to his disciples. His family occupied the first pew: Ginny, Bruce, Marta and Marilyn, and they were first to receive communion. The service concluded with the powerful hymn, "A mighty fortress is our God." Bruce remained in the chancel for a while to bless those who came to the altar. The women of Good Shepherd arranged an informal reception in the parish hall where Bruce and Ginny happily accepted the congratulations of friends. To the 1,200 communicants of his parish, he had become "Father Bruce."

# 17

# IN HIS SERVICE

Something final had happened. It was indefinable, but distinct. Bruce had crossed a bridge over a deep chasm and now he was burning it behind him. As a lay reader and then a deacon he still had had at least a toehold back in his old world, but now that was gone. Lots of people sensed it, too, and wrote to ask Bruce about it. He drafted a response.

"Beginning late in 1964, I underwent a real conversion experience of total Christian commitment, after which I was pushed more and more into the work of the church.

"I was a member of the vestry and the Brotherhood of St. Andrew, a men's prayer group, and active in the healing ministry. Then I took a course to prepare myself to be a lay reader and began increasingly to be involved in prayer groups and the prayer and healing ministries. I still felt a nagging push to do more (the Lord knows what He wants!). With encouragement from several priests I began to study for the permanent diaconate.

"Under the canon law which controls this type of dedication, a qualified layman may pursue his studies without going to seminary, in effect doing what people used to do in the study of law by reading in a lawyer's office under his tutelage. I had a couple of very good coaches whose academic proficiency in theology and the Scriptures is very high. By the spring of 1969, I was prepared to take the canonical examinations for the diaconate. These examinations cover everything that is required of seminary graduates entering the priesthood, except that for the diaconate, somewhat less depth is required in the exegesis of the Gospels and in church history.

"I was ordained a deacon in June, 1969. This is a clerical order but does not require that one give up his secular vocation or wear clericals all the time. I began spending well over half my time in the work of the church assisting our rector.

"I continued my studies under the same tutelage, digging in greater depth and in the spring of 1970, was approved by the bishop to take the rest of canonicals for the priesthood. I did so and in June, 1970, was approved and ordained. Since then I have spent at least ninety percent of my time in the duties of a priest. I am what is known as a nonstipendary priest since I refused any income from the church and do not participate in the retirement program. I am reimbursed for travel expenses when I go anywhere on a mission or for other church purposes.

"Within the Episcopal church the route that I took is known as the 'old man's canon.' It does not in any way limit my duties or responsibilities as priest and I am finding complete dedication to the work the most rewarding experience of my life."

Father Bruce absorbed a full share of religious activities as associate rector of Good Shepherd while his preaching and healing missions reached into neighboring states. The large congregation of more than 1,200 required six Sunday services and a heavy weekday schedule including the Monday night healing service which was taken over by laymen. He continued active in Friday morning prayer breakfasts of the men's group which met in members' homes.

Fellow priests in the central Florida diocese harbored doubts concerning his role for a time. His previous career and the extraordinary events of his life set him apart. How would this dynamic and forceful personality adapt to his new status? Would he become a disruptive influence in ecclesiastical councils? How much could one of his age perform in the unending demands of human need?

The clergy learned that Father Bruce is not a simple person. A firm advocate of the canons and traditions of his church, he became active in the charismatic movement that sprang into full flower in recent years. His eyes sparkled as he assured listeners that Christ lives in the hearts of those who believe. He spoke out for the clergy, defending their unique place in society, pleading for higher salaries and relief from nonreligious chores, insisting upon their right to privacy in their family life and security in their calling. Since he did not compete with other ministers for pension or parishes, he could speak with refreshing candor.

He joined the Order of St. Luke, founded in an Episcopal church in Philadelphia years before as a lay organization which conducts a healing ministry. The order became ecumenical and brought together men and women of major denominations in a common effort to relieve suffering. Bruce helped shape the central Florida chapter along regional lines while serving as one of the chaplains.

There were few visible changes except the marks left by passing years. The clear and compelling voice, direct gaze, erect carriage, quick smile, determined stride and magnetic charm remained. A small beard under his chin was new. He wore garments of gray or black instead of the khaki and green of yesteryear. The colorful ribbons and silver stars that had adorned his military uniform gave way to a silver cross suspended from a neck chain.

Less obvious but fundamental changes occurred within. For nearly five decades he fought to reach objectives and strengthen his country's defenses in war and peace, using people as tools to his purpose. The goals were stated in military and technical terms. Now people became the objectives and his abiding concern. No longer did he engage political adversaries or business rivals. He fought evil and disease to bring peace to those in pain and distress. The compulsion to excel disappeared with an even stronger motivation to help others find the redeeming grace that came to him.

Al Durrance remarked to his wife, "I find great happiness in watching Bruce mature as a priest. You know, Ruth, by ordinary standards, he was an old man when he came to us at Good Shepherd. I looked at him the other day and he is unmistakably younger. I'm sure he is not as old now as when he retired from the army sixteen years ago, incredible as it may seem. He is doing as much work as he did then and helping more people."

His ordination at sixty-eight years of age established something of a precedent. A retired naval officer, Rear Admiral Frederick J. Bell, asked Bruce for advice because he also wanted to become a priest. Bruce explained the procedure which he had followed. Bell was ordained a deacon in Indiana in March, 1971, and became a priest in September of that year. He joined the staff of the Cathedral of Saints Peter and Paul in Washington, D.C.

The Bruce Medaris story attracted the press. A sensational tabloid of four million weekly circulation reported his meeting with Virginia Lively and subsequent healing. For weeks afterward letters streamed in from the sick asking for help or for Mrs. Lively's address. The volume of mail reached such proportions that Bruce reluctantly was forced to have a lay assistant answer many letters while he replied to the more desperate cases. He tried to keep this burden from Mrs. Lively, explaining that as a volunteer in the Lord's service she lacked secretarial help and could not respond to so many requests. Again and again he reminded correspondents that God heals, not Bruce Medaris, not Virginia Lively.

"All healing comes from the Lord," he told a man in Poughkeepsie, New York, who had endured an incurable ailment for thirty years. "The miracles of healing performed in this world are signs of His hand continuing in the affairs of men. He uses all sorts of people as His instruments." A Michigan wife feared a second cancer attack and wrote him because she could find no healing ministry in nearby churches. "The perfect love of the Lord casts fear out of people," Bruce replied. "If you open to His love, He can fill you with peace. Only you can open the door." A California mother deplored the drug culture infecting youth and asked why the Almighty permitted this. "God is very much alive in the hearts of the young," Bruce assured her. "At least as many are turned on by Jesus Christ as by drugs, and their numbers are growing daily."

A women in Chicago, Illinois, despaired because physicians held out no hope for her husband stricken with bone cancer. Bruce urged her to pray. "I was healed by the mercy of our Lord," he wrote, "after the medical profession did what could be done and gave up." To a parent seeking help for an ailing daughter, he advised, "Turn to your greatest friend. If you don't know Him, you cannot talk to Him."

As he counseled those pleading for help, he remarked to

Ginny, "We've got to persuade more lay people to take up this task in the spirit of true brotherhood."

"People who hurt and don't want to be hurt are trapped in their own prisons," he explained to many. "Remember Jesus' promise: 'I stand at the door and knock, if any open to me I will come in.' Listen and obey your Lord."

To those who asked why Bruce believed so implicitly he said, "I learned the hard way what the Lord wanted me to do. Over the years, even in the absence of total surrender on my part, he kept me from doing things which were wrong and gave me answers to questions for which no one had answers. I claim no credit, the honor and glory are His."

A woman suffering from mental illness was referred by her family in desperation. Bruce learned that she believed no one cared about her which filled her with doubt as to her sanity and place with others. Persuaded that the Holy Spirit loved her, as He does all of God's children, she broke down and wept in relief.

Summoned to a hospital where a young man was dying from a massive overdose of drugs, Father Bruce brushed by a nurse as he entered the room, prayed at bedside and left, telling the nurse "he's going to be all right." Two weeks later the attending physician called. "Didn't you know that patient was clinically dead?" he inquired. "That determination was made ten minutes before you visited the room. But you should know that the young man sat up next day, spoke to his family and left the hospital three days later!"

Driven by intense conviction, Bruce gave Ginny and his parishioners cause for alarm while conducting a healing mission at St. Paul's Church in Winter Haven, Florida. He went as substitute for another cleric who was detained elsewhere. For several years Bruce was occasionally bothered by a circulatory problem caused by an obstruction in the aorta that could not be helped by surgery. During evening service he suddenly became weak, but managed to walk out to the sacristy where he sat down, bowed in pain, holding his head in his hands. His lay assistant at Good Shepherd, Florence Hood, a sprightly woman in her eighties, found Bruce with two priests standing by him.

"I can't go on," he said weakly.

Miss Hood noted that his face was marble cold. She placed her hands on his head and prayed, then turned to the younger priest and said, "You help me!"

"I haven't any experience in this kind of thing," he answered.

"Put your hands on him," she ordered. "Now recite the prayers for the sick!"

Soon color flowed into his cheeks and Bruce sat erect.

"You take care of the people at the altar rail," he instructed Miss Hood who returned to the congregation with the priests. Bruce rested a few minutes and insisted on driving back to Maitland as he had promised his wife.

"This is suicidal," their host remarked.

"No," Miss Hood said. "The Lord will protect him."

Next morning Bruce picked up Miss Hood at her home and drove back to Winter Haven, where he completed the mission.

At the invitation of Huntsville, Alabama, churches he visited the city which held such rich memories for him. He came to conduct a healing service. Executives of the space center, former military comrades and the public attended rites in Redstone Arsenal's chapel and a midtown Presbyterian church. The warmly human cleric presented a sharp contrast with the commander they had known. Eberhard Rees, who succeeded von Braun as director of the space complex, asked Bruce how he liked his new Boss. They laughed together. Then Bruce quietly answered, "He is very considerate."

Visiting his office at Good Shepherd one Saturday, Bruce found a young woman wandering about in an alcoholic stupor. He took her into the chapel and prayed. When she regained her senses Bruce listened to a sad tale of marital unhappiness. She was Christian, her husband was a Jew and they encountered seemingly impassable barriers in their marriage. A separation followed. Bruce urged her to continue seeking God's help. Weeks passed, then a letter arrived explaining that she prayed to find someone who could share her love of God. The response came from an unexpected quarter. Her former husband had visited Israel and walked the paths Jesus once trod. Now they were praying and learning together. They were remarried four months later, visited the Holy Land and found spiritual union. She joined the Order of St. Luke to help alcoholics and expressed her thanks to Bruce and the people of Good Shepherd Church for their prayers and help.

A Miami, Florida, religious editor discovered Father Bruce among clergy present at a conference on charismatic renewal held at Holy Comforter Church in that city. He asked about healing. Bruce told the reporter that increasing numbers of physicians recognize that man's relationship with God has profound effect on his physical well-being. "Many psychiatrists are coming to believe that only God can heal a deranged mind," Bruce added. The writer noted with surprise that during communion service, worshippers spontaneously broke into song. "In their response to final prayer," the newspaper reported, "many stood, hands raised heavenward and began to chant musically as they spoke in tongues." A clergyman observed that "you can tell the charismatics by their big smiles and lapel buttons which read 'Jesus Loves You.' "

Curious about this activity in a liturgical denomination, the editor questioned Bishop James Duncan of southeast Florida. "What you saw demonstrated the transcendence of God," the bishop replied. "He has freed men to talk about their religion and deepened their sense of the enormity of God's gift. I rejoice at the renewal in the church. Charisma is a gift. Traditionally and historically the church is the charismatic body in which the gifts of the Holy Spirit are found."

More unsought publicity about his personal experience brought to Bruce appeals for help from Ohio, the Carolinas, Georgia, Pennsylvania, Oklahoma, Massachusetts, Puerto Rico, Indiana, Texas, New Mexico and Alabama. Some in urgent need resorted to the telephone. Ginny wept as she listened to heart-rending accounts of human distress. A young woman called from Boston and asked Bruce to pray for a sister dying of cancer. As he spoke of God's infinite love, she said, "I can understand why the Lord chose to heal you." He advised others to seek counsel from the nearest clergyman of their faith.

Ginny shared his parish duties to the extent that her health permitted. When her breathing problem worsened she was admitted to Winter Park Hospital for treatment and rest. They sold the summer home in North Carolina, recognizing that the demands upon Bruce were so great that he could not leave Florida. She played the chapel organ, worked with other wives in parish affairs and entertained clergy wives in their new home. Bruce found a building site in a wooded area close to Good Shepherd Church where they built a lovely ranch type house, less pretentious than the Lake Maitland home, but roomy enough for Ginny's piano and a paneled study where Bruce could work at his desk. Here he taped discourses on the Gospels which, together with sermons by Good Shepherd's rector, were reproduced by volunteers and made available to shut-ins or other persons pursuing religious studies at home.

His commitments in Maitland consumed most of his time, but Bruce also maintained lively interest in national security. He addressed a world affairs forum in Daytona Beach, Florida; a prayer breakfast of the Army Materiel Command in Washington, D.C.; the Pentagon Protestant Pulpit; cadet officers at Florida Technological University and the 163rd anniversary of army ordnance in Maryland. He was elected to the Ordnance Hall of Fame as tribute to his military accomplishments.

Good Shepherd's clergy, there were now three priests, could not cope with needs of parishioners and others who sought assistance. The same, gnawing problem existed in other churches. Organizations, like Alcoholics Anonymous, which deal with specific diseases and are staffed by lay persons who want to help others, perform outstanding service and ease some of the clergy's burden. To Father Bruce, that kind of success pointed directly to recruiting lay men and women who would devote some of their time to Christian ministry. Bishop William H. Folwell appointed him chairman of an ad hoc committee to formulate a lay ministry program.

He undertook the assignment in the firm belief that priest and minister are not the same, despite the common use of the words as interchangeable. He also recognized that some clergymen entertained misgivings about the use of lay persons in ministerial roles.

"If a priest does not feel that he is different from other people," Bruce told his colleagues, "something is missing either in his choice of vocation or his understanding of his relationship with our Lord. He must feel that difference in the depths of his being and prefer his calling to anything else which life can offer.

"We cannot make a proper place for lay ministers in the community of God's people until there is general recognition and acceptance of the unique role of priest. He is the sacramentalist and that is the profound distinction between him and other men. The sacraments of confession, communion and anointing of the sick provide the continual and renewing bridge between man and his God. The priest serves as intermediary in all three between the act of man and the response of God."

Mindful of dedicated lay persons like Virginia Lively, with whom he maintained frequent contact in sharing intercessory prayers, Bruce advocated the use of laymen in the pastoral, healing and evangelistic ministries. They visited the sick, offered Christian counseling and effectively carried out other assignments given them by a priest who helped them interpret Scriptures and stepped in when circumstances required it.

"The clergy cannot do all things for all people," Bruce reminded congregations. "We must encourage priests to be just that, and not errand boys. They were not called by the Lord to become clerks, accountants and yard men."

He enlisted lay assistants from within and outside Good Shepherd parish. They kept in touch while ministering to the sick and those in need, coming back to Bruce for guidance when confronted by new situations. He kept watchful eye on the propriety of these relationships and interpreted the Gospel.

Bishop Folwell selected Bruce for an unusual and sensitive assignment. Aware that the sacrament of confession is not as widely available in the modern church as in former times, the bishop urged the 130 clergymen of his diocese to inform their parishioners of the rite. In his pastoral message, Bishop Folwell wrote: "A little over a year ago, or perhaps almost two years ago, I was talking with Father Medaris about a number of things and at that time he told me of several clergy in my diocese who sought him out for confession or counseling. Of course, he did not give me their names, but simply wanted me to know that he was being asked to serve in that capacity. On my own I had been giving thought to asking some priest to serve as confessor and chaplain to the clergy. When he told me this it seemed as though I was perhaps being led by the Holy Spirit, in response to my own prayers about the matter, to ask him to do this for me. I gave it more thought and then shortly thereafter asked Father Medaris to accept this responsibility.

"Bruce will be available at all the retreats where clergy and their wives will be present. He will establish other times to be available. There is distinct advantage in having Bruce serve in this capacity. He is retired although working full time at the Church of the Good Shepherd. He can remain completely objective and independent in this position. He is a very thorough sacramentalist with wide experience in the field of pastoral counseling and the ministry of reconciliation and absolution. I would encourage you to seek him out . . . with the full assurance of my blessing for this ministry."

When Bruce discussed confession with priests and lay persons, he reminded them that the United States Supreme Court upheld the confidentiality of this exchange between supplicant and confessor. Gradually court decisions have eroded lawyer-client and physician-patient relations until only the sanctity of the confessional remains untouched.

"Nothing is more essential to physical, mental and spiritual health than the inner cleansing that comes about through reconciliation with the Lord," Father Bruce asserted. "One of the conditions of Divine forgiveness of error is the honest recognition of what the offender did, stripped of all excuses, and frankly stated to one's confessor. The willingness of an individual to accept confession can be taken as indication of repentance because of the humility it entails."

From his work in the healing ministry, Bruce came to understand that some who believe they are sick are really troubled by guilt and receive little relief since they do not admit the underlying cause. Human ills are not always susceptible to technical diagnosis and treatment. The causative factor may remain concealed by the patient's reluctance to bare inner conflict that defies medical solution.

"Hatred, anger and resentment cause many seemingly obscure illnesses," Bruce told a young cleric. "I have prayed with victims of automobile accidents whose physical injuries were repaired, but who did not recover fully until they accepted the Lord's will that they must forgive those who caused their hurts."

Priestly duties changed the character and scope of his ministry. Until ordination as deacon in 1969, Bruce concentrated on healing. As deacon he could do more for people, assisting in church rituals, preaching and devoting more time to the sick in hospitals and homes. After entering the priesthood, the drain of personal counseling reduced the time available for healing. So he set aside one day each week for the sick. All other considerations were pushed aside, however, when he was called to the bedside of terminal patients.

As he discussed these experiences with his wife, Bruce revealed deep emotion. "There are no words to describe how rewarding it is, Ginny, to help someone who is dying to accept God's love. I have no patience with doctors or families who think they are doing the right thing by refusing to tell the patient what is happening. I know that the patient knows, many times before anyone else, what is coming. And I have seen their relief when they find someone who will discuss it with them."

The experience of one woman dying of cancer remained bright in his memory. "When I saw her for the last time and we both realized that the end was near, she told me so and said, 'But don't worry, it is all right.' She had found the real peace."

Occasionally Bruce met those who challenged his sincerity. How could he espouse Christianity, they asked, and still not renounce as entirely evil, his previous military career? He offered a straightforward explanation: "Some of God's greatest servants were involved in wars, according to the Scriptures. Some of our finest military leaders have been dedicated Christians. We must remember that evil exists in man and in the world. I know that the Lord gave me answers to problems during World War II, answers that could not have come any other way. I see no reason to apologize for my service to my country in war and peace.

"We have been a nation favored by God. So long as we remained a nation under God we were never defeated. We have never been aggressive, we do not start war. The commandment says, 'Thou shalt do no murder,' as murder was defined in Hebrew law. That is quite different from defending one's country against an enemy.

"I never felt a personal desire to kill. In war I knew that some of our enemies would be killed. It was my responsibility to help get the war over in the shortest possible time and with minimum casualties. It never crossed my mind that there was any conflict with God's will. I followed clear and direct guidance then as I did in the space business and I do not question the Lord's instructions."

As to the charismatic movement, Bruce reasoned that a lack of understanding contributed to the resistance or open animosity that the subject provoked in some people. Dictionary definitions such as "an extraordinary power, as of working miracles or speaking many tongues, said to be possessed by early Christians" added to the controversy. Group prayer, laying on of hands and speaking in tongues are outward manifestations of the movement which operates within or outside the church and crosses denominational lines.

The Protestant Episcopal Church sprang from the Church of England. In the political sense, their separation was accomplished by the American Revolution. On the other hand, in the liturgy and traditions of the church, including Apostolic succession, there never was a separation. Hence charismatics found policy supporting them in a publication of the English church, approved by the archbishops of Canterbury and York, titled *Doctrine in the Church of England 1922-1937:*

"Participation in the Holy Spirit is set forth in the New Testament as the distinctive mark of Christians which separated them off from the surrounding world; in the Christianity of Apostolic times the experience described as that of receiving the Spirit stands in the forefront of Christian life, at once as the secret of its transporting joy and power and as the source of that victory of faith which could overcome the world."

Father Bruce encouraged those who wanted to understand the movement to read Paul's message to the Corinthians and the Gospel of St. John (xiv. 15): "Jesus said unto his disciples, If ye love me, keep my commandments. And I will pray the Father, and he shall give you another Comforter, that he may abide with you forever; even the Spirit of truth; whom the world cannot receive, because it seeth him not, neither knoweth him; but ye know him; for he dwelleth with you, and shall be in you. . . ."

"What you witness in the redemption and healing of your fellow beings," Bruce said, "is the power of God operating among us as Christ promised."

The light of his countenance betrayed the Spirit within him.

# 18

# FATHER BRUCE

Massive oak trees shade the white clapboard chapel dedicated in 1883, nineteen years before Bruce Medaris was born. Flanking the chapel on the east is Good Shepherd Church completed in the year of his ordination, its stained redwood walls blending harmoniously with the older structure.

The two buildings form the southern boundary of a rectangle enclosing bright green lawn. Parish offices and church school classrooms line the remaining sides. To the rear are more classrooms, another rectangle studded with orange trees and the 500-seat Parish Hall built in 1975, "in God's time" as Father Bruce had predicted. His bright and cheerful office where he counsels those in need contains desk, chair and credenzas, file cabinets, a copy of Salvador Dali's portrait, *The Sacrament of the Last Supper*, a portrait of the Christ, the prie-dieu where Bruce prays before the image of the crucified Saviour, and a winter landscape surmounted by the words of Robert Frost: "The woods are lovely, dark and deep, But I have promises to keep, And miles to go before I sleep."

Well-worn books cover the credenza behind his desk: a leather-bound Jerusalem Bible in which he has marked many passages and tabbed its contents for quick reference; *Cruden's Concordance;* a smaller, leather-bound Bible inscribed to Bruce June 29, 1970, gift of Bishop William H. Folwell; the *People's Anglican Missal,* American edition; *Lesser Feasts and Fasts; The Choral Service; Constitution and Canons for the Government of the Protestant Episcopal Church, 1789-1970; Prayers, Thanksgivings, Litanies; A Manual for Priests,* given him by Father Al Durrance and his wife for his ordination; the *Book of Common Prayer* and *Hymnal;* a draft of the *Proposed Book of Common Prayer; Manual of Christian Healing,* a handbook of the Order of St. Luke the Physician; *Order for the Healing Ministry,* and a copy of the Revised Standard Version of the Bible, a gift from his son-in-law and daughter, the Stillings.

Behind his left shoulder stands a colored photograph of Jeff and Jani Stillings with their children, John and Jennifer, inscribed to "Very special people, Gramps and Ginna, May your lives be full of the beauty of the Lord." They are their grandchildren and great-grandchildren.

A loose-leaf binder contains "Special Services" compiled by Father Bruce, one for lighting of the paschal candle on Easter eve, another for thanksgiving after childbirth, a third for anointing with oil of catachumens and chrism, and yet another for the blessing of a house.

A book rack contains other volumes he is wont to recommend to troubled people, selecting one suited to the immediate problem: *Healing Everywhere, Sister Death, Love Song, The Christian Family, Living with God, Prison to Praise, Please Touch, Above the Noise, Kingdom of Self, Do*

*Yourself a Favor–Love Your Wife, Tough and Tender,* the American and English Bibles. There are works on church management, pastoral counseling and healing. Florence Hood keeps the office in order and makes his appointments. Father Bruce handles most of his voluminous correspondence at home, using that typing skill he acquired at Springfield High sixty years ago.

Since Good Shepherd's parishioners now support two other priests, he no longer has the same heavy schedule of services which he formerly conducted. On a typical Sunday, worshippers may find him in the little chapel that played so important a role in his salvation. As they step into the narthex, a black and white portrait of Bishop Whipple looks down from the right wall. Across the way hangs a brass plaque installed by the congregation which memorializes his founding role in establishing this place of worship in the mission district of Florida. Dark red carpet covers the solid flooring worn by generations of faithful. Hand-hewn timbers frame the doorway leading into the nave. Wooden pews line the carpeted aisle to a wooden altar surmounted by a brass cross which stands in front of a circular portrait of the Madonna and the infant Jesus. Overhead a scarlet vigil light signifies the presence of reserved sacramental elements protected in a tabernacle.

Twenty-two pews seated the congregation until the mid sixties; now both chapel and the larger church, shaped like a cross, accommodate the more than a thousand parishioners. Leaded, stained-glass windows along the chapel walls admit light. One is dedicated to J.C. Eaton, founder of Eatonville, the black community which adjoins Maitland on the west.

The congregation silently await their priest who prepares for the communion service by donning vestments in a tiny sacristy with the aid of an acolyte. Clothed in black cassock and starched white surplice, the acolyte enters the sanctuary followed by Father Bruce who reverently carries a veiled chalice which he places on the altar, then turns to the people. He begins the solemn rite that reenacts Christ's last supper with His disciples, asking God to "Cleanse the thoughts of our hearts by the inspiration of thy Holy Spirit."

After the opening prayers, Bible readings and the Creed, ushers bring the people's offerings, bread and wine to the altar where Bruce presents them to God. Turning to the acolyte holding a silver bowl, he washes his hands, stands before the cross and recites prayers for church unity, for Christian leaders, for the congregation, for those in trouble and sickness, and for the departed.

He leads the people in general confession after which he rises, faces them and holds his right hand aloft as he announces that their sins are forgiven. Now he consecrates bread and wine as he recites: ". . . in his holy Gospel Christ commands us to continue, a perpetual memory of that his precious death and sacrifice, until his coming again." The kneeling acolyte strikes a golden bell.

"For in the night in which he was betrayed," the priest continues, "he took Bread; and when he had given thanks, he brake it, and gave it to his disciples, saying, Take, eat, this is my Body, which is given for you; Do this in remembrance of me."

Once more the bell sounds as Father Bruce kneels in adoration, lifting the host for the people to see. "Likewise, after supper," he recites, "he took the Cup; and when he had given thanks, he gave it to them, saying, Drink ye all of this; for this is my Blood of the New Testament, which is shed for you, and for many, for the remission of sins; Do this, as oft as ye shall drink it, in remembrance of me."

The bell tolls a third time as Father Bruce kneels and lifts the chalice. After invoking the Holy Spirit he prays for communicants and leads them in Christ's prayer, "Our

Father, who art in heaven . . . " Following a prayer of preparation, Bruce receives communion, then summons the people to the altar rail with the words, "Behold the Lamb of God; behold him that taketh away the sins of the world." They humbly kneel as he administers first the bread and then the wine.

When all have received, Father Bruce cleanses the communion vessels and concludes with a prayer of thanksgiving, blessing the people with the words, "The peace of God, which passeth all understanding, keep your hearts and minds in the knowledge and love of God, and of his Son Jesus Christ our Lord: And the Blessing of God Almighty, the Father, the Son and the Holy Ghost, be amongst you and remain with you always."

Leaving the sanctuary he removes the vestments with a final prayer, then walks to the door and greets parishioners.

In the fourth year of his ministry, as Easter approached, a news reporter talked with Bruce about the meaning of this season to the Christian church, commenting in his account that "although seventy, Father Bruce looks twenty years younger."

"We are coming to the paradox of Holy Week," Bruce observed. "As Charles Dickens wrote in 'Tale of Two Cities' it was the best of times, it was the worst of times. We commemorate Christ's victory over death in Christianity's most meaningful celebration. Yet it is also the week of his last supper with the disciples, his betrayal and crucifixion. It begins on a joyful note with Christ's triumphant entry into Jerusalem followed by a period of deep sorrow and desolation."

He explained that on Maundy Thursday, Good Shepherd Church and other Episcopal parishes celebrated the last supper, the central sacrament of the liturgy. Of special meaning to Father Bruce, that night the rector washed the feet of vestrymen even as Christ bathed his disciples' feet. Next day, on Good Friday, all ornamentation disappeared from church and chapel as crosses were draped in black during the hours of crucifixion. The paschal candle was lighted Easter eve and on Sunday gleaming white lilies decorated church and chapel in celebration of the resurrection.

As to his personal pilgrimage of faith, he went on to say, "This has been progressive over a considerable span of time. It was in England while preparing for the invasion of Europe that I returned to God. After my recovery from cancer, I realized that it was not just my faith, but the faith of a lot of people who prayed for me and with me. For reasons of His own, the Lord decided to spare me. He just kept budging me, pushing me, until I found that I was spending more and more time in His service and less in my business. Finally, it became apparent to me that He wanted me in the priesthood.

"The Lord is in the business of transforming people. If he gets His hands on you, if you let Him, He's apt to make quite a different person out of you. People who have known me a long time say I'm very much changed. I feel differently because the whole focus of my attention and interest is what I can do for other people. I don't bother about myself. The Lord takes care of me and He's done a good job of it, better than I could possibly have done. I wish that I had had sense enough to do it immediately when I retired from the army."

As to his seemingly inexhaustible energy, Father Bruce smiled and added, "The Lord gives you the energy to carry out whatever task he expects one to perform. A great part of the ministry is to help people and especially those who hurt. I spend as much time as I can in hospitals and counseling those who seek help spiritually, mentally or physically. I've seen people healed. I've seen people who were terribly depressed, who experienced difficulties in their family, come out with a shining light of love. I've seen people who were dying enter the last days with a radiance straight from God. I've been guided myself in incredible ways."

Changes have occurred over the years in Good Shepherd's leadership. Father Suellau took up a new ministry in St. Barnabas parish in Deland, Florida. The Reverend Philip Weeks, formerly of Holy Comforter Church in Miami, and a close friend of Bruce, succeeded as the rector. He welcomed Bruce's help as associate rector and gave him special responsibilities for lay readers, ushers and the liturgies of the services. Father William Walters replaced Father Andrew Krumbaar as curate. Good Shepherd has become one of the largest and most active congregations in central Florida.

Bruce and Ginny have more family to share their love. The Reverend Eugene Stillings and Marilyn Medaris Stillings have five children. He is rector of St. James Church in Milwaukee, Wisconsin. Charles and Marta Medaris Smith live in Albuquerque, New Mexico, where she is full-time medical assistant to a prominent cardiologist, active in charismatic work and mother of four children. A graduate of Harvard and New England Conservatory, Charles teaches mathematics and is a concert organist. Lieutenant Colonel J. Bruce Medaris, II, whose example induced his parents to join the Episcopal church, is assigned to the army's weapons testing base in Aberdeen, Maryland. He is the father of three children. Colonel Medaris delighted Bruce by attend ing a men's retreat at Camp Wingman, an Episcopal facility near Avon Park, Florida, conducted by his father. Ginny maintains frequent contact with their widespread family and with her father, Clifford Smith, who at ninety-five years of age lives in Traverse City, Michigan, where his son-in-law and daughter formerly spent happy vacations.

Father Bruce instructs clergy and laity, delivering lectures on such topics as "The Whole Man" and "Brink of Understanding" to a pastoral seminar, "Release from Bondage" and "Coming into Wholeness by the Holy Spirit" for Roman Catholic Pentecostals, "Meditation and Recollection" at a diocesan conference on prayer, "Guilt and Absolution" for a Winter Haven mission, "Administering to the Sick" for lay ministers, "Transfiguration and Self-Justification" for a Vero Beach mission, "The Gospel of St. John" for his parishioners, "Healing" at a Camp Wingman retreat, "The Occult, Exorcism and Inner Cleansing" for the convention of the Order of St. Luke.

He has conducted exorcisms. A utility executive sought help after his personality changed so drastically that his wife left him and business relationships fell apart. "I need your assistance," he told Bruce, "because something is driving me to do evil things which I cannot resist." Long discussions and prayer finally relieved his torment and he found peace.

A mother fearful for the safety of her family came to see Bruce. "My children live in dread," she pleaded. "They hear voices in the night. What was once a happy home has become an evil place." Bruce took Miss Hood, his assistant, to the house. Both sensed an evil presence as they approached. They walked in to find huge African images leering from the walls. A neighbor who coveted a valuable diamond ring had persuaded the wife-mother to engage in occult practices. Bruce instructed her to destroy the images, then he cleansed the house by prayer and holy water. The neighbor fled when she saw the priest.

Living evidence of the power of prayer, Bruce encountered special need for intercession when his great friend, Wernher von Braun, became a cancer patient in 1973. He recovered after surgery and returned to his duties as vice president of Fairchild Industries only to suffer a recurrence in 1975 and again in 1976.

Bishop Folwell appointed Bruce to the Planning Commission of the central Florida diocese. Observing him in this and other capacities, noting his staunch advocacy of Episcopal traditon while encouraging charismatic activities, the Bishop commented on his work as a priest. "He has been frequently sought out by other congregations to do teaching and preaching missions," Bishop Folwell remarked. "For the most part these have dealt with the ministry to the sick or the ministry of healing. He has also been invited to many places outside the diocese to do the same kind of thing. He has been extremely faithful and indefatigable in this work."

As he did in military service, Bruce expounds his position in controversy fervently and persuasively with high courage, a trait which prompted Bishop Folwell to add, "With great affection and love for him, I believe Bruce is still the kind of fighter he must have been in order to be as effective a general as he was in the army. However, when the chips are down and a decision is made, he is a man under authority and I really respect him for this. All in all, Bruce Medaris has made a phenomenal witness to the healing power of Christ and the love of God in his life. He has literally touched thousands of lives, both directly and indirectly."

## APPENDIX I

## PERSONAL REFLECTIONS
by the Author

I first saw Bruce Medaris in action at a Pentagon conference during the Korean War. I was on duty as an army officer at Picatinny Arsenal, a research and development center for high explosives and ammunition in northern New Jersey. The arsenal commander was Colonel J. P. Harris (no relative), an ordnance expert nearing the end of a distinguished career. He took me to Washington in answer to a summons concerning Picatinny's work on a special project, an explosive device that would eject a pilot if his plane became disabled.

Uniformed and civilian officials, including a general or two, gathered in a Pentagon briefing room. Colonel Medaris conducted the meeting. He concluded that Picatinny had bogged down and decided to reassign the project to Frankford Arsenal in Philadelphia.

As we walked out of the building, I asked Colonel Harris, "Who was the officer who did most of the talking? He knew his business and dominated the discussion."

Colonel Harris smiled. "That was J. B. Medaris," he replied. "Yes, he knew what he wanted. There are two kinds of people in the ordnance corps, those who love him and those who hate his guts."

My next encounter with Bruce occurred in September, 1956. I was spending two weeks on active duty in the Pentagon as a reserve officer. Pecking at a typewriter one morning, I was interrupted by Brigadier General J. A. Barclay, a former Picatinny commander who had joined Bruce as deputy commander of the new Army Ballistic Missile Agency in Alabama. We shook hands and talked awhile, then Barclay announced: "I want you to come to Huntsville and meet General Medaris. He is looking for an information officer."

"When would you want me?"

"Tomorrow," Barclay answered.

We explained the purpose of my trip to General John Hinrichs, my temporary boss, who quickly approved. Having phoned my wife in New Jersey, I boarded a train that evening, arrived in Chattanooga, Tennessee, at 5 A.M., waited in a nearly deserted station until 6:30, and boarded a two-car local for the 125-mile trip to Huntsville.

There were few passengers. The train stopped to pick up milk cans and toss out newspapers at nearly every crossroads before pulling into Huntsville at 9:30 A.M.. A waiting sedan drove me to missile agency headquarters where General Barclay chuckled over my train experience. We soon met Bruce. I felt his personality upon entering his office. Bruce explained the agency would develop a ballistic missile to carry a nuclear warhead 1,750 miles. Much of the project was secret but he needed someone to deal with the press, army information officers in Washington, air force officers at Cape Canaveral where the rockets were tested, and industrial firms holding contracts. He seemed to know a good deal about my background and I mentally credited that knowledge to Jack Barclay.

Looking at my uniform, Bruce startled me by saying: "I want you on active duty."

"Oh no, General," I hastily protested. "I'm a civilian employee in management at Picatinny and I want to remain a civilian."

"Nope," he said curtly. "Jack, you take Harris into your office and get the army information chief on the phone. Tell him I want Harris in uniform."

As the door closed, I said, "General Barclay, I didn't bargain for this. I want to work for General Medaris and you as a civilian. I can't afford to shuttle in and out of uniform at my age (forty-seven) and have no desire to make a career in military service."

"Don't worry," Barclay answered. "I understand your position and I'm sure the army will not order you on duty over your objection."

He put through the call and talked to the general in charge of information. As Barclay surmised, the officer wanted no part of recalling a reservist. Instead he offered the pick of the army's career specialists. "I don't believe that will be necessary," Barclay remarked as he concluded the conversation. We returned to Bruce who listened to Barclay's report. "All right," he said, "you come aboard as a civilian. When can you report?"

Bruce seemed to pay little heed as I talked of my job and family in New Jersey, meanwhile thumbing a desk calendar. "I'm due in Aberdeen, Maryland, in ten days for an ordnance show," he observed. "You meet me there. That's your first assignment and I expect you here two days later."

"Yes, sir," I agreed, "but that's rather short notice for the arsenal commander. . . ."

"Don't worry about it, I'll tell him," Bruce retorted.

Colonel Ivy Drewry, the Picatinny commander, was anything but happy and considered the abrupt transfer typical of the high-handed maneuvers of the new rocket agency. Mrs. Harris showed little enthusiasm about moving to the deep South. But I was in Aberdeen ten days later and drove into Huntsville alone on schedule.

Bruce gave me clear instructions about my duties.

"Tell the truth within the limits of security," he said. "Remember that this is an all-army agency. There is no room for parochial concerns about this corps or that. Keep me out of day-to-day involvement in community affairs because I can't afford the time. And don't invite Governor (Kissin' Jim) Folsom to this command. If you do, just pack your bags and head for the nearest gate."

It turned out that Folsom differed with the general about expanding Huntsville's boundaries and tried to force army installations to pay Alabama liquor taxes. Like other commanders, Bruce refused to comply on the ground that the state had no jurisdiction over federal enclaves.

For the next three years I frequently accompanied Bruce as he traveled to both coasts and to cities in mid-America preaching the gospel of rockets and space exploration to military, industrial and technical organizations. Sometimes I traveled with Dr. von Braun on similar trips. His name soon became synonymous with outer space.

Bruce expected me to fly with him in small, twin-engine military aircraft. He was the senior army pilot and a staunch supporter of army aviation. "We fly the safest planes in the skies," he insisted. I preferred big and roomy four-engine commercial planes and managed to fly them on occasion.

Most of our flights were relatively uneventful. But there were some nerve-wracking moments. One warm spring day we took off for Chicago and flew north in silk-smooth air over Tennessee, Kentucky and southern Illinois. Bruce turned from the pilot's seat with an engaging smile and said, "You see why I like flying?" I nodded. Later as we entered Chicago's air traffic control zone, Bruce pulled up to 12,000 feet. Suddenly the right engine stopped. The plane nosed down as I looked out on endless blocks of row houses. Pilot and co-pilot opened and closed switches while I silently prayed. We glided down until the motor barked and the propellor began spinning. Bruce climbed to a safe altitude.

"We forgot to turn on the other gas tank," he called over his shoulder. A few minutes later we landed on a postage-stamp-sized airstrip on the Lake Michigan waterfront in downtown Chicago.

Wherever we traveled Bruce knew people from his contacts with business and industry dating back to World War II. His speech that night received warm applause. Next morning a violent windstorm howled over the city as we prepared to depart. Crosswinds of sixty miles an hour blew over the tiny landing field, but Bruce determined to leave because of important business awaiting him in Alabama. He gunned the engines and the plane crabbed down the runway, zigzagging as the wind pushed it toward the lake. At the last moment the aircraft bounced up within a few feet of rocks piled across the strip to repel foam-topped waves.

Bruce turned into the gale, fighting to gain altitude as powerful hammer blows drove us down. Finally the little ship broke free and soared over Chicago's skyscrapers. When we touched down at Redstone Arsenal's airfield hours later Bruce apologized, "I'm sorry we put you through that ordeal. It was rough!" The Civil Aeronautics Board issued a new restriction for the Chicago strip prohibiting takeoffs in fifty-mile crosswinds.

Repeatedly I witnessed the impact of Bruce's magnetism upon people. His bearing, delivery, voice and reasoned messages commanded attention. Frequently he concluded talks with a reference to the Deity, "with God's help" or "God willing" came as natural and fitting statements of his faith in the execution of a difficult mission. He was an inspiring leader and brilliant manager who gave subordinates specific tasks and sufficient resources, then left them to carry out their assignments. He forgave errors of commission, but not those of omission.

Mrs. Harris came south in 1957. We attended the Episcopal Church of the Nativity which was standing when Huntsville served as the first capital of the Confederacy. At midnight service on Christmas Eve, at Easter or other holy days we found General Medaris occupying a front pew, singing hymns with fervor.

As we became better acquainted Bruce added more duties. He wanted daylight saving time because Huntsville lies in the Central Time Zone, an hour behind the East Coast, and fell two hours behind when Washington and New York converted to daylight time each spring. We polled the 10,000 arsenal employees while the local newspaper, *Huntsville Times*, polled its readers. The *Times* reported a small majority opposed to the change. The arsenal poll reflected favorable sentiment. The *Times* combined the results and the arsenal margin turned the tables. Mayor R. B. Searcy and the city council adopted daylight time despite an Alabama law that prohibited it. From then until Bruce left in 1960, Huntsville was the only city in the state operating on daylight time.

Often when visiting his office I found Bruce engrossed in a book. He explained that "I'm expected to make decisions in highly technical matters, often in fields where I am not expert. But I know where to find information that will prepare me for the conference and the judgment which must follow."

Having attended some of these conferences, I became

accustomed to his habit of walking over to a window as the decisive moment approached, standing there engrossed in thought, as we supposed, then returning to say "Yes, we'll do it," or "No, I won't take that road now." Much later the realization dawned that he had prayed for guidance while pondering his decision.

We disagreed at times and I earned rebuke. Mistakes were part of the pressure situation in which we functioned, constant battling with the air force and the aerospace industry for public recognition and dollars to keep the Jupiter project alive coupled with frequent refusals of the Defense Department censors to allow the army to tell its story. The air force commander at the Cape sometimes denied permission to release information about army missiles, contending it was improper in the Cape environment. I flew back to Huntsville after these unpleasant encounters to spit out my anger to Bruce who would say, "Simmer down, that won't get us anywhere. Remember, the air force can kill us with the press down there 365 days a year so we must settle for what we can get when there is something worthwhile talking about."

The press generally accorded the army fair treatment. Drew Pearson, the well-known columnist, tried to smear Bruce with allegations that he owned lakefront property in Huntsville which was subdivided and then sold to arsenal employees. A local newspaper published the Pearson column without talking to Bruce or me. After a heated exchange with the editor I sent him a sharply critical letter. Bruce learned of my action and called me to his office, where he told me sternly that it must not happen again.

"That paper is vital to our relations with the city," he pointed out. "Furthermore, you and I cannot afford to be mad for the same reason at the same time. One of us must keep his head and that is your responsibility."

The fact was that Bruce bought mountain land at public auction twenty-five miles from Huntsville as a long-term investment in timber. The only lake in the city was in a public park.

When newspapers carried scare headlines about the Colonel Nickerson court martial, I pleaded with Bruce to talk with reporters so that they would have all the facts. He refused. He would not allow me to talk about the pending trial, insisting that Nickerson must receive just treatment. Not until the court rendered its verdict would he meet the press. Even then he said little to explain his position.

Bruce didn't court sympathy. The fact that he underwent surgery to remove prostate cancer in 1956 remained a closely kept secret. During trips to the West Coast he would disappear for an hour or two. Curiosity finally got the best of me and I asked his aide where the boss went. "He visits a university clinic where they check for any sign of cancer," he explained. After two years of close association, that was how I found out Bruce had been stricken with the disease earlier. He never mentioned it.

He liked debate. Before flying to New York with him in midwinter, I called Mrs. Harris, who was still in New Jersey at the time, and asked her to meet me in the hotel. She struggled through snow-clogged roads to reach the city. As the dinner hour approached Bruce asked his companions where they planned to eat. I broke in to say that my wife and I were going to Sun Luck's, a midtown Chinese restaurant.

"I like Chinese food," he announced, "so we'll all go."

The table of seven enjoyed an excellent dinner. Bruce talked of his distaste for television in the home as a dubious influence upon children. Mrs. Harris bristled and stated her disagreement. The exchange became more animated and I bumped her shin under the table as a signal to calm down.

"Stop kicking me!" she said angrily.

"You let her alone!" Bruce ordered. "She is doing very well without your help."

The party laughed heartily at my expense and I shut up. The argument was considered a draw, neither could change the other's opinion.

*Life* magazine wielded great influence in that era. Editors of *Life* invited Bruce and von Braun to lunch. The two men described the urgent need of a big rocket, far more powerful than any then authorized, as the only sure way to overtake the Soviet Union. The Russians were off and running in the space sweepstakes, employing bigger rockets than the United States possessed. Thus persuaded, *Life* strongly endorsed the million-pound-thrust engine required for heavy space vehicles. Within weeks the Defense Department authorized the army to undertake the project. Saturn emerged in 1960 as the biggest U.S. rocket and paved the way for an even larger version that carried astronauts to the moon. It was a classic example of mustering support for a project otherwise denied by the national leadership.

Others surmised that Bruce sought personal aggrandizement. Instead he exploited press, radio and television to communicate his ideas, above all to urge decisions that would speed up missile programs and open the door to space. On that basis he welcomed Fred Friendly, a Columbia Broadcasting System producer, and the late Ed Murrow who filmed a documentary at Redstone Arsenal and Cape Canaveral called "Biography of a Missile." The show became a hallmark of the early space age and was broadcast twice by CBS and by the British Broadcasting Corporation.

The colorful, articulate and controversial officer who engaged in high technology projects attracted television coverage. Lawrence Spivak wanted Bruce to appear on "Meet the Press." We lunched with Spivak the day before the program. He explained that he would not disclose questions in advance, but he did tell us the areas of primary interest to his panel of newsmen. Next day I watched the live telecast on a monitor in the rear of NBC's Washington studio. Bruce answered all questions; however, some of his answers were more complete than others. Consequently the panelists could ask fewer than they had planned in the thirty-minute time limit. Afterward I asked Spivak, "How did it go?"

"That man is a snake charmer," he declared. "We didn't run the show, he did." The army considered it a fine program.

What Spivak noted happened regularly when Bruce talked to newsmen. He dominated interviews, cutting off troublesome questions brusquely and responding freely to questions he liked. Reporters considered him a good subject. He made news and his statements were clear and to the point.

Bruce mastered situations. We flew to San Francisco where he delivered two speeches, one a luncheon talk to a high-powered men's club, the other a dinner of the American Ordnance Association that evening. The men's club allowed a speaker the option of talking on or off the record. Bruce elected the latter so that he could frankly discuss air force management of missile programs contrasted with the army's methods. The major difference concerned the air force's dependence upon industrial contractors while the army possessed its own resources—arsenals, etc.—to develop complete weapons systems. His remarks earned a courteous reception. No hint of them appeared in San Francisco newspapers.

That evening I sat with the press at dinner, handing out copies of the talk cleared by Defense censors. The general's aide removed the luncheon message from a loose-leaf folder and inserted the dinner speech. Midway in its delivery I was startled to hear Bruce utter several words critical of the air force. He paused briefly, turned a page as he ad libbed and resumed. The press failed to notice the break. His aide had mistakenly left one page of the luncheon talk in the folder. When he came to Bruce's room later to apologize, the general replied, "From now on only two people touch my speech folder, Gordon and I. Is that understood?"

"Yes, sir," the aide said.

His faith belonged in the private-and-personal category. Bruce and Ginny entertained their son-in-law and daughter, the Reverend Edward and Marilyn Stillings, at their Redstone Arsenal quarters. The aides who picked up Bruce each morning wondered at conversations they overheard when Bruce and his son-in-law debated theological subjects. Where had the general acquired knowledge of the Scriptures? None of us knew.

There was further evidence of faith in this complex personality when *This Week*, the Sunday magazine supplement, appeared September 13, 1959, containing a page captioned, "A General Looks at God." The magazine commented "this philosophy for the space age was written by a man who has helped its frighteningly fast development." The brief statement written by Bruce concluded that "like the growth of a child from infant to adult, man is discovering worlds new to him, but old to God."

His team scored many technical successes, bringing the Jupiter missile to operational status in three years, solving the problem of returning objects to earth from space, demonstrating the future by flying two monkeys 1,700 miles in a missile and returning them safely. But the launching of America's first satellite topped the list.

As the historic occasion neared, Bruce assigned me a three-legged stool in the Cape Canaveral blockhouse from which I could report developments to the press several miles away. I could watch activities in the firing room and listen as Bob Moser tolled off the countdown. It was the first time an information man won such a vantage point.

"You sit there," Bruce said, pointing to the stool. "There are your phone and headset. Talk softly so you don't interfere and if you become excited, out you go!"

He laughed but we both understood that if I blew up in the tense atmosphere Bruce would not hesitate to push me into a rear room.

After the missile disappeared into the night sky, I sat across from Bruce as he clung to an open phone line connecting him with the Pentagon where Secrctary of Army Brucker and von Braun waited for news. An hour and a half passed before word came that *Explorer 1* was in orbit. He scribbled that name on a yellow pad when Secretary Brucker announced it.

Seldom do reporters applaud principals at a news conference. That happened as we entered the air force theater while *Explorer* blazed its way across the heavens. When we reached the Trade Winds Hotel much later, tired and elated, Bruce walked towards his bungalow. A burly figure appeared, grabbed him around the waist and hoisted him off the ground.

"You're the greatest!" he yelled. It was Tom Dougherty, the hotel proprietor.

*Time* magazine reporters had trailed our sedan and soon knocked on the cottage door. When told of their identity, Bruce smiled resignedly and said, "Let them in." They plied him with questions for half an hour. It was nearly 4:00 A.M. when he phoned Ginny to promise that he would be in Huntsville that morning. He got up at 5:30 and flew back to Redstone Arsenal for a wild reception.

Soon after this stunning triumph Bruce visited Governor Mennen Williams of Michigan in Lansing. The governor wanted assurance that the army would continue missile production at the Chrysler plant in his state.

We left under darkening skies. The weather to the south was dismal. Turbulence increased and the plane bounced uncomfortably. Enormous masses of black clouds stretched across the sky. With its limited service ceiling, the little aircraft could not fly over the intervening storms so Bruce elected to fly another route, off the established airways at low altitude and using road maps. Torrential rain beat down on the craft. After hours of torturous flight and hearing warnings by radio of severe weather ahead, Bruce chose to land at Fort Campbell, Kentucky, to await developments. He approached the field without warning, notifying the control tower only moments before he touched down.

"Let's find out how alert they are," he remarked with a broad grin.

A sedan splashed across the water-covered runway and an unhappy officer jumped out, buttoning a slicker, to salute the visitors. Bruce explained that he was making a short, weather stop. Another car arrived and took us to the officers club where we ate sandwiches, drank coffee and listened to weather reports. A squall line passed through Tennessee and Kentucky spawning tornados as it traveled northward. As the winds lessened, we resumed the flight. Bruce commented that "we probably could have made it, but I don't believe in asking too much of the Lord."

He drew a hard and fast line between his public activities and his home, trying to protect Ginny from the swirling controversies raging between the military services as each tried to push its missile projects. Only once did he let down the bar. The CBS television program, "Person to Person," wanted to broadcast an interview with the General and Mrs. Medaris. Ginny reluctantly agreed. Technicians converted the pleasant quarters into a studio, installing high intensity lights and huge coils of cable. Viewers saw the couple in their living room as the general and his wife talked about their life at Redstone Arsenal.

Late in 1959, Bruce invited me to his quarters one evening. He told me of events that were about to happen. The new space agency, NASA, wanted the von Braun team. Bruce explored the situation with other generals and asked for my vote, whether to support the takeover or offer the team to the air force. There was much to recommend the latter alternative. The air force enjoyed larger budgets and had experience in managing large projects. NASA was relatively inexperienced in handling big tasks. On the other hand the army worried that the air force might eventually take over all of Redstone Arsenal. I voted for the air force. Bruce discussed the prospects with von Braun and several other close associates before reaching his decision. He agreed to let NASA take the team. That agency established the new George C. Marhsall Space Flight Center on the arsenal and named von Braun as its director.

Bruce held his last press conference in uniform while in New York the day after announcing his retirement. He appeared cheerful but tired and made it clear that he would remain active in some vocation. I sensed that it was the end of an era of monumental achievements in army-directed missile and space projects.

Bruce moved to Washington. We reestablished contact in 1960, when I was named assistant chief of information for the army in the Pentagon. Later Bruce became president of the Lionel Corporation in New York and invited me to join him. It was a difficult decision, but when others warned me that he might encounter difficulty in controlling the company, I chose to remain with the government.

We had little contact for the next three years. I joined the Defense Supply Agency and worked for his World War II comrade, Lieutenant General Andrew T. McNamara. Bruce ended up in Florida. We renewed our friendship in December, 1963, when NASA employed me at the Kennedy Space Center fifty miles east of Bruce's home in Maitland. His consultant role with General Electric brought him to the launch base at times. He made it a point to drop in for short visits. During one such trip in 1964, he told me of the bone cancer. I called Wernher von Braun's office in Alabama after Bruce left and relayed word of the fatal illness to Bonnie Holmes, Wernher's secretary.

Bruce seemed better when I next saw him and he met Dr. James Maxfield for the first time. Months later I was overjoyed to learn of the cancer remission.

Mrs. Harris and I attended the ordination service when Bruce became a deacon in 1969, meeting Ginny and their son, Bruce, at the church. Our pride in the man we loved became even stronger when he joined the priesthood a year later.

A disability ended my government work late in 1974. I asked Bruce then if he would let me tell the story of his life. The desire to undertake the task as a clearcut demonstration of Divine grace had grown over the years. As a matter of fact I had written some 45,000 words of a pseudobiography when he left the army and tucked the pages away in a cardboard box.

Bruce agreed and I began talking with him, his associates in Florida and Alabama, researching his papers at Florida Institute of Technology, digging through files at Redstone Arsenal, interviewing Mrs. Medaris, Marta and Marilyn, who love him dearly.

When the time came Bruce suggested that I should offer the manuscript to Logos International. He knew of the publisher's work in producing literature concerning the charismatic movement in Christian denominations. I am grateful to God, to Bruce and Ginny Medaris, to Dennis Baker, my editor at Logos; Dan Malachuk, the publisher, and Florence Hood for the result.

# APPENDIX II

Awards and Decorations
of J. B. Medaris
General Order No. 50. By command of General Eisenhower

Award of the Legion of Merit

under authority contained in Section IV, War Department Circular No. 131 dated 3 June 1943, the Legion of Merit is awarded in the name of the President to

John B. Medaris, 0258381, Lieutenant Colonel, Ordnance Corps, for exceptionally meritorious conduct in the performance of outstanding services as Ordnance Officer from 17 February 1943 to 10 April 1943. He supervised the re-equipment of II Corps after the costly battle of Kasserine Pass during which large quantities of equipment were lost. All through the advance on Gafsa, Lieutenant Colonel Medaris followed immediately behind combat forces constantly directing operations of II Corps recovery and reclamation. Inducing battlefield recovery by personal example, he exemplified the highest degree of devotion to duty.

Bronze Star Medal

6 June 1944. Awarded to Colonel John B. Medaris, 0258381, Ordnance, United States Army, for meritorious service, in England, from 20 October 1943 to 31 May 1944, as Ordnance Officer, Headquarters First United States Army, in connection with military operations against the enemy.

Soldier's Medal

10 December 1944. To Colonel John B. Medaris, 0258381, Ordnance, United States Army from Headquarters First United States Army, APO 230, by Courtney H. Hodges, Lieutenant General, U.S. Army, Commanding.

Citation

For heroism on 12 and 13 July 1944, in France. Upon his arrival at the scene of a large ammunition dump fire in the vicinity of Audoville Lu Hubert, Colonel Medaris immediately assumed control of fire-fighting groups and superbly directed their efforts in extinguishing the flames. At great personal risk, he made frequent trips in and about the blazing dump amid exploding shells to locate new outbursts of fire and to plan necessary action to bring the conflagration under rapid control. By his untiring efforts, his personal bravery, and his heroic achievement, Colonel Medaris aided materially in averting a series of disastrous fires and explosions, thereby preventing loss of life and great damage to Government property.

Distinguished Service Medal

By direction of the President, under the provisions of the

Act of Congress approved 9 July 1918 (WD Bul 43, 1918), a Distinguished Service Medal for exceptionally meritorious service to the Government in a duty of great responsibility during the period June 1944-April 1945 was awarded to Colonel John B. Medaris, 0258381, Ordnance Department, Army of the United States.

Headquarters

First United States Army

Memo to G-1 (Awards)

Subject: Supplemental Data on Colonel J. B. Medaris (15 Dec 1944 to 25 April 1945)

Colonel Medaris on 16 December immediately sensed the counter-offensive which started that day. He quickly alerted all of Army Ordnance to be ready to act. As the situation developed, Ordnance units were given the necessary instructions and were kept constantly informed of the situation. On 19 December this situation was clear enough so that complete instructions for the relocation of all of Army Ordnance was ordered. By prompt action Ordnance troops were able to continue their mission, move, yet virtually no supplies were lost to the enemy.

The battle losses incurred by the Army in the first ten days of the counter-offensive were the highest First Army had ever experienced. Colonel Medaris directed the broad policies of priorities, checked on critical details, and started steps for re-supplying the Army. By the end of January the Army was again normal from a supply standpoint. The experience and leadership of Colonel Medaris during this phase saved much equipment from being lost to the enemy, assured the best use of what the Army had, and was very instrumental in its resupply. This superior execution of heavy responsibilities was of infinite value to this Army as any less accomplishment would have had serious tactical consequences. He successfully guided Ordnance through a most difficult period.

The next month was directed to perfecting the status of supply and maintenance of equipment. Again Colonel Medaris was looking ahead to a break-through into Germany, and all Ordnance equipment would have to be in the best possible shape.

From February 23 to April 25 were the two most difficult months of the campaign. The Army moved hundreds of miles. Supply was most difficult. In every phase Colonel Medaris had led Ordnance to a successful completion. This drive into Germany has always been properly supplied with both Class II and ammunition.

Early after the crossing of the Roer River in late February, Colonel Medaris saw that the problem of locating, preserving and safeguarding captured enemy materiel would be a problem of major importance. He immediately set up sufficient personnel and resources in order to handle the problem. This gave Ordnance an early start on properly handling captured equipment and has been responsible for the proper safeguarding of much valuable property.

Colonel Medaris has constantly analyzed the tactical situation and has had an uncommon ability to foresee coming events. By the bold application of this ability he has been able to pace Ordnance service to the requirements of the Army.

Decision No. 344

Le President du Gouvernemente Provisoire de la Republique Francaise, Chef des Armes, cite:

*A L'Ordre de L'Armee*

pour services exceptionnel de Guerre rendus au cour des operations de liberation de la France

Colonel John B. Medaris, 0-258381

Etat-Major lire Armee US

Les presentes citations comportent l'attribution de la Croix de Guerre avec Palme

Par Le Colonel Missonier                    Paris, le 29 Jan 1945
Directeur du Cabinet de L'E.M.G.D.N.

Signe: Missonier                    Signe: de Gaulle

*Decret*

portant promotions et nominations dans l'ordre de la Legion d'honneur

Le Gouvernement Provisoire De La Republique Francaise

Sur Avis de Ministre des Affaires Etrangeres

Vu l'Ordonnance du 3 Juin 1943 portant custitution du Comite Francais de Liberation Nationale, ensemble les Ordonnances des 3 Juin et 4 Septembre 1944

Vu le Decret du 20 Juillet 1944 relatif aux decorations francais decernees a des Militaires etrangers,

Decret:

Article 1er—Sont nommes dans l'ordre de la Legion d'honneur

"Pour services exceptionnels rendeurs au cours des operations de liberation de la France"

Au Grade De Chevalier

De Colonel

J. B. Medaris, Ordnance Off, First Army

Article 2—Les promotions et nominations visces a l'article precedent comportent l'attribution de la Croix de Guerre avec palme

Article 3—Le Ministre des Affaires Etrangeres est charge de l'execution du present Decret.

Paris, le 3 Avril 1945

Par le Gouvernement Provisoire de la Republique Francaise
Le Ministre des Affaires Etrangeres
Signe: Didout

Signe: Charles de Gaulle

We Charlotte
by the Grace of God
Grand Duchess of Luxembourg
Duchess of Nassau
etc. etc. etc.

upon the testimony of Our Minister of Foreign Affairs and after deliberation of Our Government in Council, have been pleased and thought it proper to name

Officer
of the Grand Ducal Order of
the Oaken Wreath

Colonel John B. Medaris
U.S. First Army

Done at Luxembourg 12 October 1945

Charlotte

Certificate of the Luxembourg Government announcing the award of the Ordre de la Courronne de Chene, Degree of Officier

Authority granted to accept and wear the award, by command of General McNarney 20 December 1945

To Colonel John B. Medaris, Headquarters, 3908th Signal Service Battalion, APO 887

Order of General San Martin

15 June 1948. A communication from Francis J. Graling, Col GSC, Assistant Executive for Foreign Liaison called attention to the fact that the Order of General San Martin was conferred upon Colonel John B. Medaris by His Excellency, General Jose Humberto Sosa Molina, the Minister of War of the Argentine Republic. The Order of General San Martin is a decoration conferred by the Argentine Government only upon foreign civilians and foreign military personnel. This decoration is not conferred by the Argentine Government upon members of its military forces.

In view of this information the Adjutant General of the Army has ruled that the Order of General San Martin may not be accepted by the officer concerned but must be placed in the custody of the Department of State to be held until Congress authorizes the decoration to be accepted. The decoration with diploma was received from Colonel Medaris and forwarded to the Adjutant General 14 June 1948.

## Legion of Merit

29 October 1957. The President of the United States of America, authorized by Act of Congress July 20, 1942, has awarded the Legion of Merit (First Oak Leaf Cluster) to

Major General John B. Medaris, USA

for exceptionally meritorious conduct in the performance of outstanding services:

> General Medaris distinguished himself by exceptionally meritorious service as Commanding General, Army Ballistic Missile Agency, Huntsville, Alabama

from February 1956 to October 1957. In organizing and directing the efforts of the Army Ballistic Missile Agency, General Medaris has continually displayed the highest degree of skill in bringing about a united effort between science and industry in the accomplishment of a mission which was assigned the highest national priority. His sound judgment and outstanding technical ability coupled with his dynamic leadership and initiative are directly responsible for the eminently successful Jupiter Missile Program. His many contributions to the capabilities of the United States Army have been of unmeasurable value in attaining a strong posture of defense for our country. By his actions, General Medaris has reflected great credit upon himself and upheld the highest traditions of the United States Army.

## Navy Commendation

October 31, 1958

My dear General Medaris:

It has recently been brought to my attention that the Department of the Army has awarded you the Legion of Merit (First Oak Leaf Cluster) for your service during the period February 1956 through October 1957 while serving as Commanding General of the Ballistic Missile Agency. The Department of the Navy desires to compliment you on this well deserved award and further desires to recognize your meritorious service to the United States Navy in the interest of the Navy's Fleet Ballistic Missile Weapons System as well as your outstanding leadership in your profession.

You have demonstrated a keen appreciation and comprehension of the Navy's Fleet Ballistic Missile requirements and by your timely decisions and responsive direction of your command have made an extraordinary contribution involving the adaption of the liquid-fueled Jupiter for shipboard use. You rendered invaluable assistance to the Navy through the establishment of initial training courses and the training of Navy personnel in technical laboratories of the Army Ballistic Missile Agency thereby providing the Navy with a nucleus of personnel trained in ballistic missile systems.

Through your energetic, experienced and inspiring leadership and prompt exercise of outstanding judgment and initiative, you established an exceptional environment for highly satisfactory participation of Army and Navy personnel in a joint program. The zeal, dedication and excellent spirit of cooperation displayed by you reflect the highest credit upon yourself and the U.S. Army and are deeply appreciated.

Thomas S. Gates
Secretary of the Navy

Legion of Merit

The Department of the Air Force conferred the Legion of Merit (Second Oak Leaf Cluster) upon Major General John B. Medaris, US Army, January 15, 1960 in recognition of his leadership in the Jupiter Missile Program.

Major General John B. Medaris distinguished himself by exceptionally meritorious conduct in the performance of outstanding service to the United States from 1 February 1956 to 31 January 1960 as Commander, Army Ballistic Missile Agency and later as Commander, Army Ordnance Missile Command. During this period he demonstrated extraordinary leadership in promoting interservice cooperation of the highest order, as well as professional competence and dedicated effort in making highly significant contributions to the missile programs of the United States and the free world. Especially noteworthy was the primary role he played in the monumental development of the Jupiter weapons system adopted for deployment to selected North Atlantic Treaty Organizations. [*sic*] The selfless devotion to duty, resolute determination and singularly distinguished accomplishments of General Medaris reflect the highest credit upon himself and the armed forces of the United States. Presented by Major General Daniel Callahan, US Air Force, at Redstone Arsenal, Alabama January 15, 1960.

Distinguished Service Medal

The President of the United States of America, authorized

by Act of Congress July 9, 1918, has awarded the Distinguished Service Medal (First Oak Leaf Cluster) to Major General John B. Medaris, U.S. Army, for exceptionally meritorious service in a duty of great responsibility.

General Medaris distinguished himself by eminently meritorious conduct in the performance of outstanding service in positions of great responsibility to the Government during the period October 1957 to January 1960. As Commanding General of the Army Ballistic Missile Agency, and later of the U.S. Army Ordnance Missile Command, General Medaris directed and guided the Army missile and space activities in a conspicuously superior manner. As a result of his dedicated efforts in the engineering and scientific fields related to guided missile development, many research and development objectives have been accomplished with distinction. His brilliant leadership in all phases of the Army missile program was at all times directed in the best interests of inspired service, and materially enhanced the "state of the art" in this vital area. The broad military knowledge, selfless application and untiring devotion to duty which General Medaris constantly manifested in these scientific fields marked him as one of the nation's most outstanding authorities on these highly specialized pursuits. The many sound recommendations and valuable suggestions which he made for the advancement of national defense projects and programs resulted in the creation of the most comprehensive organization of its kind in the Free World. General Medaris' energetic direction led to the successful accomplishment of the first launching of a United States satellite (*Explorer I*), the first firing and recovery of a full-scale nose cone, the Juno lunar probe, the placing of Juno into orbit around the sun, and the first launching into outer space and return of living animals. The warm spirit of cooperation and diplomacy which he displayed in frequent discussions of complex policy matters with Congressmen, Congressional Committees, high ranking officials of the Department of Defense and other Government agencies gained consistently superior results. His voluntary sacrifice of leisure time for presentations on lecture platforms, before television cameras, on radio and at press conferences, individual interviews with magazine writers, and in personal statements developed excellent public relations which informed the public and created an intelligent understanding of the challenges, dangers and promises of the Space Age. General Medaris' distinguished performance of duty throughout this period represents outstanding achievements in the most cherished traditions of the United States Army and reflects the utmost credit upon himself and the military service.

Presented by Wilbur Brucker, Secretary of the Army January 15, 1960 at Redstone Arsenal, Alabama.

## Honors and Awards

Doctor of Science—Rollins College, University of Alabama, New Mexico State University

Doctor of Laws—University of Chattanooga, Pennsylvania Military College

Doctor of Space Science—Florida Institute of Technology

Crozier Gold Medal, General Benedict Crowell Medal—American Ordnance Association

Michael I. Pupin Medal—Columbia University Alumni

Distinguished Service Award—Jacksonville University

Fellow—American Institute of Aeronautics and Astronautics, American Rocket Society

Senior Member—Institute of Electrical and Electronics Engineers

Life Member—The American Legion

Hall of Fame—Ordnance Corps, US Army